THE SHELL GUIDE TO THE IRISH LANDSCAPE

THE SHELL GUIDE TO READING THE IRISH LANDSCAPE

(incorporating The Irish Landscape)

Frank Mitchell

Wild Ireland Library

COUNTRY HOUSE, DUBLIN, IRELAND

Cover illustration:
Glenmalure, Co. Wicklow. (Aerofilms)

First published in Ireland in 1986 by COUNTRY HOUSE.

Reprinted 1987

COUNTRY HOUSE is an imprint of
Amach Faoin Aer Teo.
2 Cambridge Villas
Rathmines, Dublin 6, Ireland

British Library Cataloguing in Publication Data
Mitchell, Frank
   The Shell Guide to Reading the Irish Landscape - (Wild Ireland library 3)
   1. Ireland - Historical geography
   I. Title II. Series
   911′.415 DA969

   ISBN 0 946172 06 4

Managing Editor Treasa Coady
Designed by Bill Murphy MSIA FBIID
Text Editor Siobhán Parkinson
Printed by Criterion Press, Dublin, Ireland
Colour Separations Kulor Centre, Dublin, Ireland

This book is supported by Irish Shell Ltd.

While sponsoring this book Irish Shell Ltd wish to point
out that the views expressed are the author's.

To Margaret and Harry Godwin

CONTENTS

LIST OF COLOUR PLATES

SOURCES FOR TEXT FIGURES

Where text figures are taken from or based on work by other writers, the sources are given here. Where no such source is given, the figures are the author's own.

Fig. 1.1 J.P.B. Lovell 1977
The British Isles through Geological Time
George Allen & Unwin

Fig. 1.2 P.A. Ziegler & C.J. Loiuwerens 1979
in *The Quaternary History of the North Sea*
Uppsala University

Fig. 1.3 M.A. Cooper *et al.* 1986
Structural evolution of the Irish Variscides
J. Geol. Soc. Lond., 143, 1

Fig. 1.4 D. Naylor & P.M. Shannon 1982
Offshore Geology
Graham & Trotman

Fig. 1.5 S.R. Kirton & J.A. Donato 1985
Tertiary dykes of Britain
J. Geol. Soc. Lond., 142, 6

Fig. 2.1 D. Gillmor 1971
A Systematic Geography of Ireland
Gill & Macmillan

Fig. 2.4 A.M. McCabe 1985
The Quaternary History of Ireland
Academic Press

Fig. 2.5 G. Singh 1970
Late-glacial Vegetational History of Lecale, Co. Down
Proc. R. Ir. Acad. B, 69

Fig. 2.6 J.G. Millais 1897
British Deer and their Horns
London

Fig. 3.6 G.R. Coope 1979
Late-glacial deposits at Drumurcher, Co. Monaghan
Proc. R. Ir. Acad., B, 79

Fig. 4.1 P.K. Rohan 1975
The Climate of Ireland
Stationery Office

Fig. 4.7 P. Woodman 1981
A Mesolithic Camp in Ireland
Scientific American 245, 2

Fig. 4.8 P. Woodman 1986

Fig. 4.9 P. Woodman 1986

Fig. 4.10 P. Woodman 1986

Fig. 4.11 R. Bradshaw 1986

Fig. 4.12 N.H. Magnusson *et. al.* 1949
Sveriges geologi (2nd edn.)
Svenska Bokförlaget

Fig. 4.13 K. Jessen 1949
Irish Quaternary Vegetation
Proc. R. Ir. Acad., B, 31

Fig. 5.1 A.G. Smith & E.H. Willis 1962
Fallahogy pollen-diagram
Gulst. J. Arch., 24-25

Fig. 5.2 S.P. Ó Ríordáin 1954
Lough Gur Excavations
Proc. R. Ir. Acad., C, 56

Fig. 5.4 E.M. Jope (1952)
Porcellanite axes
Ult. J. Arch., 15

Fig. 5.5   S. Caulfield 1983
Landscape Archaeology in Ireland
BAR Oxford

Fig. 5.7   M.J. O'Kelly 1982
Newgrange
Thames & Hudson

Fig. 5.10   V.B. Proudfoot 1969
Land Use in Goodland Townland
J. R. Soc. Antiq. Irl., 99

Fig. 5.15   G. Eogan 1964
Later Bronze Age in Ireland
Proc. Prehist. Soc., 30

Fig. 5.16   H.C. Bowen 1980
The Past under the Plough
Environment Dept., London

Fig. 6.2   B.B. Williams 1983
Landscape Archaeology in Ireland
BAR Oxford

Fig. 6.5   H. Lamb 1965
*Biological Significance of Climatic Changes
in Britain*
Academic Press

Fig. 6.6   J. Lynch 1974

Fig. 6.7   T.B. Barry 1986

Fig. 6.8   A.R. Orme 1970
Ireland
Longmans

Fig. 6.9   Röslin 1562

Fig. 6.10   Duhamel de Monceau, 1764

Fig. 6.11   Eileen McCracken 1971
Irish Woods
David & Charles

Fig. 6.12   Eileen McCracken 1971

Fig. 6.13   R. Common & R.E.
Glasscock 1964
Field Studies in the British Isles
(J.A. Steers ed.)

Fig. 6.14   M. Samuel 1984
Coppinger's Court
J. Cork Hist. & Arch. Soc., 89

Fig. 6.15   R.H. Buchanan 1973
Studies of Field Systems in the British Isles
CUP

Fig. 6.17   *Ill. Lond. News*

Fig. 6.18   National Library of Ireland

Fig. 6.19   EEC Sources

PREFACE

When we think of the landscape of Ireland, we must remember that we are dealing with only a tiny fragment of the landscapes of the world. We can think of a broad mosaic pavement of various patterns to which Ireland only provides one small tile. But the tile makes a contribution to one of the patterns, the pattern of the European continent, and for many millions of years Ireland shared in the geological fortunes of Europe, and only became the island we know today some thousands of years ago. When Europe was shaken by geological convulsions, Ireland too was shaken. At times the European area was flooded by the sea; Ireland too was submerged.

Thus the history of the rock framework of Ireland cannot be told in isolation. We cannot think of it as a geographical unit surrounded by an isolating band of water; throughout its geological history we must see it as a modest part of the European land-mass.

And we shall have to maintain the same attitude to the Irish landscape throughout prehistory and history. The seas that surround Ireland may slightly impede access to the country, but they do not isolate it from powerful influences from Great Britain and the European mainland. Today influences have been strengthened into strong bonds, as Ireland plays its part in the European Economic Community.

This book is dedicated to Margaret and Harry Godwin, friends and colleagues for fifty years. Margaret first started to look at pollen in 1931, and she and Harry were quick to realize the potential of statistical pollen-counts. Harry's studies in ecology provided the necessary background, and his research interests quickly shifted to the history of British vegetation. Where Harry led, others quickly followed, and it was a matter of great satisfaction to them both to see the subject expand so rapidly. Harry was knighted in Britain as a recognition of his work for the conservation of the British landscape. He died in 1985, but not before he had seen the setting-up of the Godwin Laboratory in Cambridge, where his research interests are energetically continued.

My endeavour in this book is to attempt to interest the many rather than to provide a treatise for the few. In any case the latter are now well provided for by such books as *A Geology of Ireland* (ed. C.H. Holland), *The Quaternary History of Ireland* (eds. K.J. Edwards, W.P. Warren), *Ireland in Prehistory* (M. Herity, G.F. Eogan) and the eleven-volume *Gill History of Ireland* (eds. J. Lydon, M. MacCurtain).

All scholars tend to pigeon-hole their results, and give specific names to events and periods of time. In order to avoid wallowing in a welter of names, I follow a chronological route as far as possible, using numbers of years to trace out events. I endeavour to explain technical names and processes as they arise in the text, rather than refer the reader to a glossary.

I wish to thank all those colleagues and friends who have been bothered by my numerous enquiries; many of them have allowed me to use photographs and figures from their publications, and also to draw on their unpublished work. For the figures and photographs that have been used, acknowledgement is gratefully made. I wish especially to thank Richard Bradshaw and Elizabeth FitzPatrick, who read the drafts of the various sections, and suggested numerous amendments and improvements.

Frank Mitchell
Trinity College
Dublin

30 June 1986

ACKNOWLEDGEMENTS

The author and publishers wish to thank the photographers whose names appear in the list of plates for permission to reproduce their pictures, and the following for permission to reproduce figures:

Dr R.H. Buchanan and the Cambridge University Press; Dr S. Caulfield and BAR Oxford; Dr R. Common, Dr R.E. Glasscock and Thomas Nelson and Sons; Dr D. Gillmor and Macmillan Ltd.; Dr A.M. McCabe and the Academic Press; Professor A.R. Orme and the Longman Group; Dr B.B. Williams and BAR Oxford; Professor . Woodman and the *Scientific American*.

To name only a few, the recent work (including published illustrations) of T.B. Barry; H.C. Bowen; R. Bradshaw; S. Caulfield; G.R. Coope; M.A. Cooper *et al.*; P. Coxon; G. Eogan; P. Flatrès; S.R. Kirton and J.A. Donato; John Lee; Joseph Lee; J.P.B. Lovell; A.M. McCabe; D. Naylor and P.M.S. Shannon; Claire O'Kelly; M. Samuel; A.J. Sutcliffe; W.A. Watts; B.B. Williams and P. Woodman was also drawn on. The author offers his sincere thanks to all.

1
GROWTH OF
THE ROCK
FOUNDATION

Before 600 million years ago
The rock structures out of which the Irish landscape has been carved have not only an extent in space, but also a history in time. Of the latter, as the famous Scottish geologist, James Hutton said so long ago, we have 'no vestige of a beginning, no prospect of an end'.

As far as the beginning is concerned, geologists now reckon that the oldest rock so far dated has an age of 3500 million years, and that the earth must have had a rocky crust stretching back still farther in time. In Ireland our oldest rock near Rosslare in Wexford has an age of 2400 million years. All these early rocks have been very much deformed and *metamorphosed* (i.e. altered significantly) by later upheavals, and it is difficult to sort out their sequence.

When geologists attempt to decipher the sequence of rock deposition and metamorphism, and hence the history of the earth, they rely on a variety of methods of dating, some physical, some biological. When molten material solidifies into rock, or is torn into ash particles by a volcanic explosion, both rock and ash will contain small quantities of radioactive elements which proceed to break down into simpler materials at a constant rate — for example, uranium breaks down into lead. If we determine the amount of uranium originally present, the rate of breakdown, and the amount of lead formed, then we can calculate for how long the process has been going on, and hence the age of the rock. This is the *radiometric* method.

The solidification process also provides another method, the *palaeomagnetic* method. The earth has a powerful magnetic field, with north and south poles; the field is not constant, but varies with time. Molten rock usually has a content of minerals, such as oxides of iron, which are influenced by the magnetic field and align themselves with it. When the rock solidifies, they are locked in position, and so record the direction of the field at the moment of solidification. Later earth movements may alter the geographical position of the rock; we can detect these by reading the magnetic record of the rock and so establish its palaeogeography.

From time to time, for unexplained reasons, the magnetic field of the earth reverses itself. Such reversals are recorded, not only in solidifying rocks, but in many other deposits, and as the reversal is simultaneous throughout the world it is most valuable in correlating geological deposits in different parts of the globe.

With the passage of time animals and plants evolved, and their hard parts changed and developed. As successive rocks were deposited, some of these hard parts were preserved in them as fossils. If the fossils in the different layers of rock can be placed in an evolutionary sequence, their relative ages will become apparent. This gives us a biological method of dating, which is of the greatest importance.

As the primeval earth formed, it seems to have passed through a liquid stage. A solid crust then began to crystallize, and for a long time the crust was thin, and was subjected to violent and repeated disturbance. But after 600 million years ago the disturbances were less profound, and with the aid of fossils and other methods of dating, it is possible to follow crustal events fairly closely. Temperature in the earth's interior remained high. Six hundred million years ago the sea covered the area we call Wales, although the Romans had earlier called it Cambria. In that sea there were many forms of animal life, and these left fossils in the local rocks, which are known as *Cambrian*. The vast majority of still older rocks have either no fossils, or only a very limited range of them, and have so far largely defeated attempts to sort them out in detail. In consequence they are lumped together as *Pre-Cambrian*, even though the period of time they represent is immensely long.

Geologists — and geographers — have long commented on the way some of the modern continents could be made to fit together. Thus South America would fit quite neatly against the west coast of Africa. Moreover we can find on the east coast of South America rock-types that would be quite at home in Africa, and similarities can also be traced in fossils of earlier periods. Scientists played with the idea of 'continental drift', though they could not imagine what forces could have moved the continents.

More recent studies have suggested the mechanism, and so we talk about *plate tectonics*. We picture the globe as covered by a series of rigid plates, which fit together like pieces in a jig-saw puzzle, though the pieces are of very different sizes; on average they are about 100 km thick, and are supported on less rigid material, which thus allows them to move relative to one another. The plate has a crust, of which there are two forms. Under the oceans we have oceanic crust, a thin uniform rind about 8 km thick, of fine-grained rock composed of minerals rich in iron and magnesium, which make it dark and heavy. If this type of rock appears at the surface on land, as it does at the Giant's Causeway in Antrim, then we know it as *basalt*. Under the continents we have continental crust, which is variable in both thickness (on average about 35 km) and composition.

It shows a wide variety of rock-types, which are generally light in colour and relatively light in weight. This is because they are composed of minerals rich in aluminium and silicon. Silicon combines with oxygen to form the mineral *quartz*, which in very thin slices (as a silicon-chip) forms the heart of a computer. Quartz is an important ingredient of the pale rock, *granite*, which occurs in the Wicklow Mountains, and is used extensively in Dublin as a building-stone.

Continental crust is less heavy than oceanic crust, and where it occurs the plate surface is at a higher level. It is therefore largely above sea-level, whereas the oceanic crust lies in the main below sea-level. But the contact between the two is not at the shore-line, as the continental crust usually extends outwards under water for some distance as a shallow *continental shelf*.

When the plates move, three kinds of relative motion are possible. In the simplest the two plates slip past one another, but if grating occurs, the consequent vibrations may cause severe earthquakes. The San Andreas Fault in California marks the contact between two plates, and movement on the contact caused the disastrous San Francisco earthquake of 1906.

In recent geological time the North American plate and the European plate have been moving away from one another, and as they diverge (Fig. 1.1a) molten rock rises up between them and solidifies on the ocean floor, thus extending the plates. By reading the magnetic print-out in the newly formed rock we can date the spreading of the sea-floor. The modern Atlantic Ocean is the product of such spreading.

The plates can also converge (Fig. 1.1b) on one another, and shrinking of the surface must follow. Buckling up may take place, or one plate may be forced down below the other and melt away when, under enormous pressures, it reaches the higher temperatures nearer the earth's interior. Original rock characteristics are drastically metamorphosed, and bodies of molten rock may be forced up to higher levels; here they cool into coarsely crystalline rocks, such as granite.

600 to 400 million years ago
When viewing our chronological route through successive events, we can picture ourselves as looking through a time-telescope. But unfortunately when we try to look at events that took place hundreds of millions of years ago, we find that our telescope is not good enough to give us a clear picture, and we can only get a hazy impression of events. As we move forward in time, our telescope improves. We will no longer have to deal in millions of years, but will be able to resolve events lasting just thousands of years.

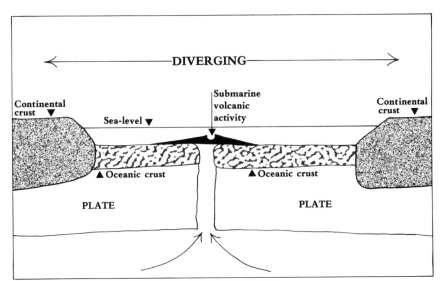

Fig. 1.1a As the plates diverge, and the oceanic plate splits, molten material rises in the crack. Contact with the cold sea-water causes it to solidify, building onto the walls of the crack, thus expanding the plate. Normally the volcanoes along the escape line are below sea-level, but occasionally, as in Hawaii, they rise above it. As a result of divergence, the sea-floor spreads, and the ocean widens or spreads.

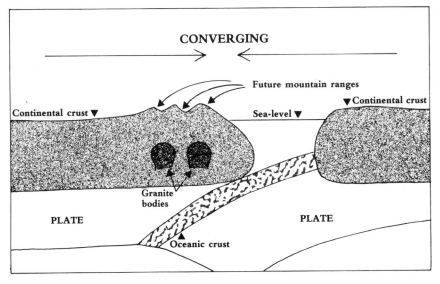

Fig. 1.1b As the plates converge, one plate is forced down below the other, whose margin buckles. These bucklings later appear as mountains. Within the continental plate masses of molten rock are forced up. On cooling they will form coarsely crystalline rock, such as granite. As a result of convergence, the ocean narrows and finally disappears.

Ultimately our scale will be hundreds — and even tens — of years.

Geologists are gradually building up a picture of the sequence of events that unrolled themselves as the years went by, and I have set these out in tabular form.

When Pre-Cambrian time ended, about 600 million years ago, a wide ocean, the proto-Atlantic, lay between the North American plate and the European plate. Off the shores of the plates there were basins with abundant marine life, a distinct North American fauna to the west, and a European fauna on the

	CLIMATE	ENVIRONMENT
Today	——— Temperate ———	——— Arable land, grassland and woodland ———
	Oscillating phases going	Forests of modern aspect appear in temperate phases
	from very cold to warm	Tundra appears in cold phases
	Frosts appear	Palms disappear; hemlock appears
65		Swamp-forests with palms
		—Erosion active as sea retreats; karst development renewed.
100		Chalk seas cover Ireland
	Warm	Sediments (some with high organic content) accumulate in various basins
200		
	Arid with temporary lakes	Eroding limestone starts to develop karstic features
		Ireland largely above sea-level; sandstones form
300		Plant debris (later changed into coal) accumulates in swamps
	Tropical marine	Warm seas (with corals) in which limestone forms flood over the land
		The landscape becomes green, as land-plants extend
	Seasonal rainfall	As the land erodes, great rivers transport large quantities of sand, which harden into sandstone
400		Ireland largely above sea-level
500		Sediments continue to accumulate in marine basins
600		Wide development of marine basins with many forms of life
		PRE-CAMBRIAN TIME
1200	Cold	(Rocks of this age give only rare signs of contemporary plants and animals)
1800		Ice in Donegal
2400		
MILLIONS OF YEARS AGO		

eastern shore. Rivers carried sediments into the basins in which animal remains were preserved as fossils. The sediments have since been hardened into sedimentary rocks.

When we study Irish fossils of this age, we find North American types north-west of a line from the estuary of the Shannon to Dundalk Bay, and European types south-east of the line. Needless to say this was for long a puzzle, but this can now be resolved by the evidence we have of a plate collision. Sometime before 500 million years ago the two plates started to move towards one

EARTH MOVEMENTS

	Today
Rift carries Greenland away from Europe; modern Atlantic Ocean nearly complete	
	65
Volcanic activity in north-east Ireland and south-west Scotland creates the framework of the Mourne Mountains and the Antrim plateau	
	100
As the North American and the European plates begin to separate, a rift — which will widen into the modern Atlantic Ocean — opens from the south	
	200
Tension creates basins around the Irish land-mass	
	300
Hercynide rock-deformation (due to plate movement in central Europe) creates the framework of the east-west mountain-ridges of the south of Ireland	
Further deformation occurs when the two halves of Ireland finally collide and are fused into one.	400
Intrusions of granite provide the framework for the mountains of Wicklow and other hills in Ireland	
The framework of the mountains of Connemara and Donegal is created.	
As the two shores get closer to one another, rocks on the western shore are intensely deformed all the way from Newfoundland, through the north-west of Ireland and Scotland and on into western Scandinavia.	
The two shores of the proto-Atlantic begin to move towards one another	500
	600
Repeated cycles	1200
of	1800
intense rock deformation	2400
	MILLIONS OF YEARS AGO

another. As the margins grew closer (Fig. 1.2), for some reason rock deformation was much more severe on the American side than on the European, and great folded structures, running north-east/south-west, were formed in what is now Newfoundland, north-west Ireland and Scotland, and Scandinavia. Subsequent denudation has left the core of these structures standing up as mountain-ranges. Caledonia was an old name for Scotland, and because of their common origin geologists call all these mountains the *Caledonides,* whether they now occur in Newfoundland, Ireland, Scotland or Scandinavia.

Shortly before 400 million years ago continental plate materials got involved in the disturbances and, becoming molten, were injected in large masses into older rocks, where they cooled slowly. Slow cooling allowed coarse crystals to develop, and it was in this way that the coarsely crystalline rock granite was formed. Dissection by denudation has left large upstanding bosses of granite, such as we see in the Wicklow Mountains (Pl. 3) and at several localities in Donegal.

Fig. 1.2 About 450 million years ago plate convergence was bringing America and Europe close together, and the early Atlantic (proto-Atlantic) ocean was being pinched out. Intense rock-crumpling on the American side ultimately resulted in a long mountain-chain running from Newfoundland through north-west Ireland and north-west Scotland and on into Scandinavia. The mountains are known as the Caledonides, *after the old name for Scotland (Caledonia), because their structure is well seen there.*

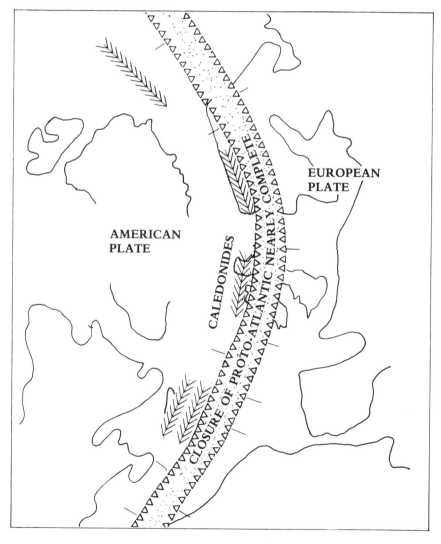

400 to 225 million years ago

Shortly after 400 million years ago the
two plates collided, and the two halves
of Ireland were welded into one.
Further rock deformation was brought
about by the shock of collision.

The area now occupied by Ireland
found itself in a totally new
environment. It was above sea-level and
exposed to atmospheric erosion. The
rivers of the period seem to have
flowed sluggishly at some times, and at
others to have swollen into torrential
floods, which transported great masses
of sand and gravel, now cemented into
sandstone, long known as Old Red
Sandstone. Such fluctuations in river
activity suggest marked seasonal
changes, and this type of climate tends
to favour rapid erosion. Some simple
types of terrestrial plants had evolved
by this time, but probably were not
present in sufficient density to form a
continuous carpet of vegetation, which
would have given the land some
protection against erosion.

Life, both animal and plant, started in
water, and it took a long struggle and
much adaptation for life to be possible
on land, where some type of supporting
skeleton was necessary. But by this
time, about 375 million years ago, some
animals had bony skeletons, and some
plants had woody tissue, and were
beginning to colonise the land.

Once more there must have been
tectonic disturbance, and either Ireland
and much of Britain subsided below
sea-level, or sea-level rose and engulfed
Ireland. In any event north-west Europe
was invaded by a great area of sea
whose waters were warm and rich in
the element calcium. Animals and plants
were able to combine the calcium with
the carbon and oxygen which were also
in the sea-water, and form supporting
skeletons of calcium carbonate (*calcite*).
Corals today build up reefs and atolls in
warm seas, but they cannot live around
the Irish coast because the temperature
is too low. They were abundant in the
Irish area long ago, and so we deduce

that the water was then warm. When
the shell-fish and the plants died, their
skeletons largely disintegrated into
calcareous debris which accumulated on
the sea-floor, though some shells did
survive more or less intact in the debris
to become fossils. Great thicknesses of
debris built up, and the lower layers
became consolidated into *limestone*.

This first stage of the sea was one of
clear water, but then sand and clay
began to be carried in. These
consolidated into sandstone and *shale*,
which lay on top of the limestone.
Ultimately the water became so shallow
that tropical forests could invade its
margins, and vegetable debris
accumulated in backwaters and swamps.
With the passage of time this debris
became transformed into *coal*. Geologists
regard this sequence of clear-water sea,
muddy sea, swamp-forest as one
sedimentary cycle, and because of the
presence of coal, call it the *Carboniferous*
period. In Ireland, alas, a better name
would be Carbonexodus period, because
subsequent denudation has stripped
away virtually all the coal that formerly
covered much of the Irish area. Limited
deposits, almost uneconomic to work
today, occur at Castlecomer and
Arigna, with two further tiny patches
at Bridgetown in Wexford, and in the
Kish Bank below the sea in Dublin
Bay.

Dramatic tectonic movements brought
the Carboniferous cycle to an end about
300 million years ago when there was
relative movement of the European and
the African plates. In central Germany
the Harz Mountains were thrust up,
and as this area was known in classical
time as Hercynia, the geological
features then created are known as
Hercynide. Disturbance was beginning to
lose force as it approached Ireland, and
its main effect was confined to the
south of the country, where a great
lateral thrust from the south caused
extensive rock deformation (Fig. 1.3,
Pl. 4). The Old Red Sandstone and the
overlying Carboniferous deposits were
folded and faulted (that is broken across

and shifted) into pleats which ran east/west. Farther north the thrust progressively died away, and its weaker effects were influenced by the older Caledonide structures, and tended to follow a north-east/south-west trend.

Following on these disturbances atmospheric denudation proceeded to whittle away the uplifted rocks. Erosion was very vigorous in the Irish area. The coal deposits quickly disappeared, and were followed by a great deal of sandstone and shale, until limestone was exposed over much of central Ireland. In the south, where the Carboniferous deposits had been thinner, the underlying sandstone was widely exposed. This was more resistant to erosion than the limestone, and soon appeared as east/west ridges separated by troughs in which some limestone had opportunity to survive.

Thus moving from north to south we have the east/west ridge of the Galty and Ballyhoura Mountains, then the low-lying limestone areas around Mitchelstown, then the Knockmealdown Mountains, then the Blackwater valley, then another sandstone ridge, and finally the valley of the Lee.

As soon as extensive areas of Carboniferous limestone had been exposed, they began to be attacked by a different process of denudation, which resulted in a karstic landscape, one type of which we see in the Burren today (Pl. 8). The essence of krastic conditions is that surface water disappears down vertical passages, instead of moving laterally as a surface stream. The carbon dioxide in the atmosphere dissolves in the water droplets in clouds, and when these fall to earth as rain, the rain is faintly acid and capable of dissolving the calcite of which limestone is chiefly composed. If the rock is broken by cracks and fissures — and earth-movements can be depended on to guarantee that it is — the rainwater will enter the fissures and enlarge them by dissolving away the rock-walls. One fissure will become a master-fissure, and a *sink-hole* will be created.

When the descending water reaches the *water-table*, that is the level below which all the spaces in the rock are filled with standing water, it begins to move laterally, enlarging its channel by dissolving the rock as it does so. If the water-table drops, the moving water follows it down, and the former channel is abandoned as a cave. As with river-flow, the level at which the water-table lies is related to the contemporary sea-level. In Ireland many sink-holes and solution-channels descend below modern sea-level, and at the time of their creation sea-level must have been far below its present position. The Blue Grotto in Capri and the drowned caves of Bermuda are modern examples of drowned solution-channels.

In normal landscape development we picture small streams in small valleys

Fig. 1.3 Section along a line running approximately from Tuam to Cork, showing tectonic features created by a lateral thrust of Hercynide age. (After Cooper and others)

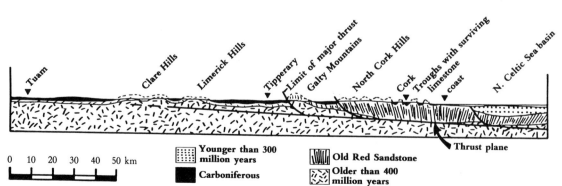

Tuam   Clare Hills   Limerick Hills   Tipperary   Limit of major thrust   Galty Mountains   North Cork Hills   Cork   Troughs with surviving limestone coast   N. Celtic Sea basin

Thrust plane

0   10   20   30   40   50 km

Younger than 300 million years

Carboniferous

Old Red Sandstone

Older than 400 million years

joining to become large rivers in large valleys, taking water and the products of erosion it is carrying to the sea in an intergrated way. In karstic landscape development surface water quickly disappears down master sink-holes, some of which develop into large closed depressions which come to dominate the landscape. Karstic landscapes are well developed and have long been studied in Yugoslavia; from there the word *karst* has entered into international geomorphological terminology.

Solution is not confined to the sink-holes and cave-channels. As the rainwater moves across the rock-surface towards the sink-holes, it dissolves some rock, and gradually frets the surface into a series of pinnacles and minarets, such as we see in tropical Africa (Pl. 9). Unfortunately when ice swept over Ireland, these spectacular irregularities were abraded away, and a rounded surface was created. The time that has elapsed since the ice disappeared from Ireland has been too short for these features to develop again, but provided ice stays away long enough, they will reappear.

In fact enormous quantities of limestone have disappeared from Ireland by the simple process of solution. In places, isolated blocks have survived: of these Knocknarea, which rises to 330 m just west of Sligo, is perhaps the most striking example. The basins of some of our largest lakes, notably Lough Ree on the Shannon, have probably been deepened by solution.

The drainage of the Shannon is one of Ireland's longstanding electoral carrots. Nearly every winter there is extensive flooding along the margins of the river, and the call goes up for its drainage. But it can only be drained — whatever magnificent engineering works may be carried out — if there is a sufficient gradient between the water-level in the basin and the water level in the sea for the flood-waters to be discharged rapidly. It may well be that the basin was lowered to its present level by

solution when sea-level was lower than it is now. Today, with a higher sea-level, there is probably not sufficient gradient for unassisted gravity discharge. Colossal pumps might be installed, but pumping would be hopelessly uneconomic. The annual pumping-season would be very short, and the land to be drained is not of high quality. The best solution would be to compensate the farmers for flood-losses, and preserve the river margins as wetlands.

It may be thought curious that I introduce discussion of karstic landscapes at this point when I am referring to events of perhaps 200 million years ago, while much of the karstic landscape that we see in Ireland today in the Burren and other places is probably of very much younger development. But there have been several successive karstic phases in Ireland, and it is not impossible that some of the features we see today are of very great antiquity.

Photograph 1 Ben Bulbin, Co. Sligo, a cliffed block of Carboniferous limestone, 525 m, rises above lower ground at about 60 m; relatively recent earth-movements may have caused the contrasting relief. The block emerged as a nunatak during the most recent glaciation, and artic-alpine plants still cling to the cliff-ledges; the flat top is buried by blanket-bog.

225 to 65 million years ago

Hitherto I have been dealing in units of hundreds of millions of years, but from 225 million years ago we have a very detailed fossil record, supported by confirming radiometric dates. This improves the focus of our telescope, and we can now handle tens of millions. I make my break at an intermediate point because of important geological events in Ireland about 65 million years ago.

The unit now entered on brought dramatic events, chiefly in the geographical location of Ireland. We have seen that about 400 million years ago the North American and the European plates were welded together along a seam that included Ireland in its course. Now the two plates were to split and diverge, and by sea-floor spreading create a new Atlantic Ocean, that would ultimately separate the continents by thousands of kilometres of water (see Fig. 1.1). When in 1858 Valencia Island was first joined to Newfoundland by cable, it was recorded that 2000 miles (3200 kilometres) of wire had been necessary; 400 million years ago the points joined by the two cable ends were quite close together.

The new rift started to open up, far south of the latitude of Ireland, about 180 million years ago. But long before that, perhaps as far back as 220 million years ago, preliminary tensional stresses began to affect the British Isles. In some places blocks of rock were dropped down into rift-basins, whose

Fig. 1.4 Basins in the Irish area, c. 220 million years ago.

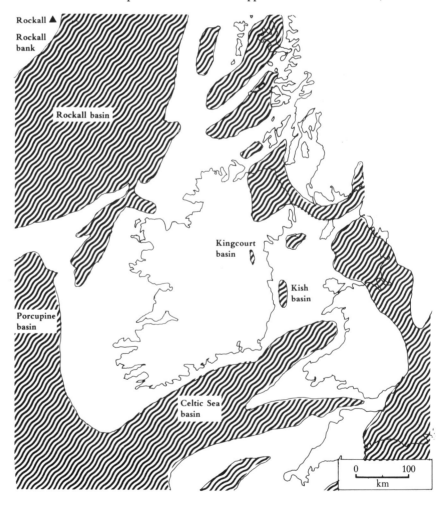

Rockall ▲

Rockall bank

Rockall basin

Kingcourt basin

Kish basin

Porcupine basin

Celtic Sea basin

0   100
km

modern equivalents are the Dead Sea, the Red Sea, the Persian Gulf, and the rift-valleys of East Africa, areas where similar tensions are operating. Elsewhere more gentle down-warping produced simpler basins.

There were extensive basins in Britain, in the Irish Sea, and on the west coast of Scotland (Fig 1.4). Basins developed to the south of Ireland in what is now known as the Celtic Sea, and to the west there are the Rockall and Porcupine basins. North-west of the Rockall basin is the Rockall bank, and from this, one tiny cone of rock projects not more than 20 m above sea-level. Small as it is, Rockall is a source of controversy in international jurisdiction; an offshore island, is it offshore of Ireland, of Great Britain or of the Færoes? The matter is not an academic one, as it brings into question oil exploration rights in the neighbouring basins.

The erosion that followed the building of the Caledonide mountains left a great deal of deposit in Ireland in the form of Old Red Sandstone. But most of the erosion products that followed the later Hercynide mountain building were carried off into the basins, where they formed New Red Sandstone. At times the sea temporarily flooded the basins, and if the sea-water evaporated away, rock salt and gypsum were deposited. The Larne basin contains valuable deposits of salt both at Larne and at Carrickfergus. The Kingscourt basin — of which only one half has survived, having been dropped down by faulting — has thick deposits of gypsum, which is the raw material of plaster of Paris and which is also widely used in the cement-making and building industries.

At a later stage some fine-grained marine sediments rich in organic debris, perhaps derived from seaweeds, were laid down. With the passage of time the organic matter transformed itself into oil and gas, and these products are being actively sought by the international oil industry. So far active drilling has been confined to the Celtic Sea and the Porcupine basins. There has been commercial success at one point, in the Celtic Sea off Kinsale, where a gas-field has been brought into production, and has already made a substantial contribution to the Irish economy.

The northern shore of the Celtic Sea was not far away, because at Cloyne, about fifty kilometres north of the productive well, we have a freshwater deposit of comparable age, say about 150 million years ago. The deposit appears to lie in karstic depressions in Carboniferous limestone, which shows that the denuded arrangement of east/west sandstone ridges and limestone valleys that we have in the south of Ireland must be of very great antiquity.

By about 100 million years ago continued erosion over much of western Europe seems to have produced a land surface of very low relief with rivers incapable of carrying substantial amounts of sediment into the sea. At that time sea-water flooded across Europe from Ireland to the Caucasus, and in it a remarkably pure form of calcareous sediment was deposited. Tiny floating organisms with calcareous shells drifted in the sea, and when they died and sank to the sea-floor, a fine oozy sediment, free from sand and clay, accumulated there. This was later consolidated and uplifted as a fine-grained white limestone, *chalk*. Siliceous debris in the ooze later coagulated as *flint*.

But the chalk which must once have covered almost the whole of Ireland — in places to a thickness of more than 100 m — has been almost completely stripped away by later erosion, and to accept that it was once there almost requires an act of geological faith. We have no problem in north-east Ireland. There, after some chalk had been removed by erosion — much of it of a karstic nature, because chalk also is a readily soluble limestone — great outpourings of basaltic lava came in time to bury the remaining chalk and so protect it from further thinning.

Over wide areas off the south and west coasts of Ireland chalk occurs on the sea-floor. But between north-east and south-west Ireland only one vestige of chalk remains. The main road from Tralee to Killarney runs through a narrow valley at Ballydeanlea, not far south of Farranfore. Here farmers found a small deposit of white limestone, which they quarried for burning in a

Photograph 2 A quarry at Magheramorne, Co. Antrim, with chalk capped by basalt. A chalk-fissure, up which molten rock moved, is filled with a dyke of basalt. Later earth-movement has moved the upper part of the dyke sideways: here we have a minor wrench-fault.

lime-kiln where it would be roasted to *lime* (an oxide of calcium), for use as a fertilizer. The deposit was noted by the Geological Survey over one hundred years ago, but as the accepted dogma was that chalk did not occur in the south of Ireland, it was not recognized as such. It was re-found in 1966 by Dr Peter Walsh of the City University in London, who not only identified it as typical chalk, but also noted that it was lying in a karstic sink-hole, which must have formed more than 100 million years ago. At Ballydeanlea the shale that was deposited on top of the limestone in Carboniferous times has not yet been eroded away; none the less many millions of years ago water percolated down cracks in the shale into the limestone, where it proceeded to create solution-cavities. These ultimately grew to such a size that in places the roof of shale was left unsupported, and collapsed down into the cavity, opening a sink-hole at the point of collapse.

Such sink-holes were standing open when the chalk-seas flooded the area, and chalk was deposited in them, just as on the surrounding sea-floor. When the area once more came above sea-level, and erosion was renewed, all the local chalk was removed, except for the fragment preserved in the pipe of the sink-hole. The tiny quarry at Ballydeanlea is one of Ireland's most remarkable, as well as most informative, sites, and should be preserved as a site of Special Scientific Interest (SSI).

65 to 25 million years ago

About 65 million years ago events were taking place to the west of Ireland, where the modern Atlantic Ocean was beginning to take shape, as Greenland drifted away from Europe. Some 5 million years later another split appeared, and the rocky platform on which Rockall later formed was left behind, as Greenland moved still farther off. We can picture the west side of Ireland as deprived of support by these movements, and sagging oceanwards, while great tensional fissures opened up further to the east. The hills and valleys of west Cork and Kerry were probably already in existence, and the sagging allowed the sea to flood their ends, and give us the indented coastline that is such a feature today. The fissures were most numerous in the vicinity of the North Channel, and here quantities of molten material welled up from below and flowed out over the surrounding countryside, in Scotland as well as in Ireland, burying it beneath great sheets of *basalt* (Pl. 6).

If the molten material should solidify in the fissure before it reaches the surface of the ground it becomes a *dyke*, and dykes trending north-west/south-east are known throughout the northern half of Ireland. Lava flows may formerly have covered much more of Ireland than they do today.

In Ireland, as well as regional lava flows, we had intrusions of molten rock, both on a large and on a small scale. Large-scale centres created the Mourne Mountains and Carlingford Mountain; on a small scale we have Doon Hill in Connemara; eruptions like those of Hawaii and of Vesuvius must have been common at this time. Similar igneous activity took place in Scotland, Wales and south-west England (Fig. 1.5). Beginning about 65 million years ago, it continued for 15 million years.

The basalts lie at the beginning of the volcanic period and we are fortunate that they have preserved a record both of climate and of vegetation, allowing

Fig. 1.5 Map of north Atlantic area about 55 million years ago showing an early stage of the modern Atlantic ocean, and outpourings and intrusions of molten rock. (After Kirton & Donato)

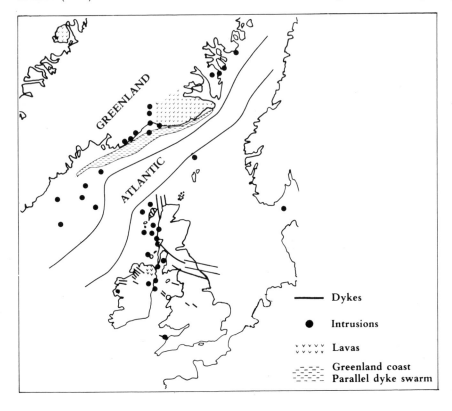

Dykes

Intrusions

Lavas

Greenland coast
Parallel dyke swarm

us to see a warm Irish landscape covered with dense tropical forest. After a first outpouring of lava there was a lull, during which the surface of the lava weathered into soil which became covered by vegation, and then a second series of flows buried and preserved the soil and the plant fossils (Pl. 7).

Molten rock is rich in silicon, oxygen, aluminium and other metals, and when the rock solidifies the metals combine with the silicon and oxygen to form complex *silicate* molecules. When weathered under cool temperate climates such as we have in Ireland today, the silicates tend to take up water while retaining the silicon and the aluminium, and turn into tiny plate-like particles of *hydrated aluminium silicate, or silicate clay*; the other metals tend to be removed in solution. But under moist tropical conditions very different changes take place; it is the silicon that is now carried away in solution, while the aluminium and the iron are left behind to take up water and become *hydrous oxide clays*, again in tiny particles; the other metals are removed in solution. If developed in sufficient quantity the hydrous aluminium oxide clay forms the ore of aluminium, *bauxite*, and its iron equivalent forms *limonite*, and in the past both of these ores were mined in the weathered inter-basaltic layer in north-east Ireland.

It is one of the ironies of the Irish economic situation that although the country has small quantities of a wide range of economically desirable substances, ranging from gold to coal, only lead and zinc occur in quantities that make economic working possible. At Aughinish Island in the Shannon estuary, Ireland has one of the largest alumina factories in the world, but the bauxite it processes comes not from Ireland, but from Guinea in west Africa and from Brazil.

The evidence of warm conditions given by the inter-basaltic soils is confirmed by the plant remains that they contain, chiefly in the form of *lignites* formed by

the alteration of lake-muds or peats in which tree-stumps and logs are embedded. Among the conifers pine (*Pinus*), cypress (*Cupressus*) and monkey-puzzle (*Araucaria*) are present, and there is a wealth of deciduous leaf debris, including leaves of alder (*Alnus*). Ferns are also present, but herbs are only poorly represented. Throughout this stage there were wide and broadly homogeneous forests in quite high northern latitudes, and the tropical woodlands of Ireland drop into place among these.

Minor earth movements had accompanied the outpouring of the basalts, and these continued in north-east Ireland after the volanic activity had ceased. The downward dropping of a large block about 35 million years ago created a depression in which a lake formed, and we can regard Lough Neagh as the modern descendant of that lake. Rivers carried clay, sand and plant debris out into it, where they accumulated to a thickness of 350 m. Again the surrounding country must have been densely wooded. Trees now confined to North America, such as redwood (*Sequoia*), swamp-cypress (*Taxodium*) and black gum (*Nyssa*) are present, together with more familiar forms, such as alder, holly (*Ilex*), lime (*Tilia*) and oak (*Quercus*). There are also types of palm (*Palmae*). The marine basins west of Mull, off the Dublin coast, in Tremadoc Bay, in St George's Channel, in the Bristol Channel, and in the Celtic Sea continued to build up sediments.

The prevailing tropical weathering had powerful effects on nearly all types of rock, and not only on those composed of silicates; quartzite alone had perhaps some chance of survival. The calcite of limestone and chalk can be directly dissolved by percolating water, and as solution proceeds the small amounts of clay that were also present in the rock will be left behind as a superficial mantle. In the case of chalk the embedded flints will disappear more slowly than the calcite, and a capping of 'clay with flints' develops. In some places we can see such material on the old chalk surface underneath the basalt, and this shows that the stripping away of the chalk by the weather had started even before the basalt was poured out. We can also see karstic features. Once the chalk had been removed, Carboniferous limestone appeared over a large part of central Ireland, and karstic attack was resumed on it.

But as the calcite of the limestone was carried away in solution, the small amount of clay it contained was left behind and gradually accumulated as a superficial mantle. As the protective layer developed, the rate at which the calcite could be removed was slowed down, and perhaps halted altogether. If there were metallic ores in the limestone, then these were also attacked by weathering, and complex hydrated compounds were left behind to form part of the protective mantle; this seems to have been the history of the valuable lead/zinc deposit at Tynagh, Co. Galway, where altered ores lay in karstic hollows; the finding of a log of cypress wood in the ore supports the suggested age of about 35 million years.

Photograph 3 Errigal, Co. Donegal a residual cone of quartzite, 750m, mantled by frost-shattered scree. At its base, 60m, beyond the cottages, ridges of moraine are banked against the lower slopes.

Over considerable areas of Ireland and of western Britain the limestone is perforated by vertical karstic pipes which contain weathered material, and in one such pipe at Ballymacadam near Cahir the fill contains pollen, which indicates woodland of the same general type as that of the Lough Neagh clays, and is presumably also of similar age. The fill must have been lowered into the pipe from a land surface at a now disappeared higher level, and questions immediately arise — How much higher? — Is the fill the last remnant of the sediment that formerly occupied a now vanished basin? — questions which are obviously of the greatest significance for the origin of the modern Irish landscape.

In Co. Clare today the limestone which has been scoured by later ice-sheets lies naked at the surface without any protective mantle of clay, and it is being dissolved away at a rapid rate. Estimates suggest that the limestone surface is currently being lowered at a rate 0.053 mm per annum; if this rate is projected backwards, it means that the surface would be lowered by 53 m in one million years, and that a layer of limestone more than 1000 m thick would have vanished during the last 25 million years.

Such rapid erosion would obviously long since have destroyed not only the Ballymacadam pipe fill but also the ore deposit at Tynagh. We are therefore driven to the position that the karstic limestone surface of the Irish midlands, ranging between 60 and 120 m in height, must be a very old one, and that it has only been enabled to survive by the former possession of a protective mantle of clay. The modern rapid rate of solution has only set in after that protective mantle had been torn away by later frost and ice.

Twenty-five million years ago there were probably very few exposures of solid rock to be seen in Ireland. The soil mantle would have been very thick and relatively uniform, because original differences due to the character of the underlying rocks would have been very largely eliminated by the vigour of the chemical weathering processes. The surface layer would probably have been brown or grey because of the presence of small quantities of decayed vegetable debris or *humus* and the absence of iron; the colour of the underlying weathered hydrous oxide clays would have been red or yellow due to the presence of fully oxidized iron; gradually this weathered clay would merge into unaltered rock below, probably at a depth to be measured at least in tens of metres. On low-lying ground, where soil drainage was poorer, there would have been a greater accumulation of humus, and a black clayey soil would have formed. The whole country would have been densely wooded by trees, many of which would have been unfamiliar to our modern eyes, and if we wish to see them growing today, we must seek them out in the mountains of eastern North America or of China.

25 to 2 million years ago

About 25 million years ago
temperatures all over the world started
to fall in an irregular way, periods of
falling temperatures being followed by
periods of recovery, but always with an
overall downward trend. At the same
time, possibly by the elimination of
some archaic forms, the flora and fauna
took on a more modern aspect.

By about 13 million years ago cooling
had reached the point at which ice-caps
could begin to form in polar regions;
though the amount of ice at the poles
has fluctuated since then, it seems that
at all times there has been some ice
present.

We have thus a period of falling
temperature, and a period of
diminishing vigour on the part of the
soil-forming agencies. But the changed
conditions could not give anything back
to the already heavily depleted soils,
and they probably altered but little.
Rainfall may have increased, and there
may have been some erosion of the soil
mantle, with increased deposition of
clays, sands and gravels on lower
grounds. There are extensive deposits of
plant remains of this age in northern
Europe, and they indicate a warm
temperate woodland, again similar to
that of eastern North America today.

We can see magnolias, sweet gums
(*Liquidambar*), black gums, swamp-
cypress and palms; the hemlock (*Tsuga*)
makes its first appearances. Some of the
conifers appear to be identical with
modern species. There are also raised-
bogs, perhaps not very different from
those we know.

One Irish deposit, again in a solution-
pipe, has an age of perhaps 15 million
years, and may fall in this period. At
Hollymount, north of Carlow town,
where the ground has a height of about
70 m, a well which was expected to hit
Carboniferous limestone at about 10 m,
went instead to a depth of over 60 m
in a pipe, i.e. almost down to modern
sea-level, before it was abandoned

without hitting solid rock. The fill
sediment was very finely divided
powdery quartz, with lignite and pollen
at some levels. As well as leaves of
heather (*Erica*), pollens of the heather
family (including *Rhododendron*) were
very common; there were some spores
of *Sphagnum* moss; coniferous trees
were represented by pollen of pine,
redwood, hemlock and umbrella pine
(*Sciadopitys*), and among the broad-
leaved trees were alder, birch (*Betula*),
hazel (*Corylus*), holly, hornbeam
(*Carpinus*) and willow (*Salix*). Palms
still survived. The plant evidence
suggests a forest, rich in varieties of
tree, growing when temperatures were
higher and seasonally more uniform
than at present. *Sphagnum* and heathers
will have been growing in wet hollows;
as these plants require acid conditions,
here again we have evidence that the
underlying calcareous limestone rock
must have been mantled by a layer of
clayey soil, out of which all lime had
been leached by deep weathering.

Hollymount lies beside the River
Barrow, at this point flowing in an
open limestone valley at a height of
70 m. But 50 km farther south where
the river is almost at sea-level a ridge of
very much older granite rises through
the limestone to lie across its path; the
river is not deflected; at
Graiguenamanagh it enters a gorge
with incised meanders whose rock walls
rise to a height of 75 m on either side.
To add to the problem, although the
gorge is 40 km from the point where
Waterford Harbour opens out into the
sea at Hook Head, spring tides flow up
through the gorge as far as
Graiguenamanagh.

How do we explain away the problem
set by the Graiguenamanagh gorge?
Some geomorphologists would claim
that there was in this part of south-east
Ireland at this time a high *planation-
surface* (a surface thought to have been
smoothed by erosion, either sub-aerial
or marine) at about 225 m, and that
the river-pattern we see today was
initiated on this surface. As the surface

Photograph 4 Landsat-2 image (13.11.76) of part of south-east Ireland, showing block-elevation of part of granite massif.

Fig. 1.6 Diagram indicating features in image, Photo 4.

wasted away through denudation, and older rocks began to be revealed below, the strength of river-flow was sufficient to cut down into the older rocks, and so maintain the flow. If the Hollymount plants were growing on this surface, then the pipe must have been over 250 m deep, and it seems impossible to think that plant debris could work its way down more than 200 m without being completely destroyed *en route*.

I reject this rather passive view, and consider that the older rocks were raised tectonically above an already low-lying landscape, and that the rivers trenched through the rising blocks. In south-east Ireland, not only the Barrow, but also the Nore and the Slaney are spectacularly indifferent to the geological structures across which they pick their way; all have cut narrow gorges through the granite ridge which seems to bar their courses. I envisage that, as the granite block was slowly raised, they trenched across it as fast as it rose, and thus by maintaining their original courses, they now found themselves leaving open country, passing through a steep-sided gorge, and emerging to open country once more. The present steepness of the gorges may be partly due to the discharge during the melting-away of the later ice-sheets of the midlands, of great quantities of meltwater through them into a sea much lower in level than that of today, but such major landforms cannot have been initiated by meltwater overflow.

I thus agree with French geomorphologists who consider that by this time, many millions of years ago, the relief of the modern landscape was already established, its river valleys were in existence, and the level of the sea was essentially of the order of that of today. In southern Brittany the corresponding sediments were deposited within already existing river valleys when these were flooded by the sea, either by a rising in sea-level, or by sinking of the land. The landscape of south-east Ireland has much in common with that of south Brittany and the rivers, such as the Barrow in Ireland and the Vilaine in France, exhibit the same paradox — their valleys are on the one hand incised into the landscape, and on the other are drowned by the sea in their lower reaches, with the result that the tide runs up them for many kilometres inland.

Several years ago Professor Herries Davies of Trinity College Dublin, when discussing the age of the Wicklow Mountains, also suggested that there might have been late tectonic movement in this part of Ireland. The mountains are eroded out of pre-existing granite. To have achieved its coarsely crystalline texture the molten granite, which was intruded 400 million years ago, must have cooled slowly below a thick insulating roof of older rock; despite such burial, granitic debris appears in the nearby Old Red Sandstone, showing that already by that early date erosion had cut down to expose at least part of the granite at the surface. If erosion had continued without interruption, one would think that at least all of the protecting cover would have been removed. But the highest point on the range today, the summit of Lugnaquilla at about 1000 m, is not of granite, but is part of the not yet completely removed roof. It seems impossible not to conclude that for much of its long geological history this part of the Wicklow granite lay at a lower level, protected by younger sediments. At a late date it was uplifted as a block, and erosion is now attacking it once more.

Images from satellites can indicate landscape features in a remarkable way. The summit of Lugnaquilla lies in the centre of the Landsat image on Fig. 1.6, the diagram under Photo 4. On the east side of the image we see the older rocks into which the granite was intruded some 400 million years ago. In the north centre we see the deeply dissected dome of granite which has been exposed by denudation. On its

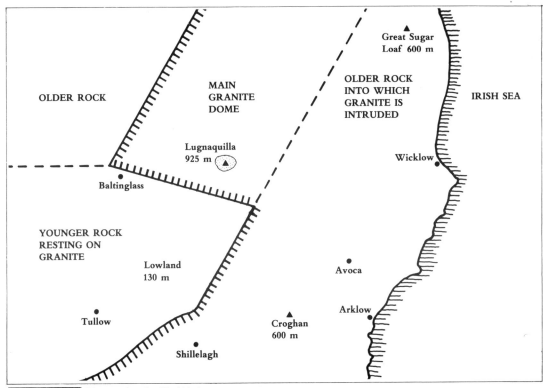

OLDER ROCK

MAIN
GRANITE
DOME

OLDER ROCK
INTO WHICH
GRANITE IS
INTRUDED

IRISH SEA

Great Sugar
Loaf 600 m

Lugnaquilla
925 m

Wicklow

Baltinglass

YOUNGER ROCK
RESTING ON
GRANITE

Lowland
130 m

Avoca

Tullow

Croghan
600 m

Arklow

Shillelagh

Western edge of uplifted block

Photograph 5 Lough Hyne, Co. Cork, is connected to the sea by the channel on the right (the picture shows high tide). We look north, and, as soil cover is thin, the east/west rock structure imposed by folding 300 million years ago can be seen. The heavily shadowed scarp may be due to later earth-movements, which raised a block of rock, and lowered the floor of the lough. In the blind arm on the left there is 'submerged' peat. In the rocky foreground there are small fields made at a time of greater population.

north-west side it rises steeply above the older rocks, separated from them by a break of slope with a remarkably straight course. To the south-west a straight-edged salient of low ground, outlined by a break in slope, thrusts into the highlands. In the lowland Carboniferous limestone, deposited 300 million years ago, rests on a weathered granite surface.

In my opinion the break in slope has resulted from recent tectonic uplift on the east, and downthrow on the west. In consequence the intact top of the granite stands at 925 m on the uplift side, while the glacial deposits and the limestone on the downthrow side lie on a surface, more than 800 m lower, to which the granite was cut down by weathering.

We probably see tectonic movement again in western Ireland where to the west of Lough Mask patches of rock 25 millions of years old lie on top of Maumtrasna at elevations between 600 and 700 m, while to the east of the lough the same rocks are buried beneath younger rocks whose karstic surface lies at an elevation of less than 70 m.

Lough Hyne, Co. Cork, suggests relatively recent subsidence. Here a small basin, which is surrounded by rock and is connected to the sea by a tidal channel, lies in terrain with some suggestion of a planation-surface at about 80 m. North-west of the lough there is a hill which rises almost to 200 m, while the present floor of the basin has in places the surprising depth of 45 m. The basin must hold a considerable quantity of recent unconsolidated debris, and the rock floor will lie at a substantially lower level. It has been suggested that the rock-basin is a corrie excavated by ice when sea-level was lower than it is at present; I can see no corrie-like features. Nor does it seem possible that it was gouged out by a flow of glacier-ice. It cannot have been created by wave erosion, nor by river erosion, for

no rivers flow into or through it. The surrounding rock is of Old Red Sandstone, so it cannot be a solution hollow. When all these agencies have been eliminated, differential movement of the order of at least 300 m, which has created a hill on one side, and a hollow below sea-level on the other, becomes a possibility (Photo 5).

We meet with a different problem when we look at the great rivers of Co. Cork, the Blackwater, the Lee and the Bandon, set in a planation-surface, with their trellis-patterns of long eastward-flowing stretches truncated by short southward-flowing discharge channels. One hundred years ago, J.B. Jukes, a distinguished director of the Geological Survey, thought that the north/south element was the older, having been initiated on a south-sloping surface of chalk, and cutting down into older rocks as the chalk vanished through denudation. As we have seen, the older rocks were deposited as two types of sediment, sandstone below and limestone above. Earth pressure then pleated these into east/west folds. Where limestone capped a ridge, it quickly disappeared to reveal a ridge of sandstone, but its removal from a trough was slower (see Fig. 1.3). Jukes thought the limestone was still in the troughs when chalk was deposited on top, and that after the chalk had gone, the later east/west tributaries pushed gradually westwards as the limestone was removed.

But as noted above, there has now been found in a low-level karstic depression in the limestone near Cloyne, a deposit which is *older* than the chalk. Thus, much limestone had been removed from the east/west troughs *before* the chalk was deposited — and of course the chalk will also have filled the troughs. It is not impossible — as Jukes thought — that the south-flowing elements of the pattern did start on a chalk-surface and succeeded in cutting through the sandstone ridges as they emerged through the chalk, thus continuing their north/south course to the sea.

I think we must agree that, granted what little we know of rates of erosion and of later earth movements, we cannot see in the Irish river systems any legacy from a chalk surface formed 70 million years ago, and that the whole relief of the modern landscape must be younger. But how much younger? At Poulnahallia, near Headford in Co. Galway, there is a karstic area of Carboniferous limestone at about 70 m above sea-level. One large depression has a layer of lignite about 5 m thick, which is covered first by blown sand, and then by glacial deposits. Pollen of palms has vanished, and pollen of hemlock has appeared, but many of the older tree forms, redwood, swamp-cypress, umbrella pine, are still represented; quantities of ericaceous pollen again suggest acid soil conditions. An age of 3 million years might be suggested. Thin patches of lignite, which give similar pollen-pictures, occur in the immediate vicinity. Here again we have our dilemma; we are told that limestone is very vulnerable to erosion, yet here no significant amounts have been removed in the past 3 million years, or even in the past 35 million years, as the picture at Ballymacadam suggests.

Across the channel at St Erth in Cornwall we get a pollen picture rather similar to that at Poulnahallia, and perhaps of the same age. Here on sandy terrain a coniferous woodland, with pine, fir (*Abies*) and hemlock, and a ground vegetation dominated by heathers surrounded a small lagoon in which a marine clay was deposited. As well as the plant fossils, the clay also had shell-fish and other marine organisms.

The clay was at a height of 40 m, but again the usual ambiguity presented itself as to whether the sea was 40 m above its present level when the deposit was being formed, or whether we are dealing with a basin which was formerly at a lower level, and has since been raised to its present height.

The rate of climatic deterioration then steepened sharply. Grasslands and open vegetation replaced the forests, and as the woodlands broke up many plants disappeared for ever from the European landscape. At a date probably about 2 million years ago severe conditions of cold established themselves in north-west Europe.

2
THE ICE AGE: 1,700,000 to 10,000 years ago

Dating methods

As we get nearer and nearer to the present day, the detail we can see with our time-telescope increases rapidly and we can begin to measure events in thousands instead of millions of years. This is because we can now use more precise methods of physical dating to assist us. As we have already seen, the earth's magnetism reverses its direction at rather lengthy, irregular intervals, and the time of such reversals can be measured by radiometric datings at favourable localities. As the period we are now measuring is shorter, our result will be more accurate. Such a locality is the famous Olduvai Gorge in Uganda.

In the past, there was a lake here and the lake-basin filled up with stratified layers of volcanic ash. Most valuable fossil material was buried in the ash, not only bones of animals but also implements used by Palaeolithic (early Stone Age) man. A later river cut a gorge down through the ash, and in the walls of the gorge a splendid sequence of deposits is revealed. If we measure the magnetism of the deposits, we can find a reversal in a layer of ash dated to about 1.7 million years ago. We can also trace this reversal in many other parts of the earth. We also of course date the early human material at the same time. So because the reversal here is most valuable for dating purposes, its date is chosen for the formal opening of the Ice Age.

It may seem curious to choose a site in tropical Africa to herald an Ice Age, but with our new precision we can hope to make our timing valid throughout the whole globe, and if we have heat in Africa we have simultaneously extreme cold in other parts of the earth.

The second method is essentially chemical. Oxygen is available in sea-water, and tiny organisms which float in the sea, *Foramenifera*, extract oxygen from the water to build up calcareous shells. There are two forms of oxygen molecule present — one lighter, one heavier — and the animals take up the two forms indifferently. If the proportions between the two forms changes with time in the sea-water, then shells of one generation will differ from later shells in the proportions of the two forms they contain. The amount of difference is very small, but can be measured by sensitive instruments. When ice-sheets form, oxygen from the sea-water is locked up in them, and the ice preferentially takes up the lighter form; consequently the proportion of the heavier form in the remaining water increases, and this change is recorded in the foramineferal shells.

When the animals die, their shells sink to the ocean floor, where they accumulate in layers, each layer recording the oxygen proportions of its day. If, again with very sophisticated equipment, we recover by coring a vertical column of sediment from the sea-floor, we can trace the varying proportions of the oxygen forms, and hence calculate the varying amount of ice on the earth's surface. We then make the assumption that large amounts of ice indicate cold conditions, and small amounts of ice warm conditions. As it accumulated, the sediment also recorded reversals of the earth's magnetic field, which are themselves dated, and when we get to sediments of less than 40,000 years of age radiocarbon dating becomes available. So we can hope to work out a pattern in time for the alternation of cold and warm conditions for the last 2 million years. About twenty changes seem to have occurred in the last 700,000 years.

Like the two forms of oxygen in the sea, we have two forms of carbon in the atmosphere. In the very rare form to which chemists assign an atomic weight of 14, called in shorthand C-14, the atom is unstable, and with the passage of time breaks down by radioactive emission at a steady rate into the more normal form of carbon. As they grow, green plants build carbon from the atmosphere into the tissues of their bodies, and so acquire a content of radioactive carbon. After their death the content of radioactive carbon gradually decays away, and if scientists measure the quantity that remains, they can tell the number of years that have elapsed since the plant died. Hence we get *radiocarbon* or *C-14 dating*, which is of such immense importance to geologists and archaeologists. But it has only a limited range, because when 40,000 years have elapsed, the amount of C-14 surviving is too small to be measured accurately. All shell-fish, as well as Foramenifera, draw carbon from the water around them to build up their shells, and after death the date of the formation of the shell can be established by C-14 dating.

These new studies of sea-floor deposits suggest that there may have been a considerable number of climatic oscillations in the not too distant geological past. In Britain at least seven cold stages are documented, but in Ireland so far there is only evidence for three. In Britain great masses of ice formed in each of the last three cold stages, but there is no record of ice before that, and opinion is now beginning to swing away from the concept that great masses of ice were the chief features of the Ice Age.

It now looks as if there was a period of cold, which was initiated a long time ago. In the Ice Age the cold intensified, but in the main it seems to have been a period of dry cold when frost processes were dominant. This dry cold was interrupted by shorter periods of two other types, in one of which meteorological conditions favoured the formation of ice, while in the other temperature ameliorated sufficiently to allow woodland to re-establish itself in north-west Europe. And so we have the new concept of 'cold stages' with frost action, in some of which ice-masses may have formed, alternating with 'warm stages', defined as having sufficient duration and a temperature adequately high for the establishment of closed deciduous woodlands in north-west Europe.

As there is no reason to think that the relatively genial climate of today is any more firmly established than that of previous transient 'warm stages', here the view will be taken that the so-called 'postglacial' in which we live is merely another 'warm stage', now named in Ireland the Littletonian Warm Stage, which will in all probability be succeeded in due course by yet another 'cold stage'.

Frost and ice in cold stages

In Ireland the deposits laid down by ice have been studied for more than one hundred years, but the study of the effect of cold unaccompanied by masses of ice is still in its infancy. Familiarity with our moist oceanic climate makes it difficult for us to picture Ireland in the dry grip of perennial frost, with a landscape typical of cold polar deserts.

Round the margins of modern ice-sheets climatic conditions are severe, and frost processes are active; such a

region and the processes can both be described as *periglacial*. But these processes are largely brought about by the energy produced by water as it expands and contracts in volume on freezing and thawing, and this freeze-thaw activity is not confined to regions in the vicinity of ice-sheets. Periglacial processes flourish best where summer thaws do not entirely melt away the frosts of previous winters, and where at some times of the year there is repeated oscillation of temperature backwards and forwards through the freezing-point of water.

If winter freezing consistently exceeds summer thaw, then an ever-thickening layer of permanently frozen subsoil — *permafrost* — will develop. Heat flow from the earth's interior will inhibit freezing below a limiting depth, but in Siberia today the permafrost may extend to a depth of 500 m. It is not known to what depth it formed in Ireland, but structures characteristic of it were

Photograph 6 Above: *Modern ice-wedge in frozen silt, near Fairbanks, Alaska (rule is 50 cm).* Below left: *Fossil ice-wedge-cast in Late Midlandian outwash gravels, Gorticross, Co. Londonderry (match-box gives scale).* Below right: *Fossil ice-wedge-polygons, probably of Midlandian age, Broomhill Point, Co. Wexford.*

formed in more than one cold stage. Marked contraction of the surface layer of the ground during the cold of winter caused tapering shrinkage-cracks to develop, and these became filled with wedge-shaped tongues of ice; if when the ice later melted foreign material took its place, an *ice-wedge-cast* was formed, and such structures are widely known in Ireland. Sometimes the shrinkage-cracks were arranged in a polygonal pattern, and *ice-wedge-polygons*, whose patterns can still be traced today, were formed (Photo 6).

If in summer the surface thaws while a still frozen layer remains below, then water cannot drain away downwards, with the result that the surface layers become supersaturated with water and highly mobile, forming the so-called 'active layer'. If the surface has a slope of even as much as 1°, the active layer will move downslope in a generally unsorted condition and when it eventually comes to rest it will form a deposit of *head*. Deposits of head are common in Ireland. If the slope is less than 1°, gravity may not be able to draw the material away, and the super-saturated material will stand in a stagnant condition. Water near its freezing-point varies in density with slight changes in temperature, and these variations will produce movements analogous to convection-currents in the supersaturated layer; under the influence of these movements, the materials of the active layer become sorted into coarser and finer units. In plan a net-like pattern may appear, with finer material in the interstices of the net, and coarser material along the strands; in section irregular columns of stones arranged with their long axes vertical underlie the strands, while below the interstices irregular material has the appearance of a basin-fill. *Polygonally patterned ground* — not to be confused with ice-wedge-polygons — is formed, and such patterned ground can be seen from Donegal to Kerry. Less regular currents churn the active layer in a tumultuous manner, and strings of stones are drawn out into irregular

bands or *involutions*. Where the ground does slope very slightly, the sorted stones may be drawn out into stripes running downhill. Both involutions and *stone-stripes* are common in Ireland.

As summer gives way to autumn, the surface of the active layer will refreeze, trapping a layer of as yet unfrozen water between the frozen ground below and the thickening rind of refreezing material above. Sooner or later this trapped pocket of water will itself freeze, and as it does so it must create space in which it can expand on changing from the liquid to the solid state. Under certain special circumstances, not yet clearly understood, the expanding water forces its way upwards, elevates the frozen surface layer with its contained soil, and so creates a dome-like space within which it can turn into ice. An ice-cored mound is thus created; such mounds are well known in arctic Canada today, and are called by the Eskimo name of *pingo*. When such a structure starts to thaw, the outer layer with its contained soil melts first and starts to slump down, surrounding the still unmelted central ice with a ring of earth and soil. When melting is complete, the former pingo is represented by a residual central hollow, surrounded by a raised rim. Fossil structures of this type are very common in south-east Ireland (Photo 7).

We have thus in Ireland ample evidence that in certain stages of the Ice Age the general aspect of the landscape must have been essentially identical with what we can see in arctic Canada and arctic Siberia today. By contrast Greenland today is buried by ice, and we have also evidence to show that Ireland too once carried an extensive ice-cover, with large areas at all levels completely buried by a very great thickness of ice.

In order that such large masses of ice may form, the amount of snow that falls in the winter must exceed the amount that can be melted away in the

Photograph 7 Above: Modern pingo, near Yakutsk, Siberia. Centre: Collapsing pingo, in permafrost with ice-wedge-polygons, near Tuktoyaktuk, NWT, Canada. Below: Fossil pingos, Camaross, Co. Wexford.

summer. The excess snow increases in thickness, and gradually consolidates into ice; a dome of ice builds up, and as the centre rises, the margins move outwards under the influence of gravity, and creep slowly across the surrounding countryside (Pl. 10).

As the ice advances it picks up the superficial weathered material that lies in its path, and thus comes in contact with the underlying rock. It is now armed with incorporated sand and pebbles and can abrade the rock, producing a surface which is in general rounded but shows on closer examination scratches or *striae*, produced as stones embedded in the base of the ice were dragged across the rock. The ice carries along not only the pebbles and clay it picked up as it advanced, but also the new material detached from the underlying rock; such material can range in size from blocks of rock several cubic metres in volume to the finest of rock-flour. When the ice deposits its load, there is usually little possibility of sorting, and rocks, pebbles, sand and clay are disgorged in an indiscriminate mixture to form what used to be called boulder clay, but is now generally named *till*. The ice sometimes moulds the till into ovoid masses aligned with the direction of its flow, and when the ice has gone a field of *drumlins* is revealed (Pl. 2). This landform was first described in Ireland, and the name is a blundered form of the Irish word for a small hill (Photo 8).

Ice *ablates* or disappears from the ice-mass in two ways, either by direct evaporation into the air from the entire surface, or by melting into water which drains away from the margins. As the meltwater flows away it carries with it some of the ice-enclosed debris released by the melting. If through a decrease in snowfall the rate at which the ice was ablating came to equal the rate at which the ice was advancing, the front of the ice would appear to stand still, and the debris that had been dispersed through a great volume of ice would all be released along the line of the

apparently stationary front. Great quantities of sand and gravel would be built up into an *end-moraine*, while the escaping meltwater would carry the clay fraction away in suspension. If the meltwater stream flowed into a lake, the clay would be deposited on the lake floor. If the rate of disappearance overtook the rate of advance, then the ice-mass became almost stationary or 'dead', and ablated away *in situ*, often producing a very confused topography of sand and gravel. Detached lumps of ice would become embedded in gravel, and when they later melted out, small lake-basins or *kettle-holes* would form (Photo 9).

Meltwater on the ice surface would sink down through fissures in the ice to its base where major discharge tunnels would gradually be established. The water in the tunnels often flowed vigorously under hydrostatic pressure, and was capable of cutting the floor of the tunnel down into the ground below the ice and creating a sub-glacial chute, with the result that on the final disappearance of the ice a segment of incised valley, usually bearing no relation to the modern surface drainage, would be exposed. Similarly changes in discharge routes might lead to a section of tunnel being abandoned by the main stream flow, and it would then silt up with sand and gravel. When the ice ultimately disappeared, the tunnel fill would emerge as an *esker*, a ridge running across country often for several kilometres, and bearing no relation to the local topography. In boggy country such ridges provided natural causeways, or *eiscirs*, and this Irish word has also passed into international geological usage (Photos 10a,b).

Where the ice-fronts abutted against hilly ground, ice-dams would hold up lakes in valleys, and great deltas would form where meltwaters discharged sand and gravel into the lake. Such deltas form important sources for concrete aggregate. There are enormous deposits of such sand and gravel near Blessington, Co. Wicklow, where an

Photograph 10 Above:
Eskers being exposed as
ice-sheet melts away,
Breidamerkurjokull,
Iceland. Below:
Bifurcating fossil eskers,
near Ballinlough, Co.
Roscommon. Discharge
water flowed from bottom
to top of picture. Note
road on crest of esker in
lower right-hand corner.

Photograph 11 North of
Galbally, Co. Limerick, a
rock ridge of Hercynide
origin formed the
watershed between the
Shannon and the
Blackwater rivers. Ice
from the midlands ponded
meltwater against the
north face of the ridge;
the ponded water over-
topped a low point on the
ridge, and as it gushed
southwards it cut a deep
channel in the ridge. The
watershed was thus
breached, and some water
which formerly went to
the Shannon now turns
south to the Blackwater.

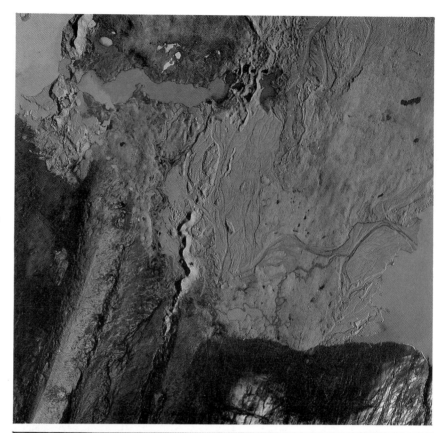

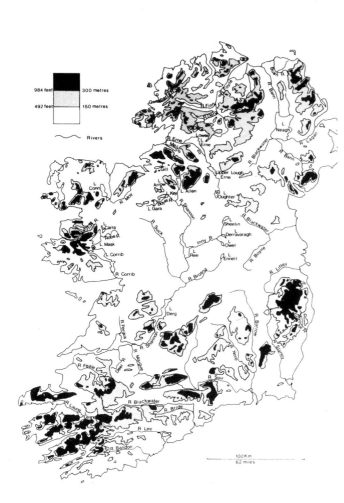

984 feet / 300 metres
492 feet / 150 metres

Rivers

100 Km
62 miles

Fig. 2.1   Major geographical features of Ireland.

Pl. 1   Ireland seen from a satellite. Grassland is green, arable land is pale-coloured, bogs are brown and high ground is pink. (MAPTEC)

entire landscape is being quarried away. Standing-water might spill from one valley across a ridge into the next valley, and a deep overflow channel might be cut in this way. There are splendid examples of such deltas and channels in many parts of Ireland (Photo 11).

Over high ground temperatures are lower than at sea-level, and snow may be able to survive on mountain-tops, when it cannot do so at lower levels. If climate in Ireland deteriorated, a north-east facing hollow in a mountain ridge would form a natural and sheltered trap for drifting snow, which would quickly thicken from a perennial snow-patch into a small lens of ice, capable of excavating a hollow or *corrie* in the rock of the hillside. Some lenses never expanded beyond this stage, but others could collect such an excess of snow that they could send a tongue of ice or *glacier* downslope. As the glacier moved along it entrenched itself into a valley with a U-shaped cross-section, in contrast to the V-shaped river valley (Pl. 12). The results of recent valley glaciation of this type are magnificently seen in the Brandon mountain-group in Kerry.

Here there was not a sufficient area of high ground for a local ice-cap to develop. Farther to the south and centring on the Kenmare estuary there was sufficient high ground, and the last of such caps formed here relatively recently. The high ground on which it lay was not continuous but was dissected into ridges and valleys, and these exercised a strong control on the directions of possible ice-movement. In places a tongue of ice forced its way across a ridge, gouging out a deep valley as it did so, as for example at the Gap of Dunloe. The ice-scoured country around the Upper Lake at Killarney gives further evidence of its erosive power, while the drumlins at Bantry, and the end-moraines around Killarney and Caragh Lake, show the materials that it transported and deposited.

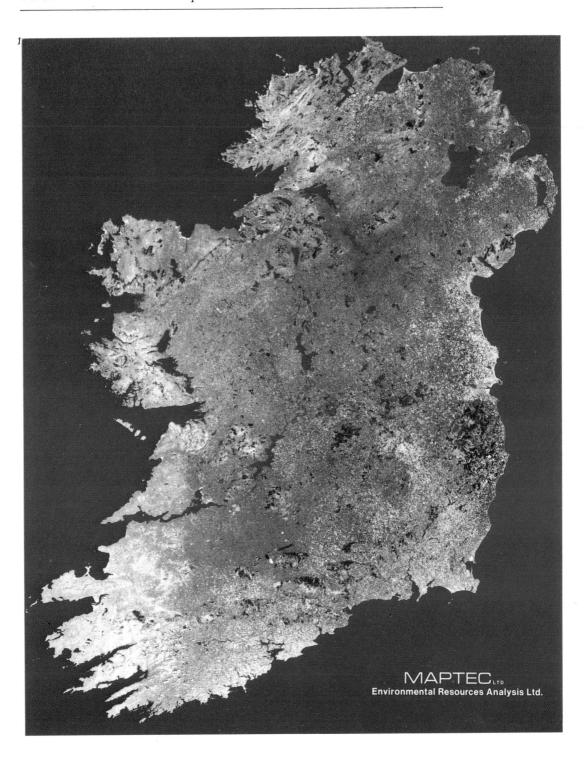

3

4

Pl. 2 Clew Bay, Co. Mayo, in winter. The quartzite peak of Croagh Patrick (765 m) is in the foreground; its scree-covered slopes are flecked with snow. In the centre are the drumlin islands of Clew Bay. Beyond are the snow-covered tops of the Nephin Beg hills. (Aerofilms)

Pl. 3 Near Aghavannagh, Co. Wicklow. Granite characteristically weathers to such rounded slopes. The blanket-bog in the foreground is planted with young conifers. Other older plantations are also seen. (Bord Fáilte)

Pl. 4 Looking north across the Mitchelstown valley to the Galty Mountains. Hercynide thrusting created east/west structures here (see Fig. 1.3). Limestone remains in the valley, but has been stripped off the mountain ridge where more resistant Old Red Sandstone stands up. (G.F. Mitchell)

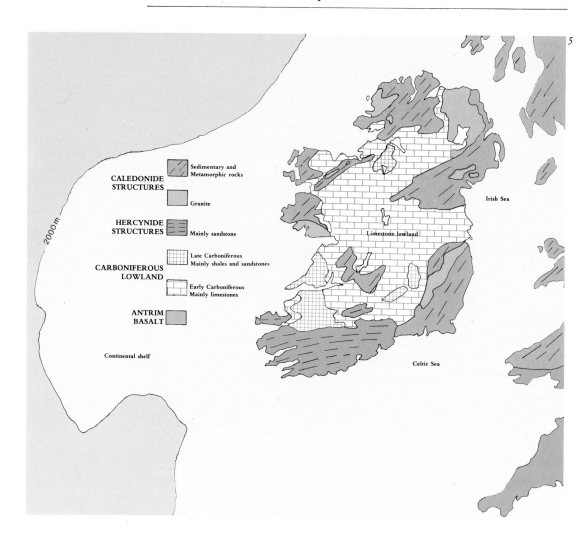

CALEDONIDE
STRUCTURES

Sedimentary and
Metamorphic rocks

Granite

HERCYNIDE
STRUCTURES

Mainly sandstone

CARBONIFEROUS
LOWLAND

Late Carboniferous
Mainly shales and sandstones

Early Carboniferous
Mainly limestones

ANTRIM
BASALT

Continental shelf

2000 m

Limestone lowland

Irish Sea

Celtic Sea

*Pl. 5   Outline geological
map of Ireland. (Dept. of
Foreign Affairs)*

*Pl. 6   Benbane Head,
Co. Antrim. On the
north coast the horizontal
sheets of basalt (which
poured out as liquid lava
sixty million years ago)
are cliffed by the sea.
Half-way down the cliff
we see a red band of
tropical soil, formed during
a lull in volcanic activity.
(Aerofilms)*

6

Pl. 7 *The hammer lies against a layer of red soil, formed when tropical rain-forest grew on the surface of a lava flow, during a pause in volcanic activity. The soil is buried by the unweathered basalt of a later flow. (G.F. Mitchell)*

Pl. 8 *The Burren, Co. Clare. Limestone, laid down in layers on the sea-floor, was in this area later raised without much lateral disturbance as almost horizontal* strata *of rock. Ice later moved over it, stripping away any projections, and leaving bare, rounded surfaces. In places the ice did deposit some of the rock-debris it had been transporting; on the lower right of the picture we see some dark-coloured remnants of such debris, which has been gullied by rain water. (Aerofilms)*

Pl. 9 Tanga, Tanzania. In tropical Africa the dissolving away of limestone by rain has gone on uninterruptedly for millions of years, resulting in deeply fretted terrain; a man shows the scale of the erosion. In the mine at Tynagh, Co. Galway, where the limestone had been protected from glacial action by an overlying layer of weathered ore, the limestone was similarly fretted. (A.J. Sutcliffe)

Pl.10 Breidamerkurjokull, Iceland. The picture looks to the melting edge of a small ice-cap. The ice is thin, and mountains can be seen standing up through it as nunataks. Central Ireland looked like this 15,000 years ago. (G.F. Mitchell)

Vegetational development in warm stages

Having summarized the developments that took place in cold stages in Ireland, we can now try to form a generalized picture of what happened in the warm episodes, which could be of minor or major duration.

When temperature rises at the end of a cold stage, the ground surface either emerges from below massive ice, or is released from the grip of frost, and soil development can start. The plants begin to return from the areas to which they had been dispersed by cold, and hardier types soon clothe the ground with vegetation. If when this point is reached the climatic trend is reversed, and the climate again gets colder, the plants will again retreat. Such minor episodes of amelioration — very many of which can be traced in the Ice Age record — have been given the rather unsatisfactory name of 'interstadial', implying a minor phase of warmth characterized by vegetation which had not developed into closed woodland, as opposed to a major episode, the 'interglacial' or 'warm stage'. Closed woodland is the climax vegetation of north-west Europe today, and if we picture that the cold of the Ice Age is over, and that we are living in the 'postglacial', then if a past stage of warmth was to merit the title of 'interglacial', corresponding in rank with the 'postglacial', it had to be of sufficient warmth and length for closed woodland to develop in it.

For classificatory purposes therefore this first phase of vegetational development will be regarded as belonging to the cold stage, which may or may not be ending, and will be called the Absence-phase (IWA) — meaning that closed woodland is absent from Ireland. If amelioration continues, and the trees return and gradually spread until they cover the whole countryside, then we enter on a true warm stage; if renewed deterioration sets in after only a short space of time, we have been merely concerned with yet another interstadial.

The events of a full warm stage are shown in diagrammatic form (Fig. 2.2); the stage is divided into phases, and each phase is given a label, e.g. IWX, in which I stands for Ireland, W stands for woodland, and X indicates the particular phase.

The return and the spreading of the trees are not simple functions of climate and of time. Even granted maximal conditions for expansion, trees will spread at different rates according to their methods of propagation. There is thus a period of immigration during which the woodlands cannot reach a position of stability, and this I call the Beginning-phase (IWB) — implying that woodland development is beginning as tree immigration proceeds. This phase opens when the first pioneer tree — in Ireland the juniper (*Juniperus*) — leads off an expansion of woodland that will continue without interruption until high forests are established.

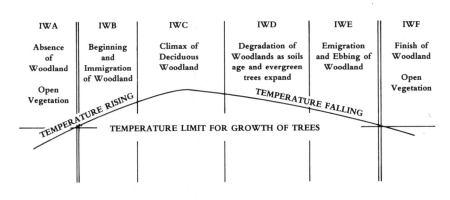

IWA	IWB	IWC	IWD	IWE	IWF
Absence of Woodland	Beginning and Immigration of Woodland	Climax of Deciduous Woodland	Degradation of Woodlands as soils age and evergreen trees expand	Emigration and Ebbing of Woodland	Finish of Woodland
Open Vegetation					Open Vegetation

TEMPERATURE RISING · TEMPERATURE FALLING

TEMPERATURE LIMIT FOR GROWTH OF TREES

Fig. 2.2 Successive phases of woodland development in a warm stage. See text for explanation of IWA etc.

Geographical barriers, such as mountain ranges and stretches of water, also affected immigration. As great ice-masses grew in cold stages they abstracted water from the oceans, and as sea-level fell Ireland would be joined to Britain, and Britain to Europe. Amelioration of climate reversed this trend, but at the beginning of the warm stage sea-level would still have been low, and immigration into Britain and Ireland would have been easy. But rising sea-level gradually reflooded the old channels, and sooner or later overland migration into Ireland was no longer possible.

The materials on which the soils of the warm stage developed had been constituted during the preceding cold stage first by the carrying away by ice or solifluction of earlier exhausted soil, and second by fresh rock being comminuted by the grinding action of ice, or by subsoil being brought to the surface through the churning action of frost processes. Thus when the warm stage opened the soil parent materials were again rich in nutrient elements, and luxuriant plant growth could quickly lead to the development of deciduous woodland. In north-west Europe deciduous trees are thought of — perhaps illogically — as giving a richer aesthetic spectacle than coniferous trees, and so woodland composed of oak (*Quercus*), lime (*Tilia*), and elm (*Ulmus*) is regarded as *climax woodland*. Accepting this outlook, we can picture this phase with tall deciduous woodlands on deep forest soils as the climax and label it IWC, the Climax-phase — with climax forest of deciduous trees.

As time progressed leaching gradually reduced the fertility of the soils, and there was a tendency to acidity, and to a replacement of the deciduous trees by conifers and heath, a process that may have been accelerated by falling temperature. Again on the perhaps mistaken aesthetic view that coniferous woods are of lower merit than deciduous, we can label this phase IWD

— the Degradation-phase — with degrading soils leading to consequent 'degradation' of the woodlands.

Sooner or later the long-term cyclical fluctuation of the Ice Age climax would start to draw the warm stage to a close, and temperatures would fall. All but the hardiest trees, in Ireland birch and pine, would be eliminated from the woodlands, and we have IWE, the Ebbing-phase — with ebbing of woodland, and disappearance of all but the hardiest trees.

A still further increase in severity of climate would cause even the boreal woods to break up, and as continuous woodland is our criterion for a warm stage, here the warm stage must end. The woodlands are finished, but some hardy herbs and grasses will struggle on in clumps which are continually shrinking in size, until even they too may be eliminated as full polar desert conditions become established. Here we move on to IWF — the Finished-phase — when the trees have fled to distant refuges, and all vegetation is on the retreat, as the rigorous climate of the next cold stage develops.

There were a considerable number of warm stages during the Ice Age and if in each warm stage the vegetational cycle and the plants which composed it had repeated themselves identically, obviously study of the plant fossils in the organic deposits of a stage could not lead to the pin-pointing of the deposit as belonging to one particular warm stage rather than any other.

But several factors worked against such simple repetition. First, the climatic conditions of each warm stage were not identical. The amount of the sun's energy received on different parts of the earth's surface does have an important effect on climate, and this amount is not constant, but is subject to several variables. The tides in the Irish Sea change every day in response to changes in the combined gravitational effects of the sun and the moon. The variables controlling the amount of solar energy received can combine with, or oppose, one another in very complicated patterns which extend over thousands of years, and each pattern has a specific climatic influence. Second, the possible migration routes of the warm stages were not identical, and animals and plants which could expand freely in one warm stage may have found their movements restricted in another. Thus there were different possibilities for vegetational developments in the different warm stages, and detailed studies may reveal key characteristics by which the particular deposits of each warm stage may be identified.

During the warm stages peats and muds slowly accumulate, trapping successive generations of pollen-grains within their deposits as they grow in thickness, and studies of the contained pollen-grains are particularly useful in revealing vegetational differences, even on a small scale. To make such a study a vertical series of samples is taken at suitable intervals from the top to the bottom of the deposit. As many types of pollen as possible are identified, and several hundred grains are counted in all. The values for the different pollens are then expressed as percentages either of their relative proportions or of the total amount (concentration) present, and the values for each sample are shown as a pollen-diagram, where the sample-values are arranged one below another, in exactly the same way as the sampled material was located in the deposit. The different values for the different pollens are expressed by bars of appropriate length. The bars may stand independently, or they may be linked to give a curve.

Within the whole column of samples a sequence, of shorter or longer length, may give broadly similar pollen-counts, indicating relatively stable plant communities throughout the period of time represented by the accumulation of the sediment from which the sequence came. The counts will be dominated by certain pollens, presumably derived from

plants that were prominent in the neighbourhood at the time, and so we can establish a type of *pollen phase* for example a hazel-pine phase, from which we draw the inference that pine and hazel were then common in the local woodlands. A second sequence of samples immediately above the first may show increased amounts of oak and elm, giving a further pollen phase, from which we can infer that relatively open woodland with pine and hazel had been replaced by denser woodland with tall deciduous trees (see Fig. 2.3).

For many years systematic pollen-counts aimed only at recording the relative proportions of the different pollens in the samples and interpretation of such figures could be very treacherous. If the amount of one pollen fell drastically in quantity, say pollen of elm due to an outbreak of disease, then the figures for the other pollens rose automatically to fill the gap, but it did not follow that the importance of the plants that produced them had increased in the local countryside. Today efforts are being made to determine the total number of pollen-grains contained in a unit-volume of a deposit, and to assess the time it took for the unit-volume to be deposited, and so form an impression of the 'absolute' amount of pollen contributed by different plants to the accumulating deposit in a given length of time. Under tundra conditions total pollen production by herbs and grasses is low, under closed woodland conditions pollen production by trees is high, and by making absolute counts it is possible to follow the expansion and contraction of the woodland cover as climate changed, as well as see how the different trees building up that cover waxed and waned in importance.

But we can only hope to make 'good' absolute counts if we can find a deposit, such as a lake-mud, which is uniform in composition and which accumulated at a uniform rate; the rate of deposition can be checked by radiocarbon datings. Our 'absolute' counts enable us to check on our 'percentage' counts, but the percentage diagram is more useful when we try to compare woodland from region to region.

In addition to pollen grains, other small fossils such as diatom skeletons and fungus spores can be identified and counted with profit. Larger fossils, wood, epidermis, seeds, insect parts, mollusc shells, often loosely called 'macrofossils', may also be preserved, and their detailed study can give a great deal of valuable information. Vertebrate bones are also of help, but because of the mobility of the typical mammal, their interpretation is often difficult.

It is thus clear that even a small amount of organic material can yield a surprising amount of information to specialized treatment, while a deposit whose thickness is measured in metres may hold a complete record of a warm stage from the first replacement of the preceding tundra, through the full development of the woodlands to their final collapse and replacement by the succeeding tundra of the next cold stage. It may also be possible to form an impression of its absolute age by determining its surviving content of radioactive carbon.*

But even after an organic deposit obviously from a warm stage has been subjected to a most meticulous examination, some ambiguity may remain as to the particular warm stage to which it should be assigned. The deposits of the cold stages also present difficulties. In all of the cold stages the action of ice and frost produced broadly similar deposits, and their appropriate assignation is difficult. The younger deposits are not neatly stacked on top of the older ones, because a younger ice-sheet could cut away older deposits, and replace them by its own ones. An ice-sheet can simultaneously deposit till in one place and meltwater sands and gravels in another, and if the ice-sheet is moving, the two types of deposit may merge laterally into one another. Life is sparse in cold stages, and fossils

are correspondingly rare. A moving ice-sheet may engulf a fossiliferous deposit, redeposit the fossils elsewhere, and so give rise to confusion.

Thus it is exceedingly difficult to sort out Ice Age deposits into their correct chronological sequence, and this difficulty obtains even within a single country, let alone on a continental or world-wide scale.

The suggested sequence of events in Ireland which follows cannot be regarded as more than tentative.

*Numerous dates based on radiocarbon age determinations (C-14 dates) are cited in this book. In recent years many efforts have been made to harmonize C-14 dates with the dates arrived at by counting the annual growth-rings of the bristlecone pine. All the dates in this book are 'raw' dates, that is to say they are the figures as issued by the dating laboratory, un-'corrected' in any way. They should be regarded as indicating an approximate age, and not a detailed date to an individual year; most are the probably accurate to about one hundred years.

The Gortian Warm Stage: 250,000 to 200,000 years ago

More than 100 years ago a distinguished Irish geologist, G.H. Kinahan, discovered 'a peaty accumulation' below a thick cover of 'glacial drift' in a river valley near Gort in Co. Galway. Pine, spruce (*Picea*) and hazel were recorded, and Kinahan considered that 'the presence of such trees in Ireland during intra-glacial times' was proved by his discovery. In 1949 the deposit was re-investigated by Knud Jessen and Svend Andersen, both experts in Danish interglacial deposits, and Tony Farrington, a Dublin glacial geologist. They confirmed that it did indeed belong to a warm stage, named then *Gortian*, very probably to the same one as that in which the famous organic deposit at Hoxne in East Anglia accumulated.

warm stage, but all these are incomplete also. However, I have put together from these partial records a schematic pollen-diagram (Fig. 2.3) to suggest the course of woodland development in Ireland through the whole stage. As the woodlands of the warm stage in which we are living have been wrecked by man's activities, it is interesting to look at an undisturbed record.

The re-investigation at Gort was done by means of a special boring, and towards the bottom of the borehole there was a change in deposit from fine sandy clay below to muddy clay above. In the sandy clay pollen of herbs and and of birch (probably the dwarf form, *Betula nana*) were common, indicating the immigration of pioneer vegetation on to still unstable soils as the

Fig. 2.3 Schematic pollen-diagram to illustrate the phases of woodland development in the Gortian Warm Stage.

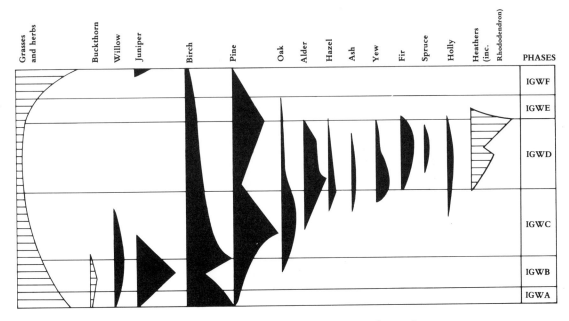

Although the Gort deposit gives its name to this warm stage in Ireland, it does not contain a record of the entire stage, as the upper part is missing, perhaps cut away by later ice, which deposited till on top of it. Bill Watts, now Provost of Trinity College, Dublin, has described other deposits which appear to belong to the same

preceding cold stage was ending. This is the Absence-phase, and on the right-hand margin of the diagram this level is marked IGWA (G being inserted to stand for Gortian) showing the approach to the Gortian Warm Stage with woodland still absent. Thus it is clear that cold conditions preceded the Gortian Warm Stage in Ireland, though we have not yet recognized deposits that belong to them.

Fig. 2.3 then shows an upsurge in pollen of juniper, presumably in response to a rise in temperature to a level sufficient to allow this tree to spread widely and to flower freely. This rise marks the beginning of woodland expansion, and the Beginning-phase (IGWB) opens the Gortian Warm Stage. Birch, juniper, pine and willow are the most important trees in this early phase.

The Climax-phase (IGWC) starts when oak appears in strength, and birch falls back. Here the climax woodland is oak and pine, with smaller amounts of alder. As the climax phase ends, hazel, ash *(Fraximus)*, yew *(Taxus)* and holly appear. The climax woods of this Gortian stage were thus very different from those of the warm stage in which we are living — the Littletonian. In these later woods elm and hazel had much greater importance.

Fir then makes its appearance, and as it increases in quantity, yew also increases. Spruce then appears.

Box *(Buxus)*, a small tree not now native in Ireland, and which we chiefly know in clipped garden hedges, spread as the larger trees disappeared. Pollen of the heather family, among which that of rhododendron is important, also appears in quantity. Here we see the trend towards soil acidity, encouraging coniferous woodland and heath, that marks the opening of the Degradation-phase (IGWD). Fir and spruce did not establish themselves in the Littletonian woodlands in Ireland, although today they are widely planted. *Rhododendron ponticum* is also here today, but only as a result of introduction in the late eighteenth century. It is clear that once introduced it found conditions ideal on Ireland's acid soils, and it has run like wildfire through woods and over upland bogs. At Killarney strenuous efforts are being made to control it. It is a classic example of a tree that had a

wider distribution in an earlier warm stage, was then driven by cold far back into Europe — it now centres to the south and west of the Black Sea, with a few outlying localities in Spain and Portugal — and has since been prevented by barriers, probably geographical in this case, from returning to areas where it formerly grew, and can again flourish after introduction by man.

Among the heaths are Mackay's heath (*Erica mackaiana*) Dorset heath (*Erica cf. ciliaris*) and St Dabeoc's heath (*Daboecia cantabrica*). Today the first two are confined to the Roundstone area of Co. Galway, while *Daboecia* occurs more widely in the same region. All have their main distribution today from south-west France to Portugal, but are found especially in the Cantabrian Mountains of Spain, where they occur in heathy woodland. There are also filmy ferns which only flourish in areas with acid soils and high rainfall. Of these the Killarney fern (*Trichomanes*) is the extreme example, as it is happiest in the spray zone of waterfalls. It used to be common in south-west Ireland, but was made almost extinct by wholesale collecting in Victorian times to supply the ferneries which were then so popular. We can safely postulate an oceanic high-rainfall climate, similar to that of south-west Ireland today, affecting all or most of Ireland.

At Derrynadivva, near Castlebar, Pete Coxon of Trinity College has carried the Gortian record almost to its end. Trees fall away, and the heathers give way give way to the crowberry (*Empetrum nigrum*). This plant seems to flourish in cold wet oceanic climates, as when the ice had finally disappeared from Ireland, and the post-glacial vegetation was endeavouring to establish itself, *Empetrum*-heaths were again well developed in western Ireland. At Derrynadivva we see the disappearance of closed vegetation (IGWE) and the establishment of tundra to herald the next cold stage.

Thus it is clear that the Gortian climax woodlands were very different from those of the current Littletonian Warm Stage, not so much in the difference in the trees present, as in the different proportions in which they were present. The later phases of the Gortian forests with fir, yew and alder and smaller amounts of spruce are, of course, unrepresented in modern Ireland, and the European woods that most resemble them today are on the southern slopes of the Caucasus. Several of the trees of those later Gortian forests have been introduced by man into Ireland — fir, spruce, hornbeam, box and rhododendron — but it is unlikely that they could have reached the country unless assisted in this way.

In all about one hundred taxa of higher plants have been identified for this warm stage, and of these about twenty are not native in Ireland today. Three that are no longer here are essentially North American in their modern distribution, and show that as the Ice Age progressed there was a progressive elimination from Europe of plants that had earlier grown freely on both sides of the Atlantic Ocean. Two water-plants, *Eriocaulon septangulare* and *Naias flexilis,* common in North America today, and recorded in the Gortian deposits, still grow in the west of Ireland.

The Munsterian Cold Stage: 200,000 to 130,000 years ago

In the Munsterian Cold Stage both frost and ice were active, but we can as yet say little about their relative importance at different parts of the stage. Head formed on an extensive scale, and there certainly was some permafrost, as shown by ice-wedge-casts on the north shore of Tralee Bay. Large ice-masses also formed, and most of Ireland was probably covered by ice in at least some part of the stage, though limited areas of higher ground in the south and west may have remained ice-free, rising as *nunataks* above the surrounding ice.

An enormous elongated dome of ice, oriented north-east/south-west, lay across central Mayo, and from it ice flowed freely to south and west (Fig. 2.4). A second elongated ice-dome, oriented east/west, lay across central Tyrone; this ice moved easily north and west over Donegal, but on the south-west met Mayo ice moving in the opposite direction. Mutual deflection took place, and the joint ice-streams moved north-west into Donegal Bay, and south-east across the midlands.

The Tyrone ice also met opposition on the north-east, where it was met by ice of Scottish origin. Scotland is larger

Fig. 2.4 General directions of ice-sheet movement in Ireland during the Munsterian (A) and Midlandian (B) cold stages. (Based on work of McCabe)

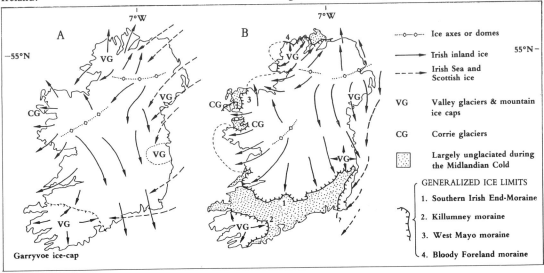

A — Garryvoe ice-cap

---o---o--- Ice axes or domes
———→ Irish inland ice
– – –→ Irish Sea and Scottish ice
VG   Valley glaciers & mountain ice caps
CG   Corrie glaciers
▓   Largely unglaciated during the Midlandian Cold

GENERALIZED ICE LIMITS
1. Southern Irish End-Moraine
2. Killumney moraine
3. West Mayo moraine
4. Bloody Foreland moraine

than Ireland, and has much higher mountains, and its ice-caps were correspondingly greater. South-west-flowing Scottish ice was powerful enough to surmount the cliffed edge of the Antrim coast, and push inland for a certain distance, before it was halted by the Tyrone ice, which turned aside to flow north and south. It is not difficult to document the Scottish ice, because in order to reach Ireland it had to cross a stretch of sea-floor. Here it picked up fine-grained calcareous marine clays and also the fossil shells that they contained, and when it melted away it deposited a till which was fine in texture and speckled with shell-debris. South-flowing Scottish ice found a ready-made exit down the North Channel and the Irish Sea basin. We can picture an enormous *mer-de-glace* flowing along between Britain and Ireland, pushing laterally inland where coasts were low, and being deflected where there were blocks of higher ground, as in the Mourne and Wicklow Mountains on the west, and in the Lake District and Snowdonia on the east. The massifs carried independent ice-caps of their own, and these added a contribution to the passing Scottish ice. Once it had passed Carnsore Point in Wexford and St David's Head in Wales the ice fanned out. In Britain it flowed along the Cornish coast to reach its outer limit in the Isles of Scilly. In Ireland it turned west along the coast to reach its limit in Ballycotton Bay just east of Cork Harbour. We can be quite positive that it did get as far as Cork because it carried with it as an erratic a very specialized Scottish rock-type. Ailsa Craig rises as a rock-cone in the Firth of Clyde; the rock which composes it is an unusual type of granite, fine in grain and containing rare minerals which give it a characteristic blue-green hue, making it easily recognizable. Ailsa Craig shed great quantities of this rock into the passing ice, and some of it was transported as far as the Cork coast, where it was recognized by a famous Irish geologist, W.B. Wright, more than eighty years ago.

Irish ice-centres were still active after the Scottish ice had ceased to advance, because on the Waterford coast shelly till of Scottish origin is covered by a till containing only Irish rocks. At Garryvoe in Ballycotton Bay where the Scottish till is at its limit, it is covered by a till containing rocks from farther west in Cork and Kerry.

The mountains of Cork and Kerry carried their own ice-cap, perhaps centred over the Derrynasaggart Mountains. To the west and south the ice flowed freely towards the sea. On the east it reached its limit at Garryvoe; on the north it abutted against ice of northern inland origin.

If we try to form a general picture of Ireland during the Munsterian Cold Stage, our main impression is of great masses of ice waxing and waning from time to time in different parts of the country, with only small patches of higher ground here and there remaining ice-free. But before it was buried by ice, low-lying ground, even along the shore of the Atlantic Ocean, was experiencing cold polar desert climate with permafrost and ice-wedges, while on higher ground conditions will have been still more severe; under these circumstances only the hardiest of plants and animals could have survived.

Where then were the temperate trees and shrubs that had clothed Ireland during the Gortian Warm Stage? They can only have survived to the south or the west. To the south conditions warm enough for their survival probably did not exist north of the Pyrenees, though they could have found refuges in Spain or Portugal. What about the west? Sea-level probably fell by substantially more than 100 m during the Munsterian Cold Stage, as water was extracted from the oceans to build up great masses of terrestrial ice, and along much of western Europe the fall exposed broad expanses of the continental shelf on which severe climatic conditions would have obtained. But off the mountains of

Kerry and Connemara the steeper slopes continue seawards, slopes that even with a lower sea-level might have continued to receive the full force of the Gulf Stream. Here ridges and valleys provided shelter, slopes drained the soils, the aspect was favourable, and oceanic waters may have provided a moderating influence. Could there have been small refuges with favourable micro-climates off these areas?

We have seen that there was a considerable range of species of heather in Gortian Ireland, and that several of the same species are in Ireland today. Have they returned from Spain and Portugal after each cold stage, or did they find refuge closer at hand? In Ireland today most of the localities for the rarer heathers lie west of the 5°C mean January isotherm, and this may be their limiting temperature. The glacial coast was perhaps 35 km west of and 100 m lower than the modern coasts where the ice-wedge-casts are now seen. The presence of the casts implies a −12°C mean January temperature, and it seems difficult to conceive of a temperature gradient of more than 15°C in such a short vertical range, and such a gradient would appear to be necessary if the heathers were to survive. In picturing such a gradient, I am assuming that the Gulf Stream did maintain its influence in the Munsterian. But it has now been shown that at the end of the last cold stage arctic waters did displace the Gulf Stream, and produced very severe climatic conditions along the Atlantic coast of Ireland. If it was the same in the Munsterian, the possibilities for survival must have been remote. On the other hand in support of the concept of a refuge off the present coast of Connemara, where the offshore slopes are steep and the heathers have their main concentration, we may note that Donegal, similar in general terrain and vegetation to Connemara, but without steep offshore slopes, is today very much poorer in heathers.

The Glenavian Warm Stage: more than 40,000 years ago

It has long been known that the depression in which the modern Lough Neagh lies is of very considerable antiquity, holding deposits that are up to 50 million years old. Some of these deposits are brown coals or *lignites,* that is to say accumulated vegetable debris which has lost only some of its volatile hydrocarbons and still retains quite a lot of woody structure, in contrast to fully matured coal which has lost almost all its volatiles, and whose woody structure has disintegrated in the shrinkage that took place when the coarse vegetable debris was compacted into dense coal.

It is now proposed to mine the lignite by open-cast workings with power-shovels, and burn it in a nearby power-station, thus making possible the production of cheap electricity, which would be of tremendous economic importance. The lignite lies below a relatively thin overburden of Ice Age deposits, and at a place called Aghnadarragh on the east shore of Lough Neagh, not far from the village of Glenavy, these have been stripped off over an area of some acres, so that the lignite can be studied more closely.

The deposits exposed are of great interest, and preliminary studies suggest that among them are some that belong to a late warm stage. As the deposits of an older warm stage have taken their name from the town of Gort, I have given a provisional name, *Glenavian,* to these deposits from the nearby village, Glenavy.

A till rests on the lignite. Above this is a gravel which has yielded a number of elephant molar teeth, pieces of tusk, some large, many small, and some broken large bones, probably elephant also.

These fossils appear to belong to the woolly mammoth (*Elephas primigenius*). We have seen that the Ice Age was not sufficiently long for significant evolutionary development to have taken place, but the elephants are a group which were undergoing rapid change at that time. The woolly mammoth had, as its name implies, a hairy coat, in contrast to the two surviving members of the once very much larger elephant group, the African and the Indian forms, which have naked skins. The hairy coat was in two layers, short woolly hair near the skin, and longer bristly hair on parts of the body. Though extinct, the woolly mammoth is well known, both because frozen carcasses have survived in Siberia, and because Palaeolithic artists made engravings of them on ivory. European evidence suggests that the woolly mammoth did not appear until the middle of a late interglacial warm stage, and this gives a pointer to the age of the deposit. Thus at Glenavy we do not have any record of the beginning of the warm stage; we only get a glimpse of its later phases.

Above the gravel there is a series of sands, and at some horizons in this there are seams of washed-in vegetable debris, in some places rolled pieces of wood, chiefly spruce and pine, in others thin layers of spruce cones. There are also fruits of hazel and yew. Beetle remains are common. The organic material was over 40,000 years old.

Higher still the sands become finer, and contain lenses of mud which was deposited in small open-water ponds under cold conditions. Cold is clearly indicated by the presence of leaves of the least willow (*Salix herbacea*), abundant in northern latitudes, and only surviving on mountain tops in Ireland, and the dwarf birch (*Betula nana*), also a northern plant, now extinct in Ireland.

At the top of the section there is till, giving clear evidence of the later advance of ice over the area.

*Fig. 2.5 The superimposed lines show the areas within which yew (*Taxus*) and hazel (*Corylus*) flourish in modern Europe. They are trees of the central European forests, and avoid northern latitudes.*

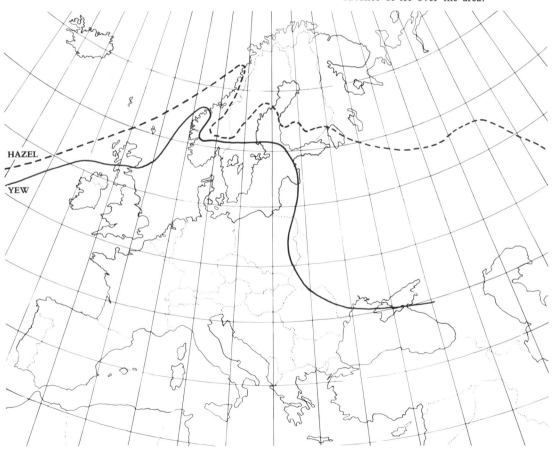

What conclusions can we draw from the limited range of fossils found at Aghnadarragh? Unfortunately most of them are not in primary position, but have been transported — though probably not very far — by running water. Yew is a tree indicative of a mild oceanic climate, intolerant of frost and limited in its distribution by winter cold. It is absent from eastern Europe, and does not go north of the Gulf of Bothnia. Hazel can tolerate slightly colder conditions, and so it goes a little farther to the east, and creeps north on the coasts of the Baltic and the Atlantic (Fig. 2.5). The beetle evidence is more definite; of the fifty forms found, many do not go north of the Gulf of Bothnia, and there is a complete absence of high northern species. The beetles suggest that temperature lay between:

July mean   + 15°C to + 18°C
January mean − 11°C to + 4°C

Armagh lies within a few kilometres of Aghnadarragh; today's temperatures there are:

July mean   + 15.5°C
January mean + 4°C

At Aghnadarragh the climate was much as today, and today yew and hazel find their home in temperate closed woodland. If — as I have already said — temperate woodland is the prerogative of a warm period, then I have to say here we are dealing with a warm stage, and not an interstadial.

I place the Aghnadarragh deposit at the point where the climax woodland of a warm stage is beginning to deteriorate and give way to coniferous forest. And this is the point at which yew is most common at Gort, and hazel is only beginning to give way. But there is insufficient evidence to equate this deposit with any particular warm stage noted elsewhere. I only say that I believe there was a Glenavian Warm Stage, and that because of the presence of woolly mammoth, it must fall late in the sequence of warm stages.

The Midlandian Cold Stage: 75,000 to 10,000 years ago

There would seem to be a consensus of opinion that the last cold stage, called in Ireland the *Midlandian,* because its deposits are well displayed in the midlands, set in about 75,000 years ago. When did it end? The radiocarbon method of dating cannot carry us back beyond 40,000 years ago, but as we move from that age towards the present it becomes increasingly accurate. The final ebbing of Midlandian cold and the beginning of the uninterrupted return of the temperate animals and plants that we have in Ireland today is dated by the radiocarbon method to about 10,000 years ago. So 10,000 years ago has been accepted as the boundary line between the Midlandian Cold Stage and the warm stage in which we are living. A raised-bog near Littleton in Co. Tipperary gave a continuous pollen-record of the local vegetation from 10,000 years ago almost to the present day, and as this is the most complete record we have of vegetational changes in the current warm stage, we call it the *Littletonian* Warm Stage.

After 40,000 years have elapsed the original content of radioactive carbon in any organic material has sunk to a level that cannot be accurately interpreted. In this book I have decided rightly or wrongly to use periods of years for dividing up the past, and I do the same for the Midlandian. And so we have:

75,000 to 40,000 years ago — events that are beyond the reach of radiocarbon, but are probably Midlandian.

40,000 to 13,000 years ago — events that are dated by radiocarbon to this interval; ice-bodies are thought to have made their last expansion about 15,000 years ago.

13,000 to 10,000 years ago — final developments between the completion of major ice-retreat and the opening of the Littletonian Warm Stage.

75,000 to 40,000 years ago
Glacial deposits are usually lacking in fossils, and can only be dated relative to datable organic deposits lying above or below them, or, in miraculous situations, both above and below. In Ireland within the area glaciated during the Midlandian Cold Stage we have several well-marked lines of moraines which must indicate important re-advances or stillstands of ice, but we have so far found only two organic horizons to help us.

Much of Co. Fermanagh is covered by drumlins which are probably of late Midlandian age. At Hollymount, near Lisnaskea, a river has cut a small cliff in the flank of a drumlin; beneath the till of the drumlin there is a silt with washed-in vegetable debris with an age of more than 40,000 years derived from a tundra landscape. The silt passes down into arctic clay, and this rests directly on unweathered till.

Another 'more than 40,000 years' date is more difficult. Over 100 years ago Mr Edward Brenan of Dungarvan saw 'giant's bones' being paraded through the streets of the town. He quickly saw that the bones could not be those of a human giant, but were elephant bones. Asking where they came from, he was directed to Shandon Cave on the outskirts of the town where limestone-quarrying was in progress. He found the cave richly strewn with bones, and the following mammals were identified:

Woolly mammoth, *Elephas primigenius*
Bear (perhaps more than one kind),
    Ursus sp. (spp. ?)
Wild horse, *Equus ferus* (Pl. 11)
Hare, *Lepus sp.*

A radiocarbon test of a horse bone indicated an age of greater than 40,000 years. A similar test on a mammoth bone failed to give a result. The date immediately raises the question, is the Shandon fauna early Midlandian or is it late Glenavian, as mammoth remains also occurred at Aghnadarragh?

40,000 to 13,000 years ago
West of Shandon, and not very far away, we have in the Blackwater valley another cave in limestone at Castlepook, close to Doneraile. The fauna was richer than at Shandon, but the bones did not lie as originally deposited, as they had been redistributed by later running water. Bones of the mammoth were very common, ranging in size from adult to unborn foetus; one bone was dated to 33,500 years ago. The cave also produced the only bones of the spotted hyena so far found in Ireland; one bone was dated to 34,400 years ago. The cave contained some recent animal bones, brought in by modern foxes, but the Midlandian fauna can probably be listed as follows:

Woolly mammoth, *Elephas primigenius*
Brown bear, *Ursus arctos*
Spotted hyena, *Crocuta crocuta*
Wolf, *Canis lupus*
Arctic fox, *Alopex lagopus*
Irish giant deer, *Megaloceros giganteus*
Reindeer, *Rangifer tarandus*
Mountain hare, *Lepus timidus*
Norwegian lemming, *Lemmus lemmus*
Greenland lemming, *Dicrostonyx*
    torquatus.

We find it hard to imagine Ireland with these animals wandering through it. What did the landscape look like under interstadial conditions? At Shandon and Castlepook we are south of the limits of Midlandian ice. The caves are in the limestone of the Blackwater valley, where there will have been both shelter and fertile soil materials, and we probably had rich grasslands with scattered copses of birch and willow, where the mammoth and the giant deer browsed and grazed, and the bear and the hyena prowled around scavenging. The tree growth cannot have been dense, because the giant deer could not cope with closed woodland. On the other hand bare tundra would probably not have provided sufficient food for the mammoth, and although the Ice Age range of the hyena went farther than that of today, it is doubtful if it pushed up into the tundra zone.

The conditions thus described are those of the typical interstadial. Had the time period been long enough and the climate sufficiently favourable for high forest to have formed then we would have been talking about interglacial or full warm stage conditions. As it is we had a shorter time interval and only open woodland.

We have a later stage of the same interstadial recorded by plant material at Derryvree in Co. Fermanagh, not far away from the Hollymount site, which is more than 40,000 years old. Here a road-straightening operation cut right through a drumlin, and underneath the till of the drumlin there was a thin layer of mud and moss-peat that contained tundra forms of plants and beetles, with a radiocarbon age of 30,500 years, 3000 years younger than Castlepook. The climate had deteriorated as the interstadial was coming to an end. The organic material rested on unweathered till, probably of early Midlandian age.

From the preceding pages it will have become regrettably clear .that in Ireland so far dated organic horizons cannot be of much assistance when we try to elucidate the waxing and waning of ice-masses during the Midlandian Cold Stage (see Fig. 2.4).

As in the Munsterian Cold Stage, but on a much smaller scale, we appear to have had an elongated western ice-dome, though with its axis a little farther to the south-east, running from Galway city to Castlerea in Co. Roscommon. We had another elongated dome to the north, lying along much the same line as its predecessor, from Belfast to Donegal town. Scottish ice advanced again, and though it did not surmount the Antrim coast, it forced the east-flowing Irish ice to turn to north and to south. It sent a lobe down the Irish Sea, depositing clay-rich till in coastal

Wicklow and Wexford, but barely managed to round the corner at Carnsore Point, failing to advance farther westwards than the Saltee Islands. In Britain it did not cross the Bristol Channel.

The Irish inland ice advanced down through the midlands (from which the cold stage takes its name) to reach its limit along an arcuate line from Kilrush on the Shannon estuary down to Tipperary town and then curving back to reach the east coast at Wicklow Head. Well-developed morainic features mark most of its course; these were first noted by Carvill Lewis, a distinguished American glacial geologist, as long ago as 1894, and were given further precision by J.K. Charlesworth, Professor of Geology in Queen's University, Belfast in 1928 as the 'South Irish End-moraine'. From its outer limits the ice shrank irregularly, sometimes maintaining a stillstand, sometimes re-advancing. As it retreated it left till, morainic mounds of sand and gravel, sheets of outwash gravels and eskers in its wake.

As we have already seen, the total amount of water on the earth is constant. If all the ice currently on the earth's surface were to melt, sea-level would rise substantially, and all the great ports of the world would be in serious trouble. Conversely if ice-masses increase in volume sea-level must fall. About 15,000 years ago sea-level fell to the lowest point reached during the last cold stage, and this must mean that very substantial masses of ice were then present on the earth. The amount of ice in Ireland also increased at this time, and the ice-margins showed a very considerable advance, reaching in the midlands a line which ran from the Shannon estuary to Dundalk Bay. To the north-west the ice must have been rather thinner, because on the whole it failed to overrun higher ground, and rather followed lower corridors wherever they offered an escape route. Thus the present sites of Galway Bay, Clew Bay, Sligo Bay and Gweebara Bay

Photograph 12 During the last warm stage the granite of the Three Rock Mountain, Co. Dublin, was partly rotted by chemical weathering to some depth. The mountain was a nunatak in the Midlandian Cold Stage, and freeze-thaw activity moved the rotted material downslope, leaving masses of solid rock standing up as tors, and rounded core-stones scattered about.

Photograph 13 Killiney Hill, Co. Dublin, also of granite, was overrun by Midlandian ice, which carried away the rotted material, and abraded the solid rock, turning upstanding blocks into streamlined roches moutonnées. The ice was moving from left to right; it cut away the upstream side of the rock in the foreground, leaving it smoothed and rounded, but plucked blocks off the downstream side, giving it sharp outlines. The rock behind shows the same shape.

were all occupied by lobes of ice. When the ice crossed Sligo Bay, it picked up shells, and deposited these in till at Belderg. The shells have an age of 17,000 years proving the late date of the ice advance. On the north-east there was again collision with Scottish ice, but when retreat set in after 15,000 years ago the Scottish ice gained some dominance, and pushed inland past Ballycastle as far as Armoy.

For some quite unexplained reason the ice of this last advance at some stage of its development moulded the underlying deposits it gave rise to into drumlins, so much so that Francis Synge of the Irish Geological Survey was tempted to call it the Drumlin Advance. Numbering thousands, the drumlins were often aligned in serried ranks, giving rise to the so-called 'basket-of-eggs' topography. In areas of lower topography they blocked the surface drainage routes and were often surrounded by standing water. Thousands of years later when separated by water and covered by dense woodland, they provided a severe obstacle to man's lines of communication. As the sea at the time the drumlins were formed was far below its present level, many were formed below modern sea-level, and are today being attacked by the waves, as in Strangford Lough and Clew Bay.

There were also small independent ice-caps in the Wicklow Mountains and in the mountains of Cork and Kerry. The southern ice-cap did not, unlike its Munsterian predecessor, get as far east as Cork harbour, but built up its end-moraine at Kilumney, west of the city. The sand and gravel at the moraine are being rapidly quarried away for building work in Cork. The ice again reached Tralee Bay, and to the south-west flowed freely seawards. It produced drumlins, and these are very striking around Bantry. There were also active corrie and valley glaciers in the Dingle peninsula and in Achill Island.

When the Midlandian ice finally

disappeared, many of the areas it had covered presented an essentially 'young' landscape, that is they showed either features associated with recent ice scouring and moulding, or features associated with ice deposition — unweathered till, steeply sloping drumlins, and sharp-sided eskers. What of the areas that were not glaciated during the Midlandian, but had been covered by Munsterian ice? In many parts of Ireland rock was left exposed at the surface of the ground. Throughout the following warm period the rock was subject to chemical attack, a type of attack to which granite is particularly vulnerable. Earth movements bring about cracking in solid rock, and very often more than one set of cracks or *joints* intersect, so that the upper layers of the granite can be pictured as a mass of closely packed, if somewhat irregular, cubes, rather than as solid rock. Water percolates along the cracks, and from them its chemical attack moves out into the stone, being especially severe at the corners of the cubes.

The upper part of the rock thus becomes a weathered mush of loose debris, which contains within itself, like currants in a cake, the rounded blocks or *core-stones* of intact rock which had survived in the centre of the cubes. The contact between the weathered rind and the solid rock below is often irregular, again due to the influence of the joint-pattern.

When the Midlandian Cold Stage came on, and freeze-thaw processes again became active, the superficial weathered debris crept away downslope. The core-stones were left behind, littering the surface, while prominences on the irregular surface of the solid rock stood up as *tors*. If a granitic area escapes being overrun by ice, as was the case with the Bloody Foreland in Donegal and the Three-rock Mountain south of Dublin (Photo 12), then the core-stones and the tors will still survive. Where the granite was overrun by ice, as was the case with Killiney Hill near Dublin,

the core-stones have been carried off, and the upstanding tors have been drastically abraded and turned into elongated rounded bosses, the elongation being parallel with the direction of ice-movement. Such bosses of abraded rock, from which the direction of ice-movement can be deduced, are known to the geologist as *roches mountonnées,* because nineteenth-century observers thought their outline resembled that of a *moutonnée,* a type of sheepskin wig then in fashion (Photo 13).

Other types of rock, though also full of cracks were not so sensitive to chemical attack. The water in the cracks expanded on freezing, and so prised off blocks and fragments which crept away downslope to accumulate as a *scree* of loose stones or *head* at lower levels. Croagh Patrick in Mayo (Pl. 2) and Errigal in Donegal (see Photo 3) are surrounded by masses of scree.

When the Munsterian ice melted away, it also had left behind it irregular deposits in a 'young' landscape. In their case their vulnerability to Midlandian freeze-thaw activity depended largely on the relative amounts of clay, silt, sand and gravel that they contained. Sands and gravels are not easily affected, and some eskers and kames of Munsterian age still stand with quite steep slopes. But where clay and silt dominated, freeze-thaw processes could mobilize the materials, and given the necessary degree of slope, great solifluction-flows would be set in motion, only coming to a halt in lake-basins, valley-bottoms and similar places where the necessary gradient was no longer available. On these stretches of flatter ground polygonal patterns and involutions would develop.

Thus in the areas, largely in Munster, where freeze-thaw and not glacial conditions dominated during the Midlandian Cold Stage, there is on the whole an 'older' smoother landscape, where sections usually show erected stones, involutions and head, whereas

farther north where there was Midlandian ice the topography is 'younger' and more irregular, and sections rarely show the churning action of frost. This concept of areas of 'Newer Drift', with steep slopes and open lake-basins, as opposed to 'Older Drift' with more gentle slopes and only rare open-water lakes, was much used by older generations of glacial geologists. The concept has rather fallen into disrepute, but I think it should not be too lightly discarded. The contrast in the two landscapes is sometimes quite striking. Midlandian ice advanced down the Shannon estuary as far as Scattery Island in midstream and Ballylongford on the south shore. Within the Midlandian limit around Ballylongford we have hummocky topography and well-drained soils; outside the limit — and with an abrupt change — we have smooth slopes of poorly drained soils, heavily infested with rushes (*Juncus* spp).

In the Midlandian Cold Stage much of the south of Ireland was never covered by ice, and most of the rest of the country was probably only physically covered by ice for relatively short periods. Was there any plant or animal life at this time? Our Fermanagh evidence from the north of Ireland shows that before 40,000 years ago at Hollymount, and 30,000 years ago at Derryvree, there was a sparse treeless vegetation of tundra type with beetles characteristic of a cold climate with very severe winters. Some of the northern plants recorded in Fermanagh, such as

Fringed sandwort, *Arenaria ciliata*
Mountain avens, *Dryas octopetala*
Mountain sorrel, *Oxyria digyna*
Least willow, *Salix herbacea*
Purple saxifrage, *Saxifraga oppositifolia*

still maintain a precarious foothold in Ireland.

The most important modern habitats for such plants in Ireland today are the cliffs and screes around the limestone blocks that rise to over 500 m in Co.

Sligo, principally those around Ben Bulbin (see Photo 1). These blocks were probably not overridden by ice at any phase of the Midlandian, and provided *nunatak* refuges at times of ice advance. Slieve League, a quartzite peak with screes that rises to 600 m on the north shore of Donegal Bay, was also a nunatak and also has northern plants. If these plants could survive on nunataks in the north part of the country, they will also have survived in suitable habitats in the ice-free areas of Munster.

Thus 'cold polar desert' is perhaps too stern a term by which to describe Ireland during the Midlandian Cold Stage, if by 'polar desert' we mean a *tabula rasa* from which all life has been swept away. At the peaks of cold there may have been very little life, but for much of the stage the landscape will have been strewn with scanty patches of arctic-alpine plants, with some beetles in ponds and patches of vegetable debris. In the interstadial represented by the Castlepook fauna conditions must have been relatively genial, at least in areas with favourable aspect and fertile, well-drained soils. If they were to live and breed in the country, the woolly mammoths must have had access to substantial quantities of fodder. It may have been possible for the hardier reindeer to survive in Ireland throughout the cold stage.

After 15,000 years ago the annual supply of snow to the ice-sheets gradually fell away, and the ice first became stagnant, and then started a long melt-out until it had totally disappeared about 2000 years later. There was only a very limited amount of plant-life, probably consisting of very sparse, scattered herbs in a landscape in which bare soil still predominated.

The absence of large mammals and of Palaeolithic man

In marked contrast to Ireland, where we have only very limited mammalian faunas, many parts of the world have rich faunas which often assist in deciphering Ice Age events. In England good assemblages are known from several warm stages, while the Irish record is almost blank. Most of the mammalian finds come from river gravels, or from cave deposits. Much of the south of England was never covered by ice, and river gravels containing mammalian bones continued to build up over a long period. In Ireland the ice cover was extensive, even in Midlandian times, and nearly every major valley outside the ice limit served as a meltwater discharge channel into a sea whose level was much below that of today, so that any earlier gravels the valleys may have contained were scoured away. Ireland has no interglacial gravels such as those in Trafalgar Square in London, which have produced abundant remains of lion, hyena, rhinoceros, elephant and hippopotamus.

The Carboniferous limestone of Ireland contains many caves, but most of the limestone is at a relatively low altitude. All the limestone areas were probably overrun by ice during the Munsterian, and by far the greater part was again overrun during the Midlandian. When the ice stagnated, and meltwater was draining downwards, many cave systems served as escape routes for meltwater, and any deposits they contained were in part grossly disturbed and in part completely carried away. Nevertheless when all this has been said, it must be admitted that there are in the Lee and lower Blackwater valleys in Cork many cave systems which it would seem could have provided shelter for interglacial mammals, and where the bones might have escaped disturbance. But despite sporadic excavation over the past hundred years, no temperate faunas, such as those that occur in the caves of Devon, have been found.

Much of the cave excavation of the late nineteenth century in Ireland was directed towards the discovery of 'Early Man', and it must at once be said that all the excavators went disappointed. In the first half of this century there was a revival of interest in the search, and various claims were made. Limestone flakes from Co. Sligo were claimed by some to be the handiwork of Palaeolithic man, but were dismissed as entirely natural by others. Kilgraeny Cave, Co. Waterford, produced human remains in apparent association with bones of the giant deer, but a later re-examination of the cave showed that the deposits in some places had been considerably disturbed. Radiocarbon dating of some of the human bones claimed to be early indicated that they were Neolithic, rather than Mesolithic or Palaeolithic in age.

A recent chance find has drawn attention to the problem once more. When examining the glacial gravel of Irish Sea origin and of Munsterian age that occurs in a big quarry near Drogheda, Co. Louth, I picked up from its stripped surface a large coarsely struck flint flake (Fig. 2.6), which showed some signs of having been rolled and abraded by running water. It cannot be claimed that the object was *in situ* when I found it, but it would strain credibility to think that someone had dropped it on the recently stripped

gravel surface a short time before my visit. Also the rolling is most easily explained if the flake belonged to the gravel, and had been rolled along with it.

On the assumption that the flake did belong to the gravel, I brought it to Gail Sieveking in the British Museum. He is satisfied that although the flake is no more than a piece of knapper's waste, it was struck by a technique that was in vogue in southern England in Palaeolithic time. Palaeolithic implements are common in the south of England, but thin out rapidly northwards; a few have been found in central England. The Drogheda flake shows that the Palaeolithic hunters pushed still farther north-westwards, out into what is now the basin of the Irish Sea. When in Munsterian time ice was advancing southwards from Scotland the flake — along with stones and other debris — was first picked up by the ice, and was subsequently washed out of the melting ice by currents which deposited it in gravel on the Irish coast.

While the occurrence of this worked flake in Co. Louth cannot be claimed to establish the presence of Palaeolithic man in Ireland, it does show that in Britain he wandered sufficiently far to the west to reach the basin of the Irish Sea.

Fig. 2.6 Palaeolithic flint flake from near Drogheda, Co. Louth: **a** *bulbar surface;* **b** *dorsal surface;* **c** *striking-platform.*

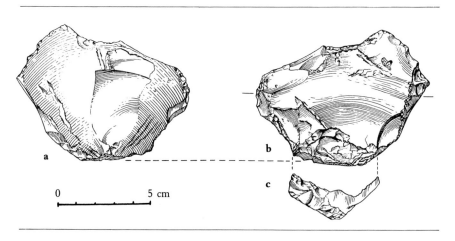

0   5 cm

3

THE END OF
THE ICE AGE:
13,000 to 10,000
years ago

**The Woodgrange Interstadial
and the re-invasion of Ireland
by plants and animals,
including the giant deer:
13,000 to 11,000 years ago**
About 13,000 years ago an amelioration
of climate set in, and as the
vegetational changes that followed have
been best documented in a pollen-
diagram from Woodgrange, Co.
Down, we can speak of the
Woodgrange Interstadial or Warm
Phase; it was no more than an
interstadial as it was followed by a
return to very cold conditions.

The vegetational developments of the
interstadial were not merely an
expansion of the plants that were
already in Ireland; there was a massive
immigration of new plants — and also
of animals. Such easy movements into
Ireland imply that land connections that
made immigration possible must have
existed. When discussing the flora and
fauna of isolated islands, the question
whether land-bridges formerly existed
or not, or whether all forms of life
arrived by chance opportunities for
migration is a very controversial one.
To me it appears that chance
opportunities must have been rare, and
that it would have taken chance a very
long time to introduce a wide range of
animals and plants. But as we shall see
shortly, in the course of no more than
one thousand years a very large number
of animals and plants entered Ireland,
and in my opinion there must have
been land-bridges to make this rapid
entry possible.

The existence of land-bridges implies a
relatively lower sea-level. Where was
sea-level as the Midlandian Cold Stage
was drawing to an end? The ice in
Ireland was only a tiny fraction of the
enormous ice-masses that were on the
earth's surface at the time, and as the
water in the ice had ultimately come
from the oceans, global sea-level was
low. Fifteen thousand years ago, when
Irish ice had its last advance, sea-level
was about 130 m, say 450 ft, below its
present level. Such a change in level
caused by the abstraction of water from
the oceans is called *eustatic*. From that
low level it rose steadily as melting ice
returned water to the sea until about
5000 years ago, when it stood about
4 m above its present level. Since then
there have been minor oscillations, not
as yet clearly understood, ending up —
temporarily at least — at the present
level.

In recent years scientists have become
increasingly interested in tracing the
history of sea-level change, and detailed
studies, chiefly on oceanic coral islands,
have made it possible to draw up a
graph of sea-level changes with time
(Fig. 3.1).

But before we leap to conclusions, two
complications have to be reckoned
with. In connection with plate tectonics
we saw that the continents appear to be
floating in a more dense substratum. If
we load an empty ship, the hull of the
ship sinks lower into the water; if we
load ice onto a land-mass, the land
sinks below the weight; when the ice
melts, the land slowly recovers. If the
sea abuts against the land-mass, their
relative levels change as the land sinks

Fig. 3.1 Outline curve to indicate possible course of sea-level during the last 40,000 years.

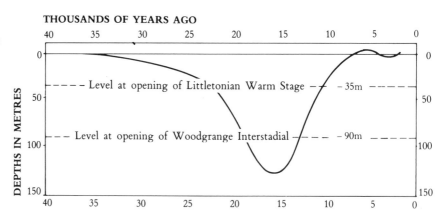

Photograph 14 Near Malin Head, Co. Donegal, Ballyhillin village lies along the curved crest of a Late Midlandian beach, raised by isostatic uplift to about 20 m above modern sea-level. From the crest the beach gravels slope seawards, with unfenced strip-fields on them. When about 5000 years ago sea-level rose eustatically about 4 m above its present level, its waves cut cliffs in the earlier beach gravels; more gravel was laid down as the waves retreated.

and rises; such relative changes are called *isostatic*.

The second complication is that when the melting ice-sheets were returning water to the sea and its level was rising as it flooded the land, waves and tides will have altered, perhaps drastically, the topography of the land-surface as they advanced. Loose deposits of sand and gravel, such as we find in eskers and moraines, will have been particularly vulnerable.

West Scotland and north-east Ireland were heavily pressed down by ice, perhaps by as much as 30 m, 15,000 years ago. As the ice melted, two things happened. The land started to rise isostatically, and sea-level started to rise eustatically. At first the rate of rise

of sea-level exceeded the land-level rise, and the waves cut narrow platforms and deposited beaches along its shore. But as time went on land-level rise became the faster, and the early beaches were carried up by continuing isostatic rise out of the reach of the waves, to become raised beaches. At Malin Head, the most northerly point in Ireland, the highest raised beach is now 20 m above modern sea-level (Photo 14).

This means that, as far as a possible land-bridge between Malin Head and Islay is concerned, we should have on our sketch-map (Fig. 3.2) in this area not a − 90 m depth-line, but a − 120 m line, because sea-floor was then 30 m below its present level when the sea-floor survey was made. The land-connection will have been

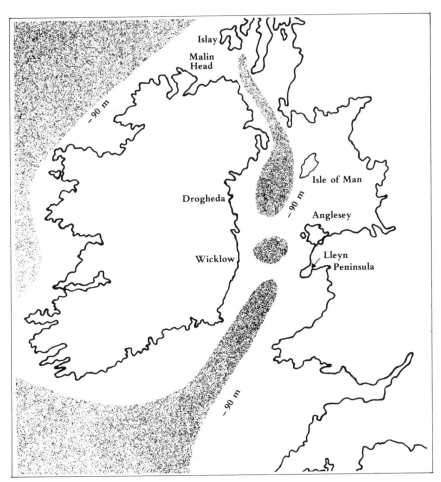

Fig. 3.2 Sketch-map to indicate possible locations of land-bridges between Ireland and Great Britain during the late Midlandian Cold Stage and the early Littletonian Warm Stage.

correspondingly narrower than the map suggests, if indeed it existed at all.

But between Wicklow and the Lleyn Peninsula, where we are far south of the main weight of the ice-mass, subsequent isostatic uplift has been much smaller, and a ridge on the sea-floor, almost certainly of morainic origin, will have stood above sea-level. North of the ridge the sea-floor drops into a basin, and then rises again to a level less than 90 m below present sea-level. The Solway Firth, Morecambe Bay and Liverpool Bay would have been dry, with the Isle of Man rising as a mountain above relatively flat ground. A ridge stretched from west of Anglesey to the east coast of Ireland. To the north of this ridge lay the southern end of a deep trough which

ran north between Down and Galloway and continued on below the North Channel almost as far as Islay. The origin of this trough, whose floor in places is 200 m below present sea-level, is not clear; it may be tectonic, it may be due to glacial erosion, or it may be due to tidal scour. There will have been a water-barrier here.

It is clear that movement into the Isle of Man presented no difficulty, because by 12,000 years ago at least eighty plant taxa had already reached the Isle of Man, and many more were pushing in; a large number of beetles and the giant deer were also present. Ireland's richest Woodgrange flora comes from a site near the Leinster coast at Mapastown, Co. Louth, and the plants — and the beetles — must have moved on easily into Ireland. The bridges of glacial material probably carried a varied pattern of soil materials, across which a wide range of plants and animals could quickly reach Ireland.

About 13,000 years ago climate seems to have improved rapidly, and plants and animals began to move in. At first there was room for all, and local conditions in soil type, elevation and exposure will have had strong influence, and many distinct plant associations will have occurred. So if I give prominence to one site, and give its name to the warm interstadial into which we are entering, it is because it is the site that was first described in detail, and it does display, at least in outline, all the characteristic features of the interstadial.

The site is at Woodgrange, Co. Down, near the east coast, and the basin which holds the deposits lies near sea-level between drumlins. It was described by Gurdup Singh, then working in Queen's University, Belfast, but who has now moved to Australia where he continues environmental studies. As climate improved, biological productivity was stepped up, and the plant cover became complete, clay ceased to be washed into the basin and organic mud formed instead. The mud was rich in pollen (Fig. 3.3) of grasses, sorrel and least willow (*Salix herbacea*); the sorrels are docks (*Rumex*) and are characteristic of heaths, grasslands and open country; as weeds they are abundant in Ireland today. Least willow is rare in Ireland today, being largely confined to mountain-tops. In northern Scandinavia today, where winter snow falls in hollows, it is slow to melt in spring, and snow-patches remain when the rest of the snow is gone. These places where snow lies late give good opportunity to sorrel and least willow, and their abundance at this time in Ireland suggests that even though climate was improving, there were still late snow-patches in spring (Pl. 15). This is the grass/sorrel phase.

Five hundred years later in the juniper phase the climate was sufficiently favourable for junipers and birches to flourish. In the north-east, as at Woodgrange, juniper was very abundant. At a few locations in the south, at Killarney and near Cashel, birches flourished. In more exposed conditions near the west coast, as at Roundstone, first described by Jessen, heaths of crowberry (*Empetrum nigrum*) were widespread.

Some of the plants recorded for this zone have today 'a remarkably southern, central or western European distribution', as Knud Jessen remarked some forty years ago. Recent detailed studies by Russell Coope of Birmingham (who has made brilliant use of beetles as climatic indicators) of an insect fauna of this zone from Shortalstown in Co. Wexford show that it closely resembles insect assemblages from England and Wales that date from about the same time. These faunas suggest a climate at least as warm as, or at times even warmer than, that in the same areas at the present day. Finds of birch fruits show that tree-birches were in Ireland at this time, and if temperature had continued to improve, birch probably would have expanded into extensive woods.

So far this vegetation sequence suggests the opening of a full warm stage, with the temperature high enough for the immigration of major trees, but at about 12,000 years ago, conditions started to deteriorate. Recent oceanic studies suggest that this deterioration was associated with a movement of cold polar water down the Atlantic coast of Europe. Production of juniper and other pollens fell drastically, and some sand and silt were washed into the lake basins. Bill Watts was the first to recognize the significance of this change; he considers that there was a serious climatic deterioration and a break-up of the plant cover, which allowed bare soil to be washed into the lake-basins.

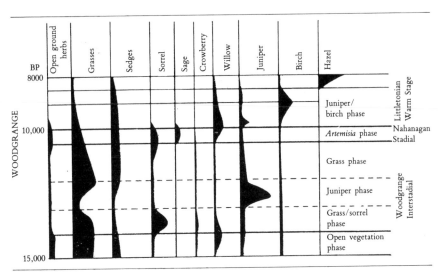

Fig. 3.3 Pollen-diagram
from Woodgrange, Co.
Down.

This break did not last long, and grasses largely re-established the plant-cover, though some bare patches may still have remained. Beetles also show that the early high temperatures were not re-established. We probably had a tundra-like grassland, with trees and shrubs confined to protected places. This grass phase lasted perhaps some 750 years, from 11,750 to 11,000 years ago (Pls. 13, 14).

It was in Ireland, during this grassland phase of the Woodgrange Interstadial, that that magnificent animal, the Irish giant deer (*Megaloceros giganteus*), reached the zenith of its success, only to be struck down, like Lucifer in full flight, by the abrupt climatic deterioration which followed. That deterioration restored freeze-thaw conditions, which broke up the plant-cover and allowed sand and clay (often containing remains of arctic plants) to be washed down into lake-basins. As a result the Woodgrange muds and peats in which the remains of the giant deer are typically found are usually sealed by a layer of sandy clay, an observation first made 250 years ago.

A letter of 1725 from Downpatrick, Co. Down, states, 'Under this appears a stratum of blue clay, half a foot thick, fully mixed with shells; then appears the right marl, commonly two,

three or four feet deep, and in some places much deeper, which looks like buried lime, or the lime that tanners throw out of their lime-pits, only that it is fully mixed with shells — such as the Scots call "fresh-water wilks". Among this marl, and often at the bottom of it, we find very great horns, which we, for want of another name, call "Elk-horns". We have also found shanks and other bones of these beasts in the same place.' The shells referred to are those of freshwater molluscs, and investigations in the same area many years later by Arthur Stelfox revealed fossil molluscan faunas of great interest, including arctic types no longer living in Ireland.

The same stratigraphy was also well known to Williams, an energetic nineteenth-century taxidermist and dealer in natural history specimens, and the illustration which he contributed to Millais's book on *British Deer and their Horns* is shown in Fig. 3.4. The method of probing is the same that was used by country folk to locate buried timbers in bogs at times when wood was short in Ireland. The stratigraphy was again confirmed in 1934 by Knud Jessen when he worked at Ballybetagh Bog in Co. Dublin, a site long famous because of the large quantities of remains of giant deer and of reindeer

Photograph 15 An artist's impression of the giant deer in life. The antlers though huge were frail, for show rather than combat. The stag would take his stand on a hillock, and slowly move the antlers up and down in order to display them fully and discourage rivals.

11

*Pl. 11 Woolly
mammoth and wild
horses. More than 40,000
years ago we could have
seen these animals near
Dungarvan, Co.
Waterford, grazing on
open tundra. (Peter
Snowball B.N.H.M.)*

12

13

14

Pl. 12 Glenmalure, Co. Wicklow. We look north up a straight U-shaped valley, cut into the granite of the Wicklow Mountains by ice moving south. The valley has been partly filled by later river gravel which gives it an inner flat floor. On the gravel in the centre of the picture we see the ruins of an army barracks at Drumgoff built in the late eighteenth century. At that time, just as in Scotland, military roads and barracks were built in upland areas to prevent rebellious forces assembling there. (Aerofilms)

Pl. 13 Abisko, Sweden. This upland country, with bushes growing where a hollow gives some protection from the wind, seen in Lapland today, gives an impression of Ireland 12,000 years ago, when the giant deer and the reindeer were here. (G.F. Mitchell)

Pl. 14 Black Head, Co. Clare. Here the limestone pavement of the Burren sweeps down to sea-level. Plants grow in the crevices, and we see mossy saxifrage and sea-pink. Both of these plants were in Ireland 12,000 years ago. (G.F. Mitchell)

Pl. 15 Abisko, Sweden. In winter a deep patch of snow fills this hollow. As spring advances, a pond gradually replaces the snow. The green leaves of the least willow (Salix herbacea) cover the edge of the pond; this plant, which is now confined to some mountain-tops, grew all over Ireland during the last cold snap, 10,500 years ago. (G.F. Mitchell)

Pl. 16 Ballynafogh, Co. Kildare. This fen is artificial, as the fen-plants are invading a canal reservoir. But it does give an impression of the Irish lowlands 9500 years ago, when wide expanses of open water had not yet been obliterated by the development of fen-peat. (D.L. Kelly)

Pl. 17 Ross Island, Killarney, Co. Kerry. These coniferous trees have been planted, but they do give an impression of the pine woods that spread widely in Ireland about 9000 years ago. There is only a narrow band of fen vegetation round the pond. (S. Ryan)

Pl. 18 Derrycunnihy, Killarney, Co. Kerry. This oakwood was probably planted, but there were also oak woods around Killarney 8000 years ago. (D.L. Kelly)

Pl. 19 Mount Sandel, Coleraine, Co. Londonderry. This Mesolithic site, dated to about 8650 years ago, gives us our oldest record of man in Ireland; it produced hearths, sites of huts, microliths, axes and bones of birds and fish. (P. Woodman)

that it had produced for Williams and other collectors. Since 1934 about thirty further finds of remains of giant deer have been investigated in the field, and in each case the remains were at the same stratigraphical horizon. Radiocarbon dating now enables us to put a date in years on the lake-mud in which the bones are entombed; a mud from Knocknacran was given an age of 11,300 years and a mud from Shortalstown 12,150 years, ages which are compatible with the Woodgrange Interstadial.

What is the record of the giant deer outside Ireland? Its ancestors appear in early Ice Age deposits in western Eurasia, but a related form appears as far away as China. In the later Ice Age the giant deer was widely spread through Europe, northern Asia and northern Africa. In western Europe, as in Ireland, it seems to have become extinct about 10,000 years ago, but there are suggestions that it survived in Syria and southern Russia almost until the birth of Christ. It was in England in interglacial time, and was also there when the giant deer was undergoing its final expansion in Ireland, though numbers in England appear to have remained very much smaller. A Swedish find was dated to 11,330 years ago.

As far as western Europe is concerned, we can picture the giant deer as a restless wanderer throughout much of the Ice Age. He could not go north to the tundras, because there he could not get sufficient nourishment to sustain him, nor south to the forests, because there the spread of his antlers would impede his movements. He lived on the intervening grasslands, which became poorer to the north, and interspersed with bushes to the south. With every climatic shift these belts of vegetation would be correspondingly displaced, and as the grasslands wandered, so the giant deer had to wander also. He was in the Blackwater valley at Castlepook about 34,000 years ago, he was then expelled by Midlandian ice, and returned for the last time in the Woodgrange Interstadial.

Fig. 3.4 *Finding bones of the giant deer.*

What did he look like? He was a splendid deer, standing about 2 m high at the shoulders, and over 3 m to the tips of the antlers. Only the male carried antlers, and these could have a span of almost 3 m, and a dry weight of about 30 kilograms. The antlers were shed annually, and had to be grown again, to a still larger size, each spring. The necessity to produce so much bone tissue so rapidly must have placed a tremendous physiological strain on the animal, and necessitated the consumption of large amounts of nutritious vegetable matter, rich in calcium. Though heavy in weight and impressive in appearance, the antlers were structurally very feeble, with elongated points mounted on the edge of a thin curved plate. They would have been useless in combat, and their only function can have been to impress. Like the Monarch of the Glen, the master stag of the herd would stand on some hillock in full view of the younger males and slowly raise and lower his magnificent antlers, and trust that at least on that occasion his status would go unchallenged (Photo 15).

What did he want? Two things, rich and abundant food, and freedom from predators. The soils of Ireland in the Woodgrange Interstadial were rich in fresh and unweathered mineral matter, especially calcium carbonate, and the plant cover must have been equally rich, at least for a short time, until the nutrient minerals had either been absorbed by the plants, or washed out of the soil by weathering. In the warmer part of the interstadial there would have been an abundance of bushes and grass, good food for the giant deer, but it seems to have been the later rich prairie grasslands, largely uninterrupted by trees and bushes, that nourished the large herds (Pl. 13).

Fig. 3.5   Localities where remains of Rangifer tarandus *(reindeer) and* Megaloceros giganteus *(giant deer) have been found in Ireland.*

A distribution-map of the remains makes this relationship with fertile soils quite plain (Fig. 3.5), even when we allow for the selective nature of such records. If an animal is to leave fossil remains, it must die in circumstances that will make preservation possible.

Those whose remains were dragged into caves by wolves or foxes, or who died near the lakes or ponds provide fossil material. In Ireland caves are in limestone areas, and lakes tend to be on the lowlands, and this must influence the pattern of fossil distribution. But the map does make abundantly clear the way that finds are concentrated in the Limerick region; today Limerick is still noted for the richness of its grasslands which make it one of the centres of the dairy industry. Records are also abundant in Co. Down, which today supplies Belfast with its liquid milk, and in Co. Meath, now an important region for fattening cattle. By contrast the mountainous regions of Donegal, Mayo and Kerry with their poor and acid soils are empty of records. The blanks in the midlands are probably due not to the lack of fossils, but to the fact that thick accumulations of peat have buried the remains beyond reach of casual discovery. Lowland areas with rich grasslands were frequented by the giant deer, and the infertile parts of the country were avoided.

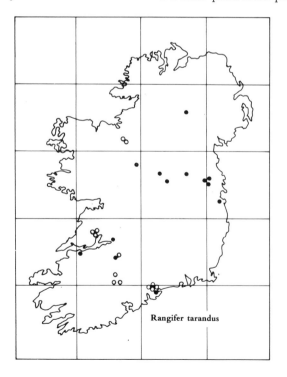

Rangifer tarandus

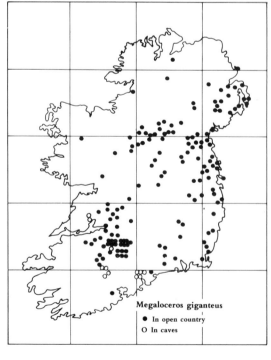

Megaloceros giganteus

● In open country
O In caves

Ponds and lakes have provided many records. Some animals were drowned. The lake-margin will have been floored by soft muds and clays, concealed beneath a floating mat of succulent water-plants. An animal might come down to drink or to feed, and find one foot becoming embedded in the mud. The struggle to extricate the trapped foot might lead to the others becoming enmired, and occasionally the desperate trampings are recorded by disturbances in the muds immediately below the skeleton. For the males the heavy antlers will have made balance especially precarious, and if the animal once went down, it will have found it hard to regain its feet. Death would quickly follow.

Male skulls with antlers are much more frequently reported than female skulls, which lack antlers. One explanation was that female skulls are mistaken for those of horses or cattle, and are neglected by the finder, whereas an antlered skull immediately attracts attention. Another suggestion was that males with heavy antlers were more likely to be trapped and drowned than females. Dissatisfied with these explanations, Tony Barnosky of the Carnegie Museum in Pittsburg recently returned to Ballybetagh, which in the past had only yielded male skulls, although the excavators were competent zoologists looking for remains of both sexes. The valley with the lake at Ballybetagh runs north/south with a sheltered slope on its western side. Barnosky excavated here and found quantities of damaged bones and antlers, and some antlered skulls which showed that death had taken place between late autumn and early spring. All remains that could be sexed were male.

In many modern forms of deer the males and females only consort together in the rutting season. In the winter females and young tend to wander in open country, while the males group together in sheltered valley bottoms, just as we have at Ballybetagh. Winter mortality is higher among males than females, because the males have exhausted themselves during the rut, and enter the winter in poorer condition than the females. Barnosky pictures the carcasses being trampled and stamped on by other deer, and so finds explanation for the damaged and scattered state of the bones he excavated. A giant deer jaw-bone that was found at the level where the mud of the grass zone was giving way to the sandier deposits above had a radiocarbon age of 10,600 years.

Predators offered little threat. There is no record of the lion (*Felis leo*) from Ireland, and this animal had probably disappeared from England long before this late interstadial began. There will have been wolves and arctic foxes, but while these will have preyed on old animals and sickly calves it is unlikely that they will have offered much threat to the herds. Man was still absent from Ireland, and there were no bands of specialized hunters like those who followed the reindeer herds in northern Europe. The giant deer must have found conditions in Ireland almost idyllic, and proceeded to expand in numbers accordingly. Conditions in England must have been very similar, and it is not easy to see why the giant deer should be so common in Ireland, and by comparison so very rare in Britain, except in the Isle of Man where numerous finds have been made.

Though records of its remains are very much less common, the reindeer (*Rangifer tarandus*) was also in Ireland at this time, and its distribution is generally similar to that of the giant deer. We have one radiocarbon date, 10,700 years ago. Many years ago I excavated remains of both animals from a lake-basin near Ratoath, Co. Meath. My pollen-counts were crude, but the muds did contain bands of silt whose full significance has now been recognized by Bill Watts. The reindeer bones lay above the silt, and so we can place the reindeer in the grass zone.

There are no records of other mammals from open country in the interstadial. Very occasional fish vertebrae have been found in the lake-muds, which is in marked contrast to the position in Denmark, where muds of similar age contain abundant fish-scales and bones. Some lake-muds were rich in shells of fresh-water mulluscs, others were completely lacking in such shells, and the late glacial migration routes of these animals are still very obscure.

The Nahanagan Stadial, the final phase of cold in Ireland: 11,000 to 10,000 years ago

It has long been known that the uninterrupted return of warmth that marked the opening of the postglacial — or Littletonian Warm Stage — in which we live, was immediately preceded by a short spell of final cold, but until recently it had not been realized both how short it was, and how cold it was. Radiocarbon has been able to tell us that the cold spell began about 11,000 years ago and that it ended about 10,000 years ago, and it therefore had a duration of not more than 1000 years. The North Atlantic ocean, which by about 13,000 years ago had become warm, suddenly became cold again, and polar water, probably with winter ice-pack and icebergs, reappeared briefly off the west coast of Ireland, and caused this severe cooling of the land climate.

Lough Nahanagan is a corrie lake at about 400 m in the Wicklow Mountains. It lies at the head of Glendasan, a valley that has been glaciated on more than one occasion. The corrie was probably occupied by a substantial ice-mass about 15,000 years ago, and a big moraine was thrown across its mouth. The modern lake behind the moraine has been developed as part of a pumped-storage generating system, and during the course of construction it was necessary to drain the lake temporarily. As water level fell, it revealed a series of very small moraines banked against the hillside. These were studied in detail by Francis Synge of the Irish Geological Survey and Eric Colhoun (then in Trinity College, Dublin, but now working in Tasmania), who found that the moraines had got lumps of organic mud embedded in them. The mud had a radiocarbon age of 11,500 years, a pollen picture that suggested the transition from the juniper phase to the grass phase and macroscopic remains of arctic alpine plants. It was clear that the mud had formed in the Woodgrange Interstadial in an earlier lake held up by the main moraine, and had been ploughed up by the ice of a smaller glacier that re-occupied part of the pre-existing corrie, and formed the small inner moraines. As this was the first site to demonstrate that the cold spell was severe enough for glacier ice to form in Ireland, the cold phase has been named the Nahanagan Stadial. In Scotland a small ice-cap formed on high ground at this time, and its ice advanced as far south as Loch Lomond. But the volume of ice formed was small, and it is unlikely that the continuing upward rise of the land by isostatic recovery and of the level of the sea by eustatic release of meltwater was seriously interrupted.

Other evidence also points to severe cold. Both at Howth in Co. Dublin, and at Old Head, near Louisburg in Mayo, solifluction moved till downslope where it buried organic deposits of Woodgrange age. There may even have been permafrost; late Midlandian outwash gravels in Co. Tyrone are penetrated by ice-wedge-casts, which can only have formed after the gravels had been deposited. They may have formed in the Nahanagan Stadial, and if so they indicate a mean annual temperature of less than −5°C. Pingos may have formed in Wexford at this time; at Camaross it was difficult to locate any early sediments in the pingo basins, but in one basin deposits had only started to form late in the Nahanagan Stadial. Pingos in Wales tell the same story. Again very severe cold is indicated.

The fossil evidence is similar. At Drumurcher, Co. Monaghan, a basin in between Midlandian drumlins yielded a muddy silt, dated to 10,500 years ago, which contained remains of about one hundred species of beetle. Many of the beetles indicated an arctic or sub-arctic regime, such as occurs today in the lower alpine regions of the mountains of Scandinavia or the tundra regions of the far north. Modern distribution-maps for four beetles (Fig. 3.6) typical of

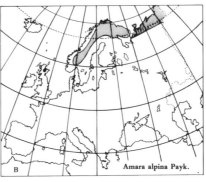

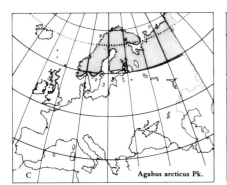

Fig. 3.6 The modern distribution of some beetles which were in Ireland in the Nahanagan Stadial.

those discoverd at Drumurcher make this clear; *Diacheila arctica* is today confined to the high north; *Amara alpina* extends south down the mountains of Scandinavia, and also occurs in the higher Scottish mountains; *Agabus arcticus* is widely distributed in the north of Europe and of Britain, and has outlying stations in Ireland; *Helophorus glacialis* was, when the climate was cold, widely distributed throughout western Europe, and still maintains a precarious foothold in the mountains of Scandinavia, the Alps and the Pyrenees.

The Drumurcher silt also yielded the first seed so far found in Ireland of the arctic poppy (*Papaver radicatum* s.l.); today the distribution of this plant is strictly arctic circumpolar, and Great Britain, too, has only produced one fossil seed, from a deposit of comparable age in Berwickshire.

In western Ireland arctic-alpine plants were growing at low levels around Killarney, and at modern sea-level at Waterville, and Achill Island. At Ashleam Bay in Achill the deposit had clearly originated in a snow-patch as sheets of least willow leaves were protruding from a sandy silt. Five grams of dry organic matter are necessary if a satisfactory radiocarbon date is to be obtained; each dry fossil leaf weighed 1 mg. I set to work and picked out 5000 individual leaves and sent them off to be dated; the very satisfactory answer was an age of 11,170 years, subject to a marginal variation of 120 years either way. By this time our time-telescope is capable of very detailed observations.

All this points to very severe conditions. On the mountains we had small glaciers in corries, on the lowlands the deposits are predominantly inorganic and may contain stones. Leaves of least willow are often abundant. Solifluction and snow-beds are clearly indicated. The plant remains suggest an incomplete plant cover, largely composed of arctic species.

Pollen of sage (*Artemisia*) is common, and we speak of the *Artemisia* or sage phase.

With the disappearance of the grasslands the giant deer disappeared also. We do not know if the reindeer survived the Nahanagan Stadial in Ireland, but he certainly survived it somewhere, perhaps far south in Europe, and from there, as the postglacial forests re-advanced inexorably northwards, driving the tundras before them, the reindeer kept pace with the tundra till it stabilized itself in northern latitudes. And there the reindeer still survives, if only by the courtesy of the Lapps and Eskimos, who have learned that it is better to manage your meat supply than to exterminate it.

It is only very recently that we have come to realize exactly how severe conditions were during the Nahanagan Stadial, and we have not yet realized the implications of that severity for many forms of animal and plant life. When we are asking ourselves if there could have been nearby refuges where some life could have survived when the Midlandian and the Munsterian ice-masses were at their maxima, we must also ask what forms could have survived the last episode of cold.

4
RESPONSE TO WARM CONDITIONS: 10,000 to 5100 years ago

It is generally agreed that under present climatic conditions (i.e. those of a warm stage) and without interference from man much of Europe would be covered by deciduous woodland. The period now under review shows such a transformation of the European scene from open tundra to closed woodland. It will be noted at once that my closing date is odd; why 5100 instead of a round figure of 5000 years ago? I do not wish to anticipate, but a large number of radiocarbon dates are now converging to show that at about 5100 years ago the amount of pollen produced by elm trees showed a drastic, if brief, fall. The cause of the fall has been much argued over, but I now join those who see this fall as the result of a wave of disease, which spread rapidly throughout western Europe. Today we are witnessing a second such wave, bringing about a decimation of the elm population. The modern 'Dutch' elm disease is caused by a bark beetle, and traces of similar attack have been found in elm trees 5000 years old. The dramatic drop in values of elm pollen 5100 years ago gives us a most valuable dating horizon.

Immigration routes

How did plants and animals get back into Ireland? Temperature was not a limiting factor, as it quickly rose to a level suitable for forest trees. What about access? Here again we enter a field of considerable debate, and again I must declare my interest. There are several points of view we could adopt:

— life had not been wiped out by cold, and plants and animals returned overland from places of refuge, probably off the west coast
— plants and animals returned via a former land-bridge, which probably lay between the present Leinster coast and Cheshire
— plants crossed a stretch of water by being carried by the wind or by birds, or by floating, either unassisted or on a log; these agencies were also available to some forms of animal life; others could swim or fly
— after man had arrived in Ireland about 6000 years ago, he introduced new plants and animals, some by design, some by accident

Let us take a brief look at the pros and cons.

Refuges: During the final cold snap we had tundra at modern sea-level near Waterville in Kerry, and snow-patches at the same level in Achill Island. Sea-level was then lower, and there would have been an offshore coastal strip, but as the temperature of the sea was very low it is difficult to see how forms of life which were not extremely hardy could have survived there. The strawberry tree (*Arbutus*) is a native of the Mediterranean, but does grow around Killarney and in other places in western Ireland today — it could not have survived the last cold snap in or near Ireland.

Land-bridges: It is strenuously claimed by some that the rapid rise in postglacial sea-level would quickly have overwhelmed any land connections that there might have been immediately after the decay of the ice-sheets, and that there was no possibility for temperate plants and animals to enter by such a route. But we know that there were oaks growing in the south of Ireland 9000 years ago, the wild boar was near Coleraine in the north about the same time, and the red deer was in the midlands near Tullamore 8400 years ago. Thus I prefer to picture organized oakwoods advancing across a land-bridge, carrying those forest animals, the red deer and the wild boar, along with them, rather than to imagine the occasional acorn floating across the sea or being carried by a pigeon across the North Channel, while groups of pigs and deer were swimming across tidal channels.

Casual introduction: Just as the team of monkeys banging away at random will eventually produce a faultless typescript of the plays of Shakespeare, so — given a long enough time — chance will introduce almost anything into Ireland. But with the aid of our pollen-diagrams and radiocarbon dates we can trace out a credible ecological development of the Irish flora. Could we do this if the times of the various arrivals were dictated entirely by chance?

Introduction by man: Man only reached Ireland about 9000 years ago, and so cannot have introduced anything that was already in Ireland by that date. But there is no doubt that man, by bringing in crop-plants and their associated weeds, domestic animals and vermin and garden plants, has greatly altered the balance of the modern Irish flora and fauna. It is at times very difficult to draw a line between what has been introduced and what is truly indigenous.

Sea-level
About 10,000 years ago cold conditions came to an end, and the Littletonian Warm Stage opened. Sea-level had continued to rise from its low glacial level as more and more of the world's ice melted, and had probably recovered to within 35 m (100 ft) of its present level, when the warm stage opened (see Fig. 3.1). Animals and plants quickly moved back into Ireland once more, and there must still have been land connections with Britain and Europe to enable them to do so. But we are faced with the difficulty that if sea-level today were to drop by no more than 35 m, a broad and continuous stretch of water would remain between Ireland and Britain.

As the ice that had formerly occupied the basin of the Irish Sea withdrew northwards, it left behind it glacial deposits of very irregular topography, which sank in some places into deep hollows, which quickly filled with water, and rose in others into high morainic ridges, which served as routeways for immigration into Ireland (see Fig. 3.2). These deposits were progressively drowned by the rising sea, and their topography was drastically modified both by wave erosion when the basin was being re-flooded, and by the strong tidal currents which developed as soon as the transverse morainic ridges were breached by the rising sea, and are still active today. Subjected to these attacks, the unconsolidated sands, gravels and clays of the ridges were quickly washed away, leaving only some truncated remnants which still project as headlands on the coasts of Louth and Meath on the one hand, and in Cumberland and the Isle of Man on the other.

For how long did the land-bridges remain available as entry routes into Ireland? Many geologists say flatly that there could not have been any land-connection after 10,000 years ago. But as we shall see shortly we now have good evidence that freshwater molluscs continued to reach Ireland until at least 7500 years ago. I accept this evidence, and so say that a land-bridge still existed at that date.

After the severance sea-level continued to rise, and about 5500 years ago it probably stood about 4 m above its present level.

Climate

At about 10,000 years ago temperature in north-west Europe reached the limit that enabled closed woodland to develop. Temperature continued to rise and probably passed the present level, for there is some evidence that about six or seven thousand years ago the average July temperatures were 1° or 2°C warmer than at present. Evidence from Lough Neagh and other lakes suggests that lake levels were lower than at the present time, and the climate may have been rather drier. This period has been referred to as the *postglacial climatic optimum*, and credit for its discovery is often given to Praeger, who towards the end of the last century noted that the estuarine clays and raised beaches formed in the north of Ireland at this time contained a molluscan fauna with species which do not live so far to the north at the present day.

Robert Lloyd Praeger (1865-1953) was one of Ireland's most distinguished naturalists, who during a long working life made many important discoveries, and increased our knowledge of field botany in Ireland very substantially, but he did not discover, and never claimed to have discovered, the climatic optimum. The attribution arose from the fact that W.B. Wright had, like many others, a great admiration for Praeger, and when in 1936 he published the second edition of his book, *The Quaternary Ice Age*, he dedicated it to 'Praeger — the Discoverer of the Climatic Optimum'. The discovery had in fact been made as long ago as 1865 by T.F. Jamieson, when he was studying the molluscan fauna of the estuarine clays of central Scotland. Praeger refers to Jamieson's work in his own paper, and would, were he alive today, be most anxious to see that honour is given where honour is due. I do not make this correction with any intent to lessen Praeger's standing. Born with a love for natural history in his blood, he qualified as an engineer, and one of his first jobs was on the excavations for dock construction in

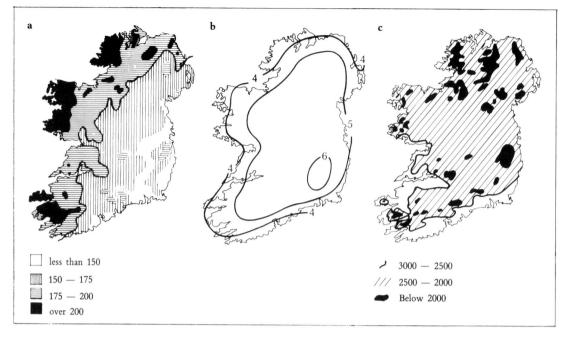

less than 150
150 — 175
175 — 200
over 200

3000 — 2500
2500 — 2000
Below 2000

Fig. 4.1 Some Irish climatic features: **a** *number of rain-days per annum;* **b** *saturation-deficit for the month of July, when the drying property of the air is greatest;* **c** *accumulated temperatures in day-degrees per annum.*

Belfast. These excavations gave a wonderful opportunity for molluscan studies, and Praeger made the most of it, and published a series of brilliant papers. However, botany called more strongly than geology, and most of his subsequent work was primarily botanical. But he never overlooked the importance of fossil evidence, and he realized that Ireland's bogs and lakes must hold great quantities of seeds and other plant parts, whose identification would throw much light on the history of Irish vegetation. He thus made, and lodged in the National Herbarium, a collection of the seeds of all the plants regarded as native in Ireland. This was done long before organized studies of fossil material were even thought of, and it must have given Praeger enormous satisfaction when, together with Tony Farrington of the Royal Irish Academy and Adolph Mahr of the National Museum, he organized Knud Jessen's visits to Ireland, and was able to see Jessen making full use of the collections of reference material he had put together many years before.

From this optimal level temperature then appears to have fallen back. It is

not easy to document the change in Ireland, but in Sweden hazel could no longer grow as far north as it had previously done. Decreases of a degree or two in both summer and winter temperatures have been suggested.

Temperature is only one parameter of climate. What are we to say about the other features of the Irish climate? Some would hold that there is no such thing as climate in Ireland, but only an irregular sequence of different weather patterns, with the emphasis on frontal systems bringing wind and rain. Ireland is an outpost in the Atlantic Ocean, and maritime influences predominate. Harsh frosts are rare; only the very centre of the country will know more than one day in the year when temperature will not rise above freezing point throughout the twenty-four hours. High summer temperatures are rare: 33°C is the highest ever recorded. The annual range is only 9°C in the south-west and 10°C in the east.

The great frequency — especially in the west of the country — of winds of moderate to severe intensity is a notable feature, and days of calm are almost unknown. The air being blown along is usually humid, and the disagreeableness of the wind strength is rarely compensated for by good drying conditions.

The amount of rainfall is not excessive, 1400 mm in the south-west and 700 mm in the east, but the number of days on which it falls is very high. A map (Fig. 4.1a) of the number of rain-days per annum will in a crude way almost also serve as a rainfall map, except that it under-represents the rainfall along the south and south-east coasts. Depressions move along the south coast and up into the south Irish Sea, bringing occasional days of heavy rain though the number of rain-days in this area is not high. Continued droughts are rare. Numerous rain-days and infrequent droughts mean that humidity will be high and evaporation low, and another map (Fig. 4.1b) shows the saturation deficit for July, the month when the most favourable values are recorded. The saturation deficit indicates the potential capacity of the air to absorb more moisture, and so gives an indication of drying conditions. In England only the eastern shores of the Irish Sea show such low saturation deficits; over the rest of that country the power of the air to absorb more moisture is very much higher. Visitors from England to the west coast of Ireland often comment unfavourably on the late hour at which the local farmers begin their hay-making operations. They overlook the fact that noon on the clock in Greenwich is eleven o'clock by the sun in Connaught, and noon summer time is ten o'clock by the western sun. Several hours of morning sunshine are necessary before the local poor drying conditions can bring the grass into a condition in which it can safely be cut or turned.

The high humidity brings about extensive cloud cover and a poor sunshine record. Plants such as the primrose and the wood-sorrel that in England grow in woods and shady places find in the west of Ireland that the clouds provide an adequate sun-screen, and live on open and treeless hillsides. People living in Ireland are not exposed to strong insolation, and if they migrate to Australia or other areas with high sunshine records they are very prone to skin-cancers and other forms of skin irritation.

Irish emigrants contrast the harshness of the Australian light with the softer colours of the Irish landscape. Australian air is almost free both from water vapour and industrial smog, and it is these two elements that give to Irish air that slightest of haziness that appeals to the Irish eye. Winds from the east increase the haziness and mute the landscape colours; winds from the north-west bring clearer air with sunshine and drifting clouds, and at once the landscape springs to brilliance. Variations in wind and cloud come rapidly in Ireland, and the never-ending change in the strength of the light and the value of the colour tones brings delight to the eye — and despair to the brush — of the artist.

The cloud cover cuts down the amount of sunshine that can actually reach and warm the soil, and growth is correspondingly slowed. The actual quantity of heat that reaches the ground can be evaluated and represented cartographically on a map (Fig. 4.1c). Such a map shows a strip along the south and south-west coast that is relatively favoured, though only to the same modest degree as the extreme west coast of England; the other parts of England are much warmer. The rest of the lowlands of Ireland receive less heat, and anywhere the ground rises, the amount of heat received drops again. Growth conditions in Ireland for many plants thus will always be slow and difficult.

We can, as seen above, make some effort to trace the course of temperature in Ireland in the past. We cannot easily pin down the other climatic features in the same way, but maritime influences will always have prevailed.

Soil development

If this were a text-book on Irish geography, we would at this point have a map which presented an outline of the soils of Ireland. But at the time about which I am speaking, 10,000 years ago, most of the soils which we know today, and which the soil surveyor can record and enter up on his field map, had not yet developed, the numerous lake-basins left behind by the ice had not been overgrown by fens, and there had been no formation of peat. Here we can only indicate the trend of soil development on different parent materials as time went by.

We have seen that the effect of cold was to refresh the soil parent material, either by the deposition of rock debris freshly crushed by ice action, or by freeze-thaw disturbance and sludging bringing subsoil to the surface where it replaced, or at least diluted, the materials that had been deeply weathered during the preceding warm stage. At the opening of the Littletonian the replacement of a dry cold climate by a warm moist one meant first that water was now free to bring about chemical changes, second that the high humidity reduced evaporation, and third that vigorous plant growth both by its foliage above ground, and by the humus that its decaying debris was contributing to the upper layers of the soil below ground, checked water from flowing away along the surface, and encouraged it to sink down into the ground instead.

Soil formation is a very complex process, or series of processes, in which leaching (or washing out), enrichment, redeposition and transformation all play a part. In Ireland, where the principal movement of water is downwards, leaching predominates in the surface layers, which tend to grow more acid with time. The application of lime to the surface will halt or reverse this tendency, and at least for the past 750 years farmers have been engaged in this process. Shelly sand can be collected on the shore, or calcareous clays (*marls*) can

be dug from pits and spread on the land. Limestone can be roasted in kilns — and the abandoned lime-kiln is one of the characteristic features of the Irish countryside — slaked with water, and spread. Today ground limestone is more popular. Farmyard manure or seaweed used to be used extensively to replace lost organic material; today chemical fertilizers are dominant. As a result of all these activities man has, in many places, profoundly altered the soil.

The course the soil-forming process will take is influenced by texture, by primary base status and by organic activity. As the water moved down from the surface it could carry easily soluble substances (including humus) in solution, and the very fine insoluble clay particles in suspension, and so remove or *leach* material from the surface layers, giving rise to the *leached-* or A-horizon of the pedologist. The materials carried down from above tended to be deposited below in an *enriched-* or B-horizon, while the as yet unaltered material below is styled the C-horizon. In this way the three main soil horizons began to appear.

To begin with everything was C-horizon, and in some areas there was little change, particularly if the primary material was rich in clay particles. Bodies of water that had been dammed up by ice often filled up with finely divided clays, and such glacial lake clays are not uncommon in Ireland. The upper Carboniferous shales of north Kerry, Clare and Kilkenny, and the tills derived from them, are very rich in clay; in Leitrim the drumlins are built up of stiff clayey till; on the south-east coast Midlandian ice moving in from the basin of the Irish Sea incorporated large quantities of marine clay in its till.

Because the spaces between the clay particles are very small, movement of groundwater through such materials is extremely slow, and there is in consequence no development of soil horizons; a wet water-logged soil,

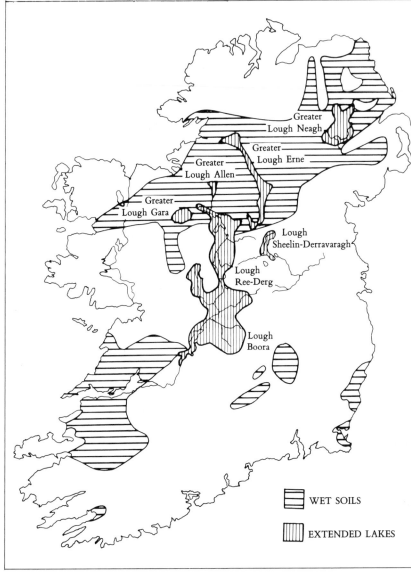

Fig. 4.2 Map to show areas where the very high primary clay content causes the soil to remain poorly drained and wet at all times. At the opening of the Littletonian Warm Stage the lakes on the lowlands were much larger than they are today; the map endeavours to indicate the extent of these lakes before they were reduced in size by the growth of fens and bogs.

Greater Lough Neagh

Greater Lough Erne

Greater Lough Allen

Greater Lough Gara

Lough Sheelin-Derravaragh

Lough Ree-Derg

Lough Boora

WET SOILS

EXTENDED LAKES

known as a *gley*, results, irrespective of the chemical composition of the parent materials. Decomposing plant material may accumulate on the surface of the soil; if the plant layer remains thin, i.e. does not thicken into peat, then the soil is described as a *peaty gley*.

By means of a map we can attempt to indicate the initial distribution about 10,000 years ago of poorly drained and well-drained soils, and also the much greater extent of lakes at this time, because they had not yet been overgrown by fens and bogs (Fig. 4.2).

If on the other hand the parent material was poorer in clay and coarser in texture, water could move downwards, and a well-drained soil, more favourable to plant root systems, could gradually develop. As the Littletonian proceeded, trees returned to the country, and gradually a high forest of deciduous trees built up climax woodland where the primary soil materials allowed such development. If there were open-textured parent materials on limestone the establishment of the forest went hand in hand with the development of a *brown forest soil*. The surface layers of such a soil consist of an intimate mixture of well-decomposed humus and mineral matter. But because of the way man subsequently interfered with the woodlands, there are no typical brown forest soils in Ireland today.

If change has only been slight, the surface humus will have disappeared, and the soil becomes a fertile *brown earth*, which in Ireland is quite often shallow.

Where the parent glacial material was not strongly calcareous, the chemical action of the groundwater could be more marked, and there was a tendency for substances to be leached out of the top layer — the A-horizon — and carried away in the groundwater, or deposited lower down in the profile in the B-horizon. If iron was washed down, the A-horizon tended to be bleached to a paler, ashy colour, a feature described as *podzolic*,[*] while the B-horizon, because of enrichment there, took on a strong brown colour, and we have a *brown podzolic* soil. Human interference does not appear to have affected these soils greatly.

In many parts of Europe where the parent material was calcareous and had some content of clay, or of minerals that would break down into clay on weathering, then the movement or flow of groundwater down the profile over a long period of time would gradually carry clay particles down out of the A-horizon, and deposit them in the B-horizon, which thereby became progressively enriched in clay. We have thus the soil called the *grey-brown podzolic*; it is so-called on account of its colour, bleached above and deeper below, because in addition to the movement of clay, other substances including iron have been lost from the A-horizon, bringing about podzolization, but in fact its diagnostic criterion is the added clay in the

B-horizon. Studies of fossil soils buried beneath raised bogs in Ireland show that the accumulation of clay has increased with the passage of time. Today grey-brown podzolic soils are widely developed on the calcareous deposits of the last glaciation in the midlands, where they form very fertile soils. Ten thousand years ago the movement of clay was only beginning, and the soils must then have had a rather different character.

But we also have in Ireland another type of soil which is very rich in clay some little distance down from the surface, which we can call a *pseudo grey-brown podzolic*. The quantity of clay present is much too great to have arisen from the transformation of other minerals in the A-horizon, and must be a feature inherited from the glacial material on which the soil subsequently developed.

If the parent material was not more than feebly calcareous and of mixed texture, the soil formed resembled the brown earth in that it did not develop marked horizons, but it was more acid and of lower fertility than the brown earth, and is known as an *acid brown earth*. Woodland clearance probably did not affect it markedly, and today, provided its fertility is improved by adding limestone and fertilizer, it gives a good agricultural soil.

If the parent material is non-calcareous and rich in sand, marked leaching will take place, and iron, aluminium and humus will all be removed from the A-horizon, which will become very pale in colour and be left in a highly acid condition. Because of the strongly bleached appearance the soil is called a *podzol*. The materials leached from the A-horizon are precipitated in the B-horizon, where the iron often forms a continuous impermeable layer, known as *iron-pan*. Water cannot move down through such a layer, and the soil surface becomes water-logged in consequence. Though experimental work suggests that podzolization can

[*]Based on the Russian *pod*, meaning *under*, and *zola*, ash.

take place very quickly, there is no doubt that many of the Irish podzols developed slowly over a long period of time. Such infertile and poorly drained soils are widely distributed, especially in the west and on higher ground. As with the gley, a thin layer of plant debris may accumulate on the surface, and the soil then becomes a *peaty podzol*. Peaty podzols have a very special importance in the history of the Irish landscape, because they provided the substratum on which blanket-bogs later developed.

Base status and texture are not the only factors affecting soil development. Topography, including altitude, slope and aspect, is also very important. In low-lying areas rivers are sluggish, and there may be lakes of varying sizes. On higher ground temperature is lower and winds are stronger, and these factors influence plant growth, especially tree growth. In many parts of the temperate world trees grow at heights much higher than the highest Irish mountain-top, and the absence of trees from higher ground today is partly due to the activities of man and partly due to the spread of blanket-bog. We can picture three main landscape units: (1) the lowlands, which are given an arbitrary upper limit at 150 m (approximately 500 ft), which is the height above which tillage is rarely practised in Ireland today; (2) the uplands above 150 m (often today covered by blanket-bog); and (3) what can be conveniently called the 'wetlands' and will include rivers, lakes, fens, raised-bogs, and extensive areas of gley soils on the lowlands. These three landscape units had different patterns of vegetation, and their later uses by man differed widely, and wherever it is appropriate they will be discussed separately. But we must remember that the difference between them is not fixed and immutable. If climate improved, tillage might move higher up the mountain slopes; if climate deteriorated and blanket-bog spread, fertile lowland areas might be turned into infertile wetlands.

Return of the flora and fauna

We can now retrace our steps to about 10,000 years ago, and ask ourselves what will happen when the Littletonian thermostat is given a vigorous upward turn? In the Nahanagan Stadial we had plants and animals requiring open habitats, but capable of surviving relatively adverse climatic conditions. Now these must face rising temperature and strong competition; some will survive the change and hold their own, others will become extinct in Ireland, a few will find refuge on cliffs or on mountain-tops. Where are their competitors? We can picture them strung out across continental Europe, as well as down the Atlantic coast of France, standing in their places like the starters in a handicapped gold rush. When the 'off' is given, they spring into action, each determined to stake out his claim. And this is a race against the clock, because there is not more than 2500 years to go before a water-barrier will have to be crossed if they are to reach Ireland, the Outpost of Europe, as Grenville Cole called it many years ago.

Professor David Webb of Trinity College, who is a leading authority on the flora of Europe as well as that of Ireland, has recently discussed the flora of Ireland in its European context, and the account which follows draws heavily on his work. Professor Webb places main emphasis on land-bridges, but he also calls in survival for some plants which occur in Ireland, but not in Britain.

Professor Webb has kindly given me a table of the number of wild plants in the countries of north-west Europe as follows:

France	3500
Britain	1172
Belgium	1140
Denmark	1030
Ireland	815
Isle of Man	576

The poverty of Ireland is immediately

apparent, as is the richness of France. But France is in a different league to the other countries; it is almost a sub-continent, ranging from the English Channel to the Mediterranean and varying in elevation from sea-level to almost 5000 m. Belgium and Denmark show that low-lying land on the European side of the English Channel can muster about 1100 wild plants.

Britain is much larger than Belgium, Holland and Denmark put together; it has a large area of high ground as compared with the Ardennes in Belgium; and it has a much wider climatic range. East Anglia is akin to the continent, while the west coast is markedly oceanic. We should expect a much bigger tally for Great Britain, and in consequence must regard its flora as also impoverished, though not to the same degree as that of Ireland. Only the early wave of returning plants was able to reach Ireland before it was cut

off; the Isle of Man, with its very restricted range of habitats, was up a side-road; later waves got to Britain, and after Britain was severed from the continent northern Europe continued to receive stragglers, who might have reached the British Isles had they been quicker off the mark.

We can picture the process as a steeplechase (Fig. 4.3). Those plants that did reach Ireland presumably used the Channel land-bridge. They met their first fence at a line between Tyneside and Exeter, drawn many years ago by the distinguished Welsh archaeologist, Sir Cyril Fox. This line separates lowland Britain with its soft rocks, base-rich soils and low rainfall from highland Britain with its harder rocks, less fertile soils and higher rainfall. Seventy-five of the plants that had entered Britain did not advance across the line, and so had no opportunity to reach Ireland.

Fig. 4.3 The Littletonian plant steeplechase.

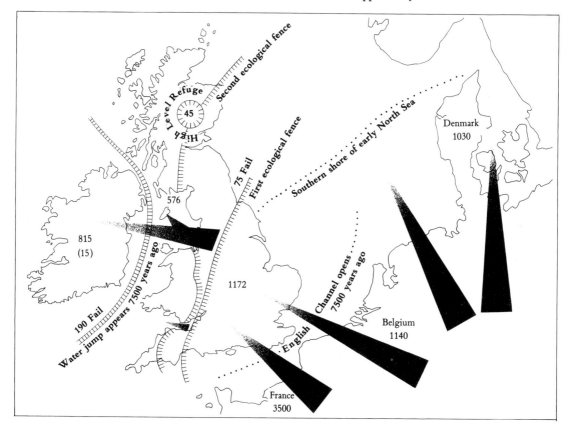

Still farther west these highland factors become more extreme, and so still less attractive to incoming plants. An interrupted fence was erected here, but through its gaps fertile lowlands around the Bristol Channel and on the Cheshire coast could be reached. In the latter area we are on the eastern end of our postulated land-bridge, and I picture that the Cheshire plain was the bridge-head for further orderly advance into Ireland. There will have been an advance party of plants of open country, but the trees quickly followed.

And with the trees came the shrubs, lianes and herbs which tolerate and sometimes require the cover of deciduous trees, together with the mammals and other animals of the woods.

Freshwater molluscs appear to have accompanied them. Not far west of Dublin, near Newlands Cross, there is an extensive deposit of tufa containing freshwater molluscs. These are being studied by Richard Preece of Cambridge with most exciting results. He is also studying a comparable deposit in Wales, and this not only has the same age of about 7750 years ago, but has also an almost identical faunal sequence. The molluscs must have moved into Ireland from pond to pond as successive ecological groups, and not at random on the feet of birds, or other transporting agency. When washing the material to separate the shells from the matrix of the tufa, a flint implement and teeth of a field-mouse (*Apodemus sylvaticus*) also appeared.

But if the molluscs got here, freshwater fish did not, as it is generally agreed that non-migratory freshwater fish (such as pike, perch and bream) were introduced into Ireland by man. It is thought that during the last glaciation all freshwater fish disappeared from Britain and Ireland. When the rivers of south-east England were still part of the Rhine system, they were re-colonised from Europe, but by this time Ireland had already been cut off from Britain.

The migratory fish, salmon, trout and eel, returned to the Irish river systems early in postglacial time. The migratory habit is related to water temperature, and becomes more pronounced under cold conditions. The pollan (*Coregonus autumnalis*) of Lough Neagh, the shad (*Alosa fallax killarniensis*) of the Killarney lakes, and the char (*Salvelinus alpinus*) of several lakes probably used to come and go, but were trapped in inland waters when conditions changed.

But we must return to the plant steeplechase. For the late-comers the breaching of the Irish Sea bridge had introduced a water-jump, and there were many casualties here. Professor Webb reckons their number at about 190, that is plants whose distribution in Britain suggests that there is no apparent reason why they should not have succeeded in Ireland, had they managed to reach it.

Webb also excludes another group, about forty-five in all, who would have had nowhere to go, had they reached Ireland. These are the plants of the high mountains of Scotland, a refuge habitat which has no equivalent in Ireland. This group is a little tricky because it includes some northern plants which were present in both Britain and Ireland in late-glacial time, but have become extinct in Ireland. The habitat they require has disappeared from Ireland, though it still survives in highland Scotland. The arctic birch (*Betula nana*) is such a plant. In Britain the group may thus be late-glacial survivors, rather than early postglacial immigrants.

There is also another very problematical group, that is plants — some fifteen in all — that have restricted distributions in Ireland, but do not occur in Britain at all. Of the fifteen, eight occur in the north-west of the Iberian peninsula. We have already noted three heathers: St Dabeoc's heath (*Daboecia cantabrica*) occurring in Connemara, and also in outlying stations not far from the French west coast, Mackay's heath

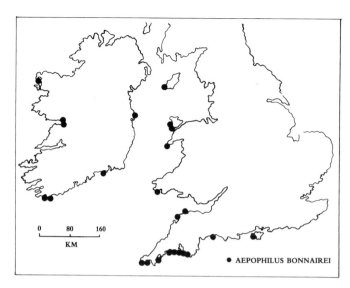

0   80   160
KM

● AEPOPHILUS BONNAIREI

Fig. 4.4 The modern distribution of Aepophilus bonnairei, *a shore-dwelling bug, which is most likely to have reached Ireland in early Littletonian time by moving along a continuous coastline that stretched from the Atlantic coast of France to Ireland.*

the route. A convincing demonstration is the modern distribution of a shore-living bug, *Aepophilus bonnairei* (Fig. 4.4). The modern headquarters of this insect, which lives in rock-crevices near low-tide-mark and can neither swim nor fly, are on the Atlantic coast from Morocco to Portugal. It could not have survived the cold of the Nahanagan Stadial in the British Isles, and when warmth returned at the beginning of the Littletonian Warm Stage it marched north up the French coast, skirted the embayments that then occupied the English Channel and the south of the Irish Sea, and made its way on to the Atlantic coast of Ireland. The orchid (*Neotinea*), found only in the Isle of Man and in western Ireland, hints at the same route.

Today we can only study the variety and distribution of the Irish flora and fauna as we see it before us, but we must always remember that since plants and animals first arrived they have been influenced by changing climate, pushed aside by expanding bogs, and grossly interfered with by man.

Naias is an inconspicuous, totally submerged water-plant. A small form, *N. flexilis*, still lives, though it is rare, in lakes in western Ireland and Scotland, with one outlying station in the English Lake District. But about 6000 years ago, when summer temperatures were slightly higher than they are today, it was widely distributed in Scotland, and in Scandinavia extended further to the north than it does today. The larger form, *N. marina*, today survives in the British Isles only in the Norfolk Broads, but it was widely distributed in Britain and Ireland around 6000 years ago. On today's distribution we might think that *Naias* had reached Ireland by an Atlantic route; the fossil record lets us see that both forms are probably of north European origin.

The Scots pine (*Pinus sylvestris*) probably died out in Ireland in the early centuries of the Christian era. Six

(*Erica mackaiana*) in Connemara and Donegal, and Mediterranean heath (*Erica erigena*) in Connemara with one outlying station near Bordeaux.

Two are saxifrages, London pride (*S. spathularis*) and its close relative, *S. hirsuta*, chiefly in the south-west. The sixth is the large-flowered pinguicula (*P. grandiflora*), found only in the south-west. The seventh, the strawberry tree (*Arbutus unedo*), also of the heather family, is Mediterranean, and has an outlying station in Brittany; in Ireland it is confined to the west. The eighth is an orchid, *Neotinea maculata*, chiefly in Clare and Galway; an outlying station has recently been found in the Isle of Man.

There is also an animal, the spotted slug (*Geomalachus maculosus*), which is restricted to the south-west, where it is quite conspicuous on wet rocks after rain.

While the absence of these species from Britain is hard to explain, I cannot feel that this group either survived off western Ireland or made its way from north-west Iberia to Ireland entirely by chance. I believe there was a west European coastal strip along which the group made its way to Ireland. Some stragglers were left behind to indicate thousand years ago it must have been widespread in Ireland, because in many places where peat has been cut we can see a sheet of pine stumps at the base of the bog. It was probably wetter conditions that enabled the bog to invade the pine forest. If another change brought about a drier bog surface, then the pine could invade the bog, and produce still another distribution pattern (see Photo 24).

Man has been the chief disturber of natural distributions. He introduced new plants and animals to compete with the indigenous forms, and has brought about further gross change by cutting down forests, draining wetland and mechanically removing peat. When there were primeval woods in Ireland, there were woodpeckers here also, as bones found in Clare caves show; when the woods vanished, the woodpeckers also vanished.

The different animal groups also show deficiencies, as great as or greater than those of the plants.

THE LAND MAMMALS OF IRELAND AND GREAT BRITAIN COMPARED

Species native to Ireland

Extinct	3
Native in Britain also	11
Naturalized in Britain	0
Absent from Britain	0
Total:	14

Species native to Britain

Extinct	4
Native in Ireland also	11
Naturalized in Ireland	3
Absent from Ireand	14
Total:	32

Similar shortfalls are recorded among the birds (Ireland 354; Britain 456) the reptiles (Ireland 1; Britain 4), and the amphibians (Ireland 2; Britain 6).

Professor Webb's figures show that Ireland has about 70% of the plants that occur in Britain. The same comparison has recently been made for groups of insect and other invertebrates occurring in terrestrial and freshwater habitats, and here Ireland has about 65% of the British number. It would therefore seem that the barriers which impeded access to Ireland operated with rather similar force on a wide range of plants and animals.

Early development of woodland: 10,000 to 8500 years ago

The current, or Littletonian, warm stage is, we believe, merely another interregnum in continuing cold, and we can follow its development — as far as it has proceeded — in the same way as we followed earlier warm stages. Figure 4.5 shows the phases of woodland development into which it can be divided, and also two curves, one to indicate the movement of temperature and the second to indicate the movement of sea-level.

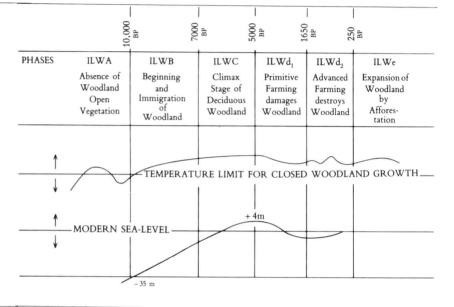

Fig. 4.5 Phases of woodland development in the Littletonian Warm Stage in Ireland.

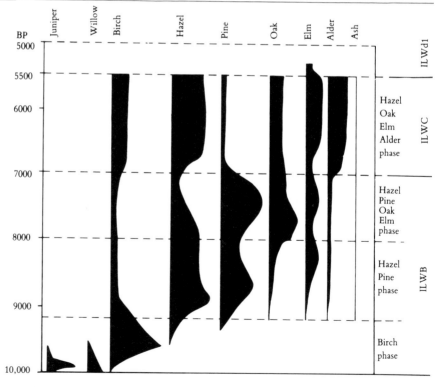

Fig. 4.6 Schematic pollen-diagram to illustrate the early development of the Littletonian woodlands in Ireland.

We can also draw a schematic pollen-diagram (Fig. 4.6) to indicate the order in which the trees arrived in Ireland, and give some indication of their relative importances, as shown by the amounts of pollen they produced. The amounts indicated are 'raw' figures, that is to say they are the numbers counted, and ignore the fact that some trees are much more lavish producers of pollen than others, and so give an impression that they were more important in the woodlands than their numbers warranted. It is possible to introduce corrections to allow for the relative pollen productions of the different trees, but that has not been done in this simple diagram.

As we have already seen, the Littletonian Warm Stage opens at 10,000 years ago when rising warmth brought the Nahanagan Stadial to an end. The beetles of the Nahanagan Stadial suggest a July average temperature of only 10°C, such as is found in the Scandinavian Mountains today, and they are rapidly replaced by relatively thermophilous forms which indicate a July average of 15°C, which is the same as that of today. Temperature was therefore not a limit on the movement of plants and animals, and immense migratory movements must have begun.

The first response of the flora to warming was a development of rich meadows with grasses, docks and meadowsweet. The meadows were quickly invaded by juniper, and within 250 years juniper scrub had replaced the meadows over wide regions. About 9500 years ago tree willows began to overshadow the juniper scrub, and these in turn gave way to tree birches, and Littletonian Ireland had its first woodlands. Aspen (*Populus tremula*) was also present, and — at least in the Burren — guelder rose (*Viburnum opulus*).

We have thus a birch phase which lasted till about 9250 years ago, by which time pollen of hazel is appearing in the pollen counts, and thus indicating the arrival of this bush or small tree. The expansion of hazel was rapid and complete in some areas, and slower and less overwhelming in others, and differences in soil and in aspect must have had considerable influence. In some areas the lake-muds are full not only of hazel pollen, but also of fragments of hazelnuts, and here there must have been dense hazelwoods.

The pine was moving into Ireland at about the same time as the hazel, and its spread also seems to have been irregular. It appeared early in the south-west, and only reached Donegal about 1000 years later. Soil differences may have kept the hazelwoods and the pinewoods apart from one another, but they both produced pollen abundantly, and we have a hazel-pine phase from about 9000 to about 8500 years ago (Pl. 17).

Fig. 4.7 Twenty microliths, the commonest form of flint artifact at Mount Sandel, are seen here at their actual size. They fall into four categories. Scalene triangles (a-d) were arrow-tips or the barbs and cutting edges of composite implements. Rods (e-h) may have been used in food preparation. Obliquely trimmed blades (i-l) could have been small knives. Needle points (m-p) may have been the tips of arrows or other projectiles. The microburins (q-t) are not tools but waste products.

The first appearance of man: c. 9000 years ago

Just south of Coleraine in north-east Ireland, high bluffs dominate the lower reaches of the River Bann at Mount Sandel. This very strategic site has been occupied by man throughout the millennia, and Peter Woodman, now Professor of Archaeology in University College, Cork, has shown that it is here that we have the earliest record of man in Ireland, in camp-sites that may go back as far as 9000 years ago. The site appears to have been occupied by people who used small flint points or microliths (Fig. 4.7), and small axes struck from flint pebbles, or from flakes off such pebbles. The microliths were probably set as barbs in a harpoon-like implement. These people had no knowledge of agriculture, and so they must have lived by hunting and fishing; they had no knowledge of the art of making pottery, and so they had not attained the level of Neolithic culture. By the time they reached Ireland the country had been re-smothered in trees, and they could not range wide prairies in search of herds of big game, as the Palaeolithic hunters had done. They seem to have had axe-like implements of chipped or roughly ground stone, but they either could not, or did not, use these for forest-clearance as the later Neolithic people used their hafted polished stone axes to open up cultivation-patches in the woodlands. They were hunters and fishers of Mesolithic (between Palaeolithic and Neolithic) status, restricted by their inability to clear large areas to roaming along the shores of lakes and rivers and along the coasts, hunting small game and catching fish, and collecting nuts and seeds, as seasonal opportunity offered (Pl. 19).

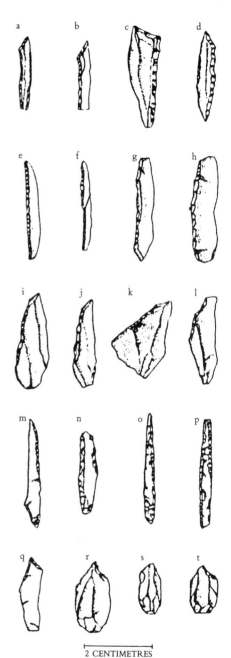

2 CENTIMETRES

Wild pigs seem to have been the largest animals they captured, and they probably had dogs to assist the chase. They took salmon, trout and eels from the river, and nearer its mouth sea-bass and flounders. Of birds there were four edible forms, pigeon, duck, grouse and capercaillie, and one bird of prey, the

goshawk. The capercaillie is a bird of pine forests, and it may then have been common in the early Irish pinewoods; it became extinct in the eighteenth century. The goshawk, also now extinct, was never a common bird, and it is curious that its bones have been found not only at Mount Sandel, but at a later Mesolithic site on Dalkey Island, Co. Dublin, and at the Early Bronze Age site of Newgrange, Co. Louth. Could it have been used in falconry, rather than killed as a bird of prey? The Mount Sandel site was rich in hazelnuts, which must have been freely available in the nighbouring woods. There were also charred seeds of the white water-lily (*Nymphaea alba*). These seeds were eaten by Mesolithic man. Charred seeds of the yellow water-lily (*Nuphar lutea*) were found on a late Mesolithic site on Lough Derravaragh, in Co. Longford.

Mount Sandel came to be noticed because archaeological debris was lying on its flanks. A second site appeared without warning and was excavated by Michael Ryan of the National Museum. A large area of raised-bog, known as Boora Bog, near Tullamore, Co. Offaly, is being developed by Bord na Móna. Usually the basal layers of the peat are left in position, so as to assist eventual reclamation. At one point, where a lake had formerly existed, all the peat was removed. A gravel ridge carrying an early Mesolithic site and a massive beach were exposed. Here was proof that there had been large lakes in early postglacial Ireland (see Fig. 4.2). The original Lough Boora was quite broad enough for strong winds to whip up considerable waves; when the waves reached the shore, they built up a substantial storm beach. There would have been a lagoon between the beach and the ridge, and obviously the top of the ridge overlooking the lagoon would have been a very attractive site for Mesolithic fishermen.

In north-east Ireland where deposits of chalk still survive, *flint*, a siliceous concretion, usually pale, which develops in chalk, was freely available as raw material for implements. At Lough Boora there was no flint, but the local limestone also had concretions, which were black and are known as *chert*. From this microliths very like those at Mount Sandel were worked, and there were also ground axeheads of slate. The

Fig. 4.8 Known Sandelian material. (Based on Woodman)

C-14 dates centred on 8400 years ago, of the same order of age as Mount Sandel.

Food debris was also much as at Mount Sandel, but in addition to pig, red deer and hare also occurred. There were bones from ducks and small fish, and again hazelnuts.

The whole settlement was then swallowed up, as bog vegetation developed and grew upwards, gradually blocking the local drainage system. The original Lough Boora shrank in area as bog growth constricted it, but its level was raised, and its final remnant was left 'perched' high above its first level.

Professor Woodman has recently picked up similar microliths along the River Blackwater, chiefly in the vicinity of Cappoquin. The microliths can be taken as the signature tune of the first wave of Mesolithic people, and a distribution-map (Fig. 4.8) shows where such implements have been found in Ireland. I call these first inhabitants the Sandelians, from their best known site (so far) at Mount Sandel.

Where did these first Irishmen come from? Microliths and axes are found in Mesolithic sites in Denmark, and we cannot overlook Denmark in our search for the original home of the first men to reach Ireland. There is also an early Danish Mesolithic, and this spills over into eastern England, where it perhaps finds its finest flowering at Star Carr, occupied about 9500 years ago. This wonderful site, discovered by John Moore and excavated by Grahame Clark, was on the margin of a lake which was then at a rather lower level, and the damp conditions created by a later rise in the water-table had enabled bone and wood to survive. So here we had, what we have yet to find in Ireland, a Mesolithic dwelling-site with all its appurtenances. There were antler harpoons, both finished and unfinished, and as if this was not enough, carefully cut antler head-dresses, which were used either as stalking-aids in actual hunting, or in ceremonies intended to promote success in the chase. There were also containers made out of birch bark.

The Star Carr folk had an impressive range of implements of flint and stone. Their axes (and adzes) were made from pebbles, not flakes, and are known as core-axes; in addition to variously trimmed flakes and microliths they also had the burin, a chisel-like and invaluable tool, especially for the cutting and working of bone.

In Denmark, lavish Mesolithic burials have been found; rows of shells in the grave suggest that the bodies were buried in garments richly embroidered with patterns of shells.

In Britain many Mesolithic sites occur on the uplands in the Pennines, placed perhaps where the lower forests were thinning out. This type of site has not yet been found in Ireland. An upland site at Filpoke Beacon in Co. Durham, dated to about 8750 years ago, has microliths very similar to the Irish ones, and it may have been one of these upland English groups that wandered westwards across the land-bridge. Some may have turned aside to what is now the Isle of Man, where microliths and other implements with Pennine affinities also occur. It is a nice thought that they may not have realized they were moving on into new territory. The woods were moving west, bringing the red deer and wild boar with them; it was natural for the Mesolithic hunters to keep in step.

20

Pl. 20 Bog of Allen, Co. Kildare. The raised-bog surface is purple, because the ling (Calluna) which grows densely on it is in flower. We can picture the growing bog as a glacier, slowly spreading over the surrounding green countryside. (R.F. Hammond)

21

Pl. 21 Camderry, Co. Galway. On this raised-bog we see a hummock of bog mass (Sphagnum imbricatum) on the right, and a pool on the left Cross-leaved heather (E. tetralix) and bog asphodel (Narthecium ossifragum) grow on the hummock. The insect-eating sundew (Drosera intermedia) and white beak sedge (Rhynchospora alba) grow round the margin of the pool. In the pool there are another moss (S. cuspidatum) and bog-bean (Menyanthes trifoliata). (C. Douglas)

22

23

24

Pl. 22 Glenamoy, Co. Mayo. Monotonous blanket-bog covers the landscape. The hills on the coastline to the north stand up like nunataks. The peat island in the pool is better drained, and is covered by tall ling (Calluna). (G. Doyle)

Pl. 23 Behy, Co. Mayo. Blanket-bog overlying the partly collapsed wall of a cairn which contained a megalithic tomb. (G.F. Mitchell)

Pl. 24 Shanid, Co. Limerick. This splendid rath has a high, platform-like, central area, and two protective banks and ditches. (L. de Paor)

Further woodland development: 8500 to 7000 years ago

By 8500 years ago the oak and the elm were beginning to overshadow the hazel on the heavier soils, and the amount of hazel pollen falls. The pine may have been forced back onto the sandier and drier soils, but it continued to produce very substantial amounts of pollen, which indeed tended to increase in quantity. At this time the climate in general may have been rather dry. Under these circumstances the alder, a tree of wet soils, may have been restricted to the margins of lakes and rivers, and this may be why its pollen makes only a trifling appearance in the pollen record. Ash will have been in the country, but was perhaps confined to dry limestone soils, a habitat which was not sufficiently extensive to enable the ash to make an effective contribution to the pollen rain. The yew will also have been in Ireland, but its pollen is relatively fragile and difficult to recognize in fossil form, and has hitherto been largely overlooked by many workers, including myself. More recent studies show that it was much more important in Ireland than has hitherto been supposed (Pl. 18).

We thus picture Ireland as having been in a state of vegetational turmoil for some 3000 years. The drama began when the pioneer trees, juniper, willow and birch, invaded the open meadows. The taller hazels and pines then overshadowed the earlier trees. Hazel in turn had to give way to the forest-size oaks and elms, while pine was displaced from the better soils. The establishment of the high forest brought about a position of some stability, which ran for about 1500 years until alder began to carve out an ecological niche for itself.

A visitor to Ireland at this time would have seen endless sheets of trees interrupted only by the water of lakes and river-channels. Such country has almost totally vanished, though some fragments do survive in the valley of the Lee; much more is now submerged

beneath the waters of a hydroelectric scheme (Photo 16).

These are the trees that did reach Ireland; what others fell by the wayside? It is not easy to understand why the small-leaved lime (*Tilia cordata*) failed to reach Ireland, as it accompanied the oak and elm in their advance as far as south Wales, and Ireland had plenty of limestone soils on which to receive it. The hornbeam (*Carpinus*) and the field maple (*Acer campestre*) did not advance seriously beyond south-east England. The beech (*Fagus sylvatica*) is more of a problem; after introduction by man in the eighteenth century, it spread widely throughout Ireland, where it finds the moist conditions very much to its taste.

Photograph 16 The Geeragh, near Macroom, Co. Cork, now drowned beneath a reservoir. Here the Lee expanded into a network of streams and wooded islets, uninvaded by grazing animals. Much of lowland Ireland looked like this before fens and bogs clogged the waterways, and man and his animals damaged the woodlands.

It had reached south-east England before 7000 years ago, and its continued advance ought to have been rapid. Even if there was a water-barrier between Britain and Ireland, beech capsules float and birds feed eagerly on its small edible nuts.

Did other trees arrive, and then fail to survive? It is commonly pictured that climate at the opening of the Littletonian Warm Stage was relatively continental, and this may have meant that killing-frosts occurred later in spring than they do today. Within the range of plants that a botanist recognizes as a single species, there will be forms or *ecotypes* that have different ranges of tolerance for various factors, and it may have been that only those tree ecotypes that were sufficiently frost-hardy were able to hold a permanent position in the Irish woodlands.

It is one of the paradoxes of the modern Irish spring that some introduced trees, such as the horse chestnut (*Aesculus hippocastanum*) and the sycamore (*Acer pseudoplatanus*), which today are natives of more southern lands, put out their young leaves earlier than the native oak and ash, and are taking advantage of the sunshine while the Irish trees are still in bud. It may be that the modern Irish trees are the descendants of ecotypes that held back their leaves until the late killing-frosts were over, while other forms that put out their leaves earlier were eliminated. In the more oceanic Irish climate of today, the horse chestnut and the sycamore escape killing-frosts, and are able to flourish.

Photograph 17 The raised beach at Cushendun, Co. Antrim, which contains Mesolithic flint implements in Larnian style has been isotatically uplifted to 8.5 m above modern sea-level.

The second wave of human invasion, c. 8000 years ago

About 8150 years ago the Irish Mesolithic implements alter completely. Microliths almost disappear and heavy blades struck from large pieces of flint (*cores*) appear. The edges of the microliths had been carefully re-worked, but the sharp cutting-edges of the blades were used without any modification. Did the earlier group of people, the Sandelians, disappear, and were their successors, who for reasons shortly to become clear we call Larnians, of entirely different stock? The problem is compounded because, just as we find it hard to find ancestors for the Sandelians, the Larnians stand in equal isolation: we cannot find a source for them either. And the difference between the implements is so great, that we cannot see the Larnian style develop from the Sandelian. Larnian sites are common on the west shore of the Irish Sea (Fig. 4.9) and this suggests that the Larnians were good coastal navigators.

We see the newcomers first at the north-west corner of Lough Neagh where the Lower Bann makes its exit towards the sea, and a little later on the east Antrim coast at Cushendun. The oldest charcoal from Peter Woodman's excavations at Newferry on the Bann is 8150 years old. Many years ago Hallam Movius excavated implements from estuarine gravels and silts in the raised beach at Cushendun (Photo 17), and charcoal and wood collected at the same time have now been dated by radiocarbon to an age of 7500 years. The sites provide a well-defined if restricted range of implements, among which the microlith, so common at Mount Sandel, is very rare. Typical implements are common in the raised beach gravels at Larne, Co. Antrim, where they have long been collected and studied, and it is from this town that the name Larnian comes.

We get a tantalizing Mesolithic glimpse at Newlands Cross, west of Dublin.

About 8000 years ago springs were trickling from the local limestone; pond-snails lived in the water, and a thick deposit of shells and *tufa* (calcium carbonate deposited from the limy water) was formed. When collecting shells for study, Dr Richard Preece of Cambridge, as has already been noted, dug up a worked piece of flint, and seeds at the same level had an age of 7700 years. Though the flint is not a typical Larnian implement, it shows that Mesolithic man was here at the same time as the Larnians were.

In Ireland we can see parts of the Larnian way of life, but not as yet the full sequence. Lough Neagh was then at a lower level, and there were sand-banks and bars both at Toome Bay, where Lough Beg is cut off from the main lake, and at Newferry where the Lower Bann flows out of Lough Beg. Fishing parties taking seasonally running salmon and eels occupied the sand-banks, and almost certainly smoked fish there. After about 7000 years ago the Bann became more prone to seasonal flooding, and each year the water-meadows which flanked the river accumulated thin sheets of diatom-frustules which gradually built up into a thick layer of diatomite. In places the diatomite contains large spreads of ash, and some of these produced clusters of leaf-shaped flakes which the excavator, Hallam Movius, suggested might have been hafted together to form some sort of multi-pronged fishing implement — such as is still all too frequently (and illegally) employed in many parts of Ireland.

Flint was very valuable for the manufacture of implements, and this was easily obtained on the Antrim coast, where not only are there outcrops of chalk, but the glacial deposits and beach gravels are full of derived flint nodules. Larnian groups would visit the shores, and give a preliminary dressing to suitable flint blocks, leaving sheets of debris behind them. Sea-level was still rising, and the knapping-floors were overwhelmed by

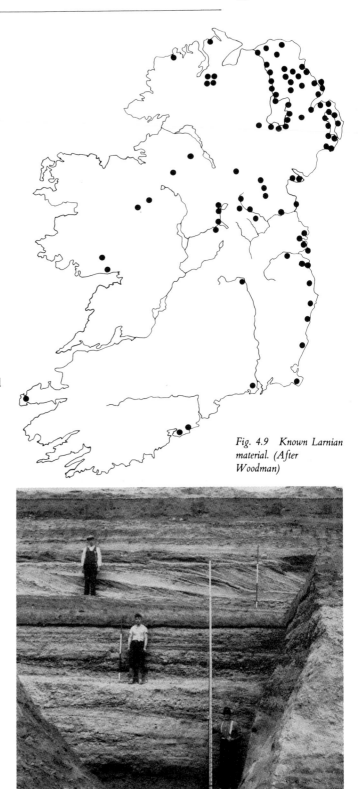

Fig. 4.9 *Known Larnian material. (After Woodman)*

the waves, and the debris embedded in beach deposits and spits, now raised above modern sea-level. Curran Point in Larne Harbour — which has been much built over — is such a spit and has long been famous for its content of man-worked flints. Excavating here in 1935 Hallam Movius opened up a pit 5 m square and 5 m deep, and from it he obtained over 15,000 pieces of humanly struck flint, but unfortunately relatively few finished implements. Sustenance was easy on the sea-shore, because both fish and shell-fish were readily available, and where the camp-sites were high enough to escape destruction by the sea, kitchen-middens of oyster, limpet, periwinkle and other shells have survived. It would not have been possible to cure shell-fish, crabs and lobsters, but sea-fish could have been salted and dried in the way that continues in Iceland to the present day. There great acreages of wooden fish-racks are employed in the drying and smoking of cod and other fish, and a substantial trade is carried on in the export of such preserved fish to Nigeria and other African countries which are short of protein. Porpoises and small whales would occasionally be stranded, or might under favourable circumstances be driven ashore, and after they had provided an immediate feast the rest of the flesh could be smoked, as mutton is smoked in Iceland today. This was how the coastal Aborigines of Australia were living when white folk first arrived there, and we are fortunate to have some paintings from which, if we ignore the difference in climate, we can form some impression of the Larnian way of life (Photo 18). Most early peoples had light boats, and in the currachs of the Atlantic coast of Ireland, we can imagine we see the descendants of Ireland's first boats (Photo 19).

To build boats a knowledge at least of simple carpentry is needed, and the Larnians must also have had implements of wood, bone and antler, but of these almost nothing has survived. At Toome Bay on Lough Neagh some pieces of

worked wood had got broken and were then used as firewood, but of the charred scraps it was only possible to say that they clearly had once been worked for some special purpose. A kitchen-midden on the shore of Dundalk Bay produced two small bone points, which were probably used as fish-gorges; a cord was attached to the point, not in the centre but towards one end; the point was baited and lowered into the water; an approaching fish would be given full opportunity to draw the bait well into its mouth; a quick jerk was then given to the cord, in the hope that the point would turn at right angles, so that its ends would jam in the sides of the fish's mouth, and enable the fish to be drawn from the water.

Most implements were made by a flaking process (Fig. 4.10). Suitable rounded pebbles of flint would be collected on the sea-shore or from glacial gravels; one end would be struck off, and a flat surface produced; by striking blows at the perimeter of this surface, elongated flakes would be detached; two forms of these were most sought for, parallel-sided blades or knives, and leaf-shaped flakes, to be used as pointed knives, or mounted in a shaft to serve as arrow- or spear-heads. The Larnians were aware that a thin edge could be strengthened by removing small flakes at right angles to the edge, by the so-called 'retouching' or 'reworking' technique, and flakes were turned into scrapers and borers. In the same way one edge of a flake could be blunted, so producing a 'backed' knife. Core-axes were occasionally made, by striking flakes off a chosen pebble until it was reduced to the desired shape. Flat pebbles, either elongated or rounded, were used for pounding or scraping, with the result that the edges either flaked away or became faceted.

The Larnians do appear to have made small clearings in the woodlands, and the axes may have been of use here. If we make very detailed pollen-counts at

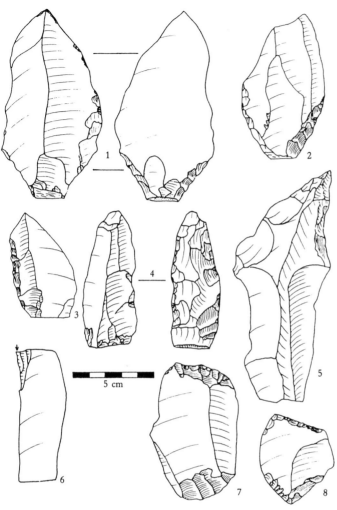

Fig. 4.10 *Larnian implements from Lough Kinale.*

1. *Leaf-shaped flake*
3. *Backed knife*
4. *Blade*
5. *Pick or borer*
6. *Burin*
7/8. *Scrapers*

that an artificial clearing would attract deer into positions where they could be easily trapped or shot.

Dependent as they were on hunting and collecting for their proteins and their carbohydrates, the Larnians must have led a semi-nomadic existence as the seasonal pattern of abundance of various foodstuffs led them on from one location to another. Such a pattern of life dominated the Maoris of the extreme south of New Zealand at the time when they first came in contact with white settlers. The Maoris had a wider range of implements than the Larnians, but were like them essentially food-collectors. For carbohydrate they largely depended on bracken rhizomes, and on the starchy roots and young stems of the *Cordyline* (still known in New Zealand as the cabbage tree). They had a permanent village site, from which foraging parties travelled to places where they could live comfortably for several weeks, gathering and preserving seasonally abundant foods. For one such group the following yearly pattern in search of protein has been recorded — September and October, up to Tuturau for lampreys at the Mataura Falls; November, on to the Waimea Plains to get eels; December, back to Tuturau to dry food; January, to the coast to catch fish and collect seaweed; February, making seaweed bags; March, to the offshore islands; April, catching and smoking seabirds; May, return from the islands; June, bringing presents of smoked seabirds to friends and relatives; July and August, catching forest birds.

At a later Larnian stage, about 5400 years ago, the same type of activity was taking place on the lakes in the Irish midlands. On the shore of Lough Derravaragh, just where the Inny enters the lake, there were extensive fens which were visited by people living in Larnian fashion. Chert outcrops on the shores of the lake, and this was used for the manufacture of implements. There will have been open channels in the fen through which the river entered

critical levels in deposits associated with Mesolithic activities, we can see small irregular movements in some values that suggest that some artificial interference with the woodlands was taking place. A seasonal camp-site may have been semi-permanently fenced, and a stockade would have been necessary to keep wolves and foxes, and an occasional wandering bear, at bay. Such a camp-site would from time to time be abandoned, and it would soon be noted that deer came to browse on the young trees and bushes that started to recolonize the site. Deer haunt the margins, rather than the depths of the forests, and it would be quickly realized the lake, and water-lilies growing in the open water beyond the edge of the fen. In the fen-peat there were the ashes and charcoal of numerous isolated fires, and associated with these were chert flakes, hazelnut shells and charred and uncharred seeds of the yellow water-lily (*Nuphar luteun*). We can picture parties of Larnian folk coming here in Maori style in early autumn, setting traps for fish in the fen-channels, collecting and perhaps parching water-lily seeds, gathering hazelnuts and giving a preliminary dressing to blocks of chert, carrying away the semi-worked pieces to be finished elsewhere.

As already noted we urgently need to find residential sites, where we shall find the tools with which sophisticated objects in wood and bone were fabricated, and not just the waste fragments which were discarded by the thousand. And we need wet sites, where organic materials and objects fashioned from them will have survived, together with food debris and other potentially informative rubbish.

One swallow does not make a summer, and one worked flint does not make an archaeological site, but the flint from Newlands Cross is the only one so far to come from a 'wet' site of this age in Ireland, and even a limited excavation there to see if there is an occupation-site nearby would be of the greatest importance.

Climax-phase of woodland: 7000 to 5100 years ago

In organic deposits which were accumulating about 7000 years ago, the pollen-counts show a dramatic change at this level, which must reflect a radical alteration in the woodlands. Alder rises from the meagre values it has hitherto shown, and pine falls back to a much lower level. Related changes can be traced throughout north-west Europe, and it may be that the climate had become more oceanic and wetter, enabling alder to form fen-woods on the damper soils, and forcing pine more exclusively onto the poorer soils. Temperatures remained high, with, as already noted, July temperatures perhaps 1° or 2°C warmer than at present.

Dense, tall, deciduous woodland dominated by alder, oak and elm occupied the better lowland soils, with birch and pine still probably holding their own on the uplands. The Climax-phase of woodland stability, a hazel-oak-elm-alder phase became established, and then persisted for about 2000 years until it was dramatically altered, by a wave of elm disease, just like the wave that is now sweeping western Europe, apparently due to the same cause, attack by a bark-beetle which gives entry to a fungus.

Our evidence for a severe attack by disease is given by an important reduction in the amount of elm pollen reaching lakes and bogs; after the fall pollen values rise again, sometimes to their former value. The cause of this oscillation is a matter of acute controversy. Neolithic farmers started to reach Ireland about 5500 years ago; armed with polished stone axes with good cutting-edges mounted in wooden handles, they undoubtedly opened up clearings in the woodlands, where cereals, grasses and herbs replaced trees. Local pollen production was thus disturbed, and we can see this disturbance in our pollen-counts.

Elm trees grow on good soils, and it was natural that the first farmers should

Fig. 4.11 Relative pollen-abundances of elm, pine and hazel in Ireland 5250 years ago.

Hazel: *Common in centre, most common in north centre.*

Elm: *Common in centre, most common in east centre.*

Pine: *Rare in centre, most common along western seaboard.*

(After Bradshaw)

be attracted to these soils, and clear away the trees. For many, including myself, this was the reason for the fall in pollen values. Others claimed that the first farmers must have been limited in numbers, and could not possibly have removed enough elm trees to cause the fall in pollen values. Young leaves make succulent fodder for cattle, and many primitive farming people cut leafy twigs off the trees and feed them to their stock; it was claimed that if such pruning of elm trees was severe, then the trees would fail to produce pollen. But again the question of farmer numbers arises. Climate was turned to for an explanation; if temperature was falling, then the elms would not do so well, and their pollen production would fall. But after the fall, the values for elm pollen rise again, and so it seems climatic deterioration cannot be the cause.

But while the debate has been raging, the number of radiocarbon datings for the elm-fall has been quietly increasing. The fall is now not only the most dated pollen horizon in the postglacial of Britain and Ireland, but also, within the limits of the radiocarbon method, the most synchronous. Twenty Irish dates lie between 5300 and 4600 years ago, and the mean would be about 5100 years ago. I now accept that the brief but dramatic fall in values for elm pollen was caused by a wave of disease which was at its most severe 5100 years ago.

We cannot overlook the fact that natural soil development must have been a factor in the establishment of the climax woodlands. But when we try to trace out the history of soil development in Ireland, we come up against the problem that man himself has been interfering with the soils for at least half the time that has been available for soil development, because it was about 5500 years ago that the natural progression was broken by man starting to clear trees away, in order to create clearings for his farming operations.

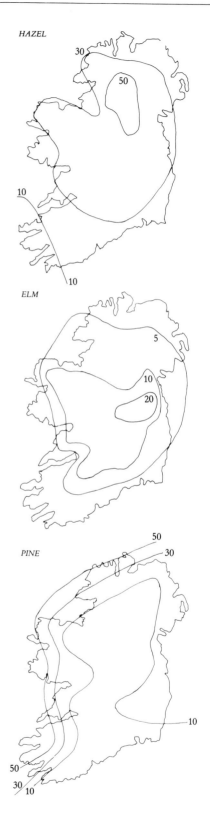

HAZEL

ELM

PINE

The opening 5000 years of the Littletonian Warm Stage must have seen a hand-in-hand development of the forests and of the soils on which they grew. The early shallow-rooted birches were progressively displaced by bigger and bigger forest trees with deeper and deeper rooting-systems, and deep soils will have formed. It was a very intimate relationship, because if on the one hand the more deeply penetrating roots and their accompanying microflora and fauna promoted soil development, on the other the inherent texture and base status of the soil in turn affected the competitive powers of the different tree genera, and thus influenced the composition of the woodlands. Due to the variety of Ireland's basic rock structure, and to the different flow-paths followed by different ice-masses, the parent material of the soils developed on glacial deposits varied widely, and so the forest pattern could not be monotonously uniform — as our pollen-diagrams often suggest — but presented a mosaic of different ecological systems, each in response to the local factors. Thus we can take a point in time, say 5250 years ago, just before the invasion of the elm disease, and try to determine from pollen values a fundamental woodland pattern for the country (Fig. 4.11). We thus see that elm was most common on the good soils of the midlands, and especially in the east where rainfall was lower; that hazel, which had formerly been common almost over the whole country, was now rare in the south-west, and most abundant in the north centre; while pine had almost completely withdrawn from the centre of the country, but was still very common along the western seaboard.

It is hard for us to picture the majesty and silence of those primeval woods, which stretched from Ireland far across northern Europe. We are accustomed to an almost treeless countryside, and if we can find anywhere some scraps of 'native' woodland, we are disappointed by the quality of the trees. For thousands of years man has been roving the Irish woodlands seeking 'good' timber for houses, ships and other uses. As a result all the well-grown 'good' trees have long since disappeared, and what are left are the progeny of 'bad' trees, rejected by earlier carpenters. If we visit the National Museum, we can see a dug-out canoe, still 18 m in length and 1.5 m across. We would find it hard to find in Ireland today an oak tree from which such a large canoe could be hewn. Similar fossil oaks are revealed from time to time in the English fenlands; they have straight trunks up to 27 m without side branches, indicating a forest height far greater than in today's British woodlands. In relict natural woodland in Poland, oaks with long unbranched trunks and small crowns still stand to a height of 26 m. In the museum we can also see wooden shields, 1 m in diameter, worked from a slice taken from the trunk of a well-grown forest alder. We could not find in Ireland today a single alder tree capable of supplying a blank for such a shield. Only in some remote parts of Europe can we recapture something of the vanished dignity of the Irish forests.

Fig. 4.12 Four stages in the development of a typical Irish raised-bog.

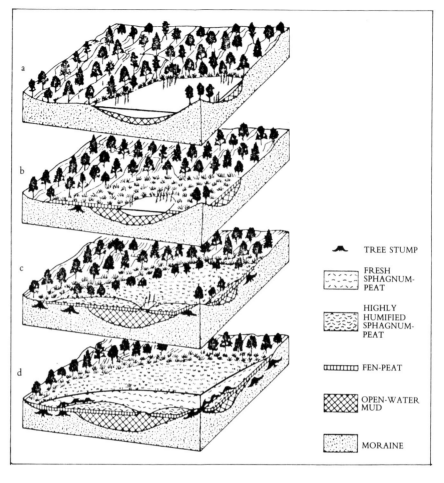

TREE STUMP

FRESH SPHAGNUM-PEAT

HIGHLY HUMIFIED SPHAGNUM-PEAT

FEN-PEAT

OPEN-WATER MUD

MORAINE

a *An open-water lake lies in morainic country which is covered by forest; an island of moraine rises in the lake, on whose floor open-water mud is accumulating.*

b *Fen plants, originally growing round the lake-edge, whose decaying debris builds up fen-peat, extend in two directions: out into the lake as accumulating mud makes its margins shallow, and inland into the forest, burying the tree-stumps with its peat.*

c *The same process continues, and as the fen-peat thickens, its surface becomes less rich in nutrients, and is invaded by the acid bog community, dominated by Sphagnum-moss. Nourished only by rain-water, the bog community slowly builds up a dome-like mass of highly humified Sphagnum-peat. As the bog grows, the local water-table rises, and the fen-peat creeps still higher up the surrounding slopes, killing more trees as it advances. The flanks of the dome of peat are relatively dry, and some trees can grow there.*

d *Some change in conditions allows the Sphagnum-peat to form more quickly, and the dome, now composed of fresh Sphagnum-peat, grows up still higher. The trees on the flanks of the older raised-bog die, and are buried by peat. The island, which had been getting smaller and smaller as bog growth continued, is finally overwhelmed by peat, and its trees disappear.*

First development of peat:
c. 9000 years ago

Throughout the period of the Beginning-phase (ILWB), from 10,000 to 7000 years ago, the great stretches of open water that were established after cold conditions had ended were being progressively reduced in area by the growth of marginal fens and marshes. This was the first link in a chain of development that led to the building-up of raised-bogs (Fig. 4.12). Plants capable of spending their entire life largely submerged, such as bladderworts (*Utricularia*) and hornwort (*Ceratophyllum*), established themselves in shallow waters, and as their debris together with silts and clays further reduced the depth, plants with floating leaves such as the pondweeds (*Potamogeton*) and the water-lilies (*Nuphar, Nymphaea*), colonized the margins. Soon the margins were invaded by the reedswamp plants, the bulrush (*Schoenoplectus lacustris*), the reed (*Phragmites communis*), the sedge (*Cladium mariscus*) and many others, and the accumulating vegetable debris, gradually consolidating into fen-peat, built itself up to water-level. In the fen, species of *Carex* (sedges) and of grass are dominant, and there are flowering plants, such as marsh cinquefoil (*Potentilla palustris*), marsh marigold (*Caltha palustris*), cuckoo-flower (*Cardamine pratensis*) and meadowsweet (*Filipendula ulmaria*). At Ballyscullion Bog, Co. Antrim, first investigated by Jessen, and later re-investigated with the aid of radiocarbon dating by Alan Smith, such fen-peat was forming at least 9000 years ago (Pl. 16).

If the water-table remained constant in level, willows and birches might invade the margin of the fen; as peat rich in sedge and wood debris began to build up, the wooded area would extend and other trees such as pine might invade its drier surface, and gradually a thick layer of wood-peat was formed. Such a development took place at Ballyscullion Bog, as is shown in the cross-section drawn up by Jessen (Fig. 4.13b).

If the water-table rose, the drainage of the surrounding slopes would be worsened, and the fens and fen-woods could creep up the surrounding slopes beyond the limits of the primary basal fen. Bob Hammond of Bord na Móna examined such a situation in the great areas of bog that now occupy much of the central lowlands of Ireland, and I have constructed a sketch-section to summarize his results (Fig. 4.13a). I have to say that the construction is my work, and I hope that it does not do injustice to Hammond's evidence. Here over a wide area there had been an early lake, and the open-water lake-mud is seen at the base of the section. On the right-hand of the section wet fen-wood is seen growing directly on the local glacial deposits 8500 years ago, and when the lake margin was invaded by fen vegetation, the fen spread in both directions building fen-peat out over the lake-muds on the one hand, and up the slope on top of the wood-fen-peat on the other. On the left-hand side of the section, where the slope is steeper, the wood-fen-peat took a longer time to extend upwards, and its base is correspondingly younger, having only started to form about 5000 years ago.

Lakes continued to shrink as fens and fen-wood extended, and as the fen-peat thickened, the plants on its surface found it more and more difficult to maintain their necessary supply of inorganic material from the underlying mineral soil, and the way was open for plants that could thrive on minimal amounts of inorganic nutrients to colonize the surface of the peat (Fig. 4.13a).

The moss *Sphagnum* was ideally suited for this purpose, for it can grow vigorously when nourished only by rain and by the very small amount of nutrient material contained in the rain. *Sphagnum* has a remarkable capacity for capturing and storing rain-water. Many of its cells are like small hollow boxes with an aperture through which water can enter as into a trap; it is then held

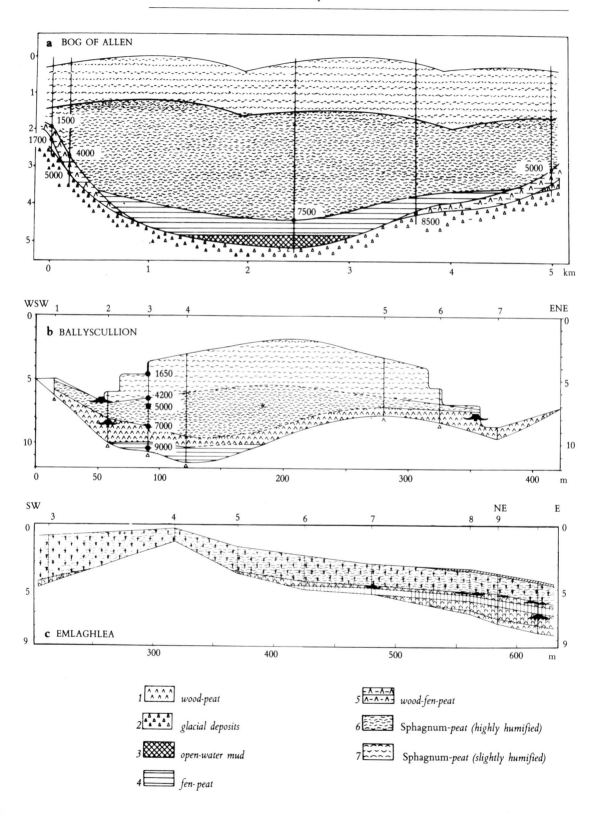

a BOG OF ALLEN

1500
1700
4000
5000
5000
7500
8500

0   1   2   3   4   5 km

WSW   1   2   3   4   5   6   7   ENE

b BALLYSCULLION

1650
4200
5000
7000
9000

0   50   100   200   300   400 m

SW

3   4   5   6   7   8   9   E
                                                         NE

c EMLAGHLEA

300   400   500   600 m

1 ^^^^ *wood-peat*   5 ⌐⌐⌐ *wood-fen-peat*

2 ▲▲▲ *glacial deposits*   6 ▒▒▒ *Sphagnum-peat (highly humified)*

3 ▨▨▨ *open-water mud*   7 ∿∿∿ *Sphagnum-peat (slightly humified)*

4 ≡≡≡ *fen-peat*

in the trap until needed for further growth. We can picture that the fen-surface was irregular and that rainfall was increasing. Pools will have formed in the fen hollows, and vigorously growing *Sphagnum* species, such as *S. fuscum*, will draw on the water, and build themselves up into a small mound or hummock. There is a limit to the height of the hummock, whose top becomes very sensitive to periods of dryness. As soon as the top becomes reasonably dry, it is invaded by lichens and by ling (*Calluna vulgaris*). As rain continues, the hummocks themselves now provide the high points between which water gets trapped, and shallow pools form between them. Aquatic *Sphagna* which grow submerged, such as *S. cuspidatum*, invade the pools and build up a muddy layer which shallows the pools. The deer-grass (*Trichophorum cespitosum*), the cotton-grass (*Eriophorum angustifolium*), the white beak-sedge (*Rhynchospora alba*), and the sundews (*Drosera* spp.) — which supplement their nutrient supply by catching insects — come in round the margin of the pond until the hummock-building *Sphagna* take over, and a new hummock rises over the former pool, while the tops of the old hummocks await flooding to form the next generation of pools. As the hummocks and pools scattered over the bog-surface replace one another cyclically, capillarity carries the water-table up with them, and the *Sphagnum*-peat rises into a dome or raised-bog nourished only by rain-water, forming the so-called ombrogenous-bog (Pls. 20, 21).

Such is the hummock/pool picture of raised-bog growth. But the picture is probably an over-simplification. Other studies suggest that the *Calluna*-occupied hummocks may persist, and maintain a vertical growth through a considerable thickness of peat, while the pools between them fluctuate in size. In some bogs the pools have a linear arrangement, lying at right angles to the slope of the bog surface; if the bog has expanded due to the uptake of additional water, the pools may lie in

tears in its surface. Given constant climate, will the bog dome attain a certain degree of convexity, and then come into a stillstand phase?

The bog can only grow because the rate of accumulation of vegetable debris exceeds the rate of decay. Most of the decay appears to take place in the top 20 cm, because below that level conditions are waterlogged, anaerobic and acid, with the result that only very few decomposing organisms can operate. If growth is slow, there is time for attack on the surface materials, which partly break down or *humify*, producing brown degradation-products which culminate in jelly-like or liquid humic acids. If growth is rapid, the plant debris passes quickly beyond the reach of decay, and can survive in a remarkably undamaged condition. Efforts are made to correlate the degree of decay, or *humification*, with climate, strong humification being equated with relatively warm, dry conditions, and weak humification with relatively cool, wet conditions.

If climate moves towards warmth and dryness, the pools dry up, growth slows down, trees invade the bog margins, humification proceeds, and a rind of well-decayed peat covers the bog. If cold wet conditions return, the bog surface is flooded, the trees are killed and their stumps buried, and fresh unhumified peat starts to build up (see Fig. 4.12).

Raised-bogs, which were building up highly humified *Sphagnum*-peat, had certainly started to form, both in the midlands and in the north of Ireland, not less than 7000 years ago. It was at about the same time that alder started to expand in the Irish woodlands, and both phenomena may be due to increased wetness, which enabled water-tables to rise and allow the fens to expand, and the alder to establish fen-woods. Because the *Sphagnum*-community can flourish when nurtured only by rain, it is tempting to think that increased wetness meant increased

*Fig. 4.13 Sections through Irish bogs. **a** Schematic cross-section of large raised-bog complex in the Irish midlands to illustrate its progressive expansion as time elapsed. (Based on work by R. Hammond) **b** Cross-section of the raised-bog at Ballyscullion, Co. Antrim, as drawn up by Knud Jessen, with added radiocarbon datings by Alan Smith.*

***c** Cross-section through blanket-bog at Emlaghlea, Co. Kerry.*

rain, and that this was the factor that triggered off the growth of the ombrogenous raised-bog. But the inhibiting factor that prevents the development of the *Sphagnum*-community may not be rainfall below a certain level, but rather the inability of the *Sphagnum*-community to oust other communities as long as the latter are continuing to receive at least the minimum amount of inorganic nutrients necessary for their growth. In other words it was the thickening of the fen-peat, to the point where the roots of the fen-plants could no longer draw sufficient inorganic nutrient to make healthy growth possible, that gave the *Sphagnum*-community its opportunity.

Two lines of evidence point in this direction. Raised-bog peat seems to find it impossible to start to form directly on inorganic soil; there must always be an insulating layer of fen-peat, which has in many cases a peaty podzol soil at its base.

Thus a peripheral band of fen vegetation always lies between the plants of the mineral soil and the plants of the raised-bog community, and unless the band advances secreting the insulating layer beneath itself, then the raised-bog cannot expand laterally, though it can grow upwards into a dome. The fens that lay in the poorly drained ground between drumlins often provided nuclei for raised-bog growth, and from such nuclei the surface of the bog would rise like a rising tide to surround and eventually engulf the drumlins. But at all times a ribbon of fen, whose plants drew their nourishment from the drainage water from the mineral soil of the drumlin, lay between the slopes of the drumlin and the rising dome of the bog (see Photo 31).

Today we have the impression that raised-bogs are very rare or absent near the coasts of east and south-east Ireland and that this reflects the dryness of these regions (Fig. 4.14). But even here we can find the townland name

'Redbog' usually associated with low-lying ground, and here there will formerly have been raised-bogs which were cut away for fuel in days when the population was much higher than it is today. Few parts of Ireland have an annual rainfall of less than 750 mm, but although an area of the midlands between Athlone and Birr has no more rain than this, it is an area that is buried beneath some of the largest and deepest raised-bogs in Ireland.

The raised-bog system, once its growth had been initiated, may have been more or less self-perpetuating. It could trap water directly from the air, and build its own water-table up above that of the surrounding countryside. As it expanded it built up a natural dam across valleys which had previously been free to discharge surface water. The raised-bog can be likened to an enormous bag of water, and though we have very little knowledge whether there is a slow circulation of water within the bag, or whether water leaks out of the bag into the surrounding countryside, it is obvious that such a mass of saturated material may well have important effects on the water-table in the area surrounding it. The drainage of the neighbouring woodland floors may be further impeded, and the ground made still wetter.

If we picture the raised-bog as a water-filled bag, we can immediately see that damage to the bag can cause irreparable damage to the whole bog-structure. Conservationists find it extremely difficult to convey this concept to those who would 'develop' a bog, whether on a small or a large scale. One cannot develop one half of a bog, and conserve the other. Small hand-cutting at the edge of a bog allows large quantities of water to escape; the bog-margin drops in level and becomes drier; the local pools disappear and the bog-surface becomes heather-clad and incapable of growth. The large-scale developer wants to cut a drain to separate what is to be developed from what is to be conserved, and cannot see that the drain

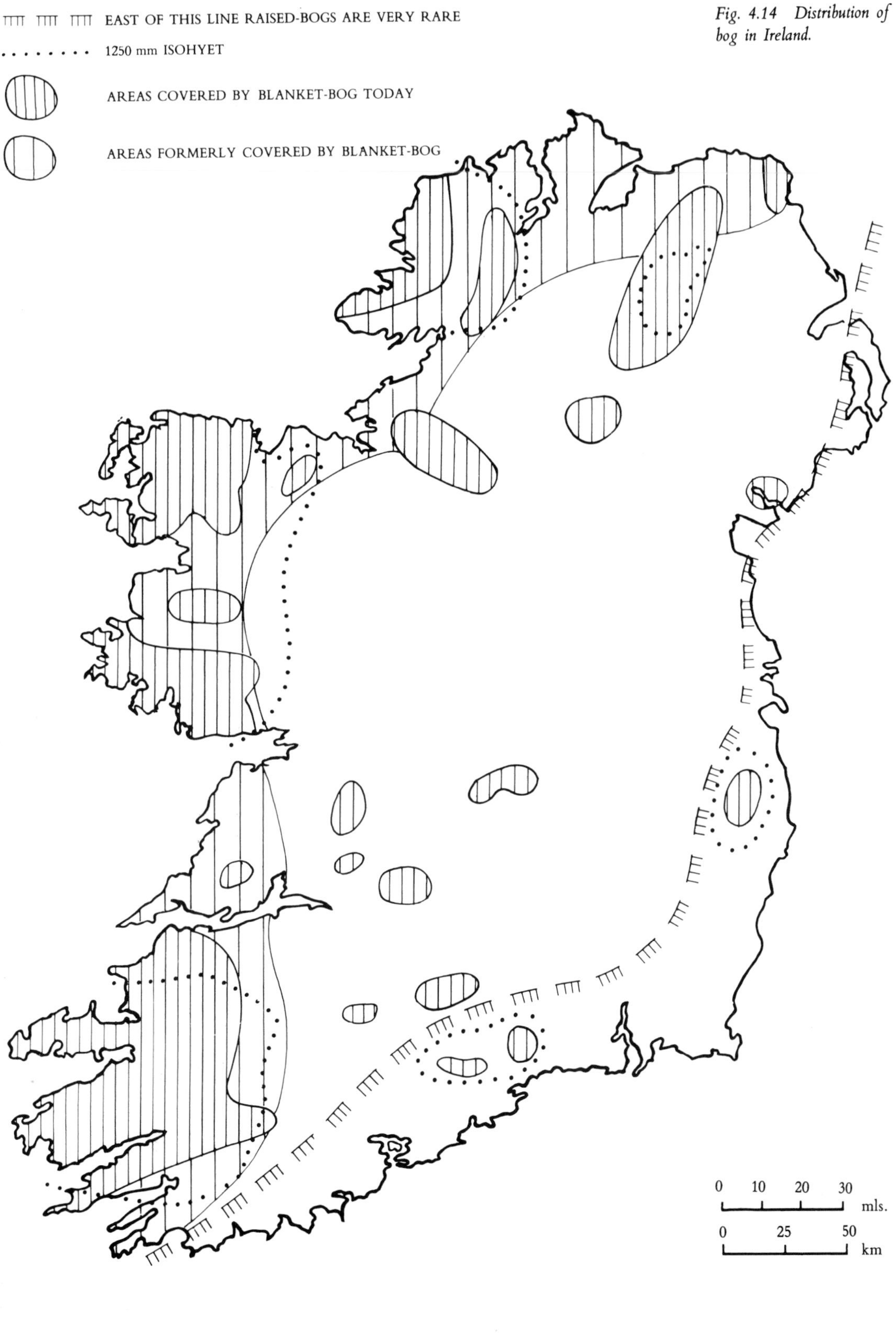
EAST OF THIS LINE RAISED-BOGS ARE VERY RARE
1250 mm ISOHYET
AREAS COVERED BY BLANKET-BOG TODAY
AREAS FORMERLY COVERED BY BLANKET-BOG
0 10 20 30 mls.
0 25 50 km

Fig. 4.14 Distribution of bog in Ireland.

will start a haemorrhage which will influence the whole bog. Continued drainage will drop the whole bog surface by several metres.

Whatever may be the complicated factors that initiated bog-growth, domes of highly humified *Sphagnum*-peat had started to develop at least 7000 years ago. Climate was still relatively favourable, and bog-growth was slow. This type of accumulation continued till at least 5000 years ago.

In the next chapter we shall see how the first farmers affected the woodlands when they arrived in Ireland about 5500 years ago. But the acme of the Irish forests had probably passed with the climatic optimum. On the lowlands the expanding bogs were starting to engulf them like an inexorable tide. On the uplands increased exposure was probably enforcing a retreat to lower levels.

5
THE FIRST FARMERS: 5700 to 1650 years ago

The Neolithic farmers and their megalithic tombs:
5700 to 4000 years ago

The Neolithic way of life, with its domestic animals, its cultivated crops, its pottery and its polished stone implements, began in the Middle East, and had reached south-east Europe before 7000 years ago. Our first record of Neolithic activity in Ireland is at Ballynagilly in Co. Tyrone 5700 years ago. How did knowledge of farming make a 'great leap forward' and spread apparently without difficulty throughout the whole of north-west Europe, so that it had reached even into Ireland almost 6000 years ago? One can only suppose that the conditions of the 'climatic optimum' greatly favoured agriculture, and that the farming population was constantly increasing and radiating outwards. In central Europe farming was on open plains, and as soon as the forests of the north-west were reached, agricultural practices must have changed substantially. Woodland had to be cleared, and soil exhaustion came more quickly under the leaching effect of western rain. When the patch was exhausted there was still virgin forest ahead, and so you moved on. Can we picture a wave of agriculture advancing ever northwards and westwards through the woodlands, just as a fairy ring of toadstools advances outwards in a meadow?

Humphrey Case has discussed the problems of Neolithic migration in a very enlightening way, and he points out that communal movement implies the transposition of men, women, children and infants, together with breeding and milking livestock and seed-corn. Such an Odyssey could only take place at a certain time of the year, probably between August and November, when the crops had been harvested and there was still good grass and leaf-fodder along the route. The route to be followed would have been well prospected because once the crops had been sown, a limited number of able-bodied men could have gone out in scouting-parties, carrying some food but also existing in Mesolithic style by hunting and food-gathering. But sooner or later a water-barrier would cause a temporary halt.

From the chalk-cliffs of Calais the identical lands across the English Channel could easily be seen, and such a crossing was not too daunting or difficult for scouting-parties, but what about the livestock, the cattle, the sheep and the pigs? Until recently currachs (see Photo 19) were built in western Ireland with nothing more than lengths of timber, wooden pegs, rods of hazel or willow, hair twine and hides, though today more modern materials are used. These boats are about twenty feet in length, and in calm weather can carry up to twelve people, or a tonne and a half of potatoes, or a cow with its legs tightly roped together.

Case discusses the type of boat that might have been available to Neolithic travellers, and comes to the conclusion that lightness and manoeuvrability were more important than size. A currach-type boat about thirty feet (10 m) in length, with eight oarsmen and a helmsman, carrying about three tonnes gross weight might have been near the ideal size. With space for the crew and two dogs, and bedding for the stock, its load for a sea passage might have been two adult cows and two calves, or about six pigs, or ten sheep or goats. Because of the difficulty of watering stock on a voyage, such trips must of necessity have been short. Skinbags or vessels containing water would add to the load of an already overcrowded boat; in any case the cattle would have been lying trussed on their sides, and could only have been given water with considerable difficulty. Case thinks that stock if well watered beforehand might hold out for two days, but that they would get restless and dangerous as their thirst developed. They might also die quickly from a build-up of gas in the rumen. It is clear that sea voyages would have to be planned with some care, and that undue hold-ups had to be avoided.

We speak of not putting all our eggs in one basket, but this is exactly what Neolithic folk were doing as they loaded their stock and their seed-corn into their skin boat on the shore of the English Channel or the Irish Sea. They could not have afforded not to know exactly where they were going, and what the beaches, tides and currents would be like at their landfall. Case thinks that there must have been a lot of coming and going, the location of elm-rich woodlands where the soils would be fertile, and perhaps the establishment of stock and crops on the far shore, before the final migration of the whole community. There was too much at stake to take a chance on *terra incognita*. Given these considerations it is tempting to think that the first landings in Ireland must have been on the coasts of Antrim and Down, which are clearly visible from Britain. Scouting-parties may well have reported that here alone in Ireland there were ample supplies of flint. Tidal currents run strongly in the North Channel, but the distance is short, and advantage

could be taken of spells of fine weather.

In an earlier discussion of the return of animals and plants to Ireland after the Ice Age, I referred to the influence of man. As the currach carried man and beast to Ireland, its floor would have been soiled by a litter of hay debris with grass and weed seeds mixed with animal dung. After the cargo had been discharged, the currach would have been turned upside down for storage, even if it was not cleaned out, and the litter would have fallen to the ground; what better way could we have for the introduction of new plants to Ireland? Some workers picture small mammals as also being introduced in this way, but even if they did get into the currach, I imagine they would have been noted during the voyage, and quickly killed.

Once safely ashore, there was much to be done. Woodland had to be cleared to provide plots for cultivation and paddocks for grazing. The cleared areas had to be surrounded by stockades. Above all, the breeding stock had to be protected from their numerous enemies. First of these were the animal predators, the wolf, the lynx, the fox, none of which had seen slow-moving domesticated animals before, and would regard them as natural gifts from the gods. Second, there were those less lucky immigrant farmers who had lost some of their vital stock on the voyage, or whose bull was sterile, or whose heifers were barren, who were desperate and would stop at nothing. And then there were the Larnians, amazed by the newcomers, with their strangely different way of life. What were the contacts — hostile or friendly? I believe that friendly trading relations were established, and that the higher standard of living of the farmers raised that of the aborigines, who at first rapidly increased in numbers, and then were assimilated into the Neolithic communities. Both the coastal Larnians in Co. Dublin, and the lakeside settlers in Co. Westmeath, are dated after the arrival of the Neolithic people: they may have established fishing villages in the vicintity of Neolithic settlements, and traded fish for corn.

Sixty years ago the late Professor Macalister thought that we had no evidence of an extensive Neolithic way of life in Ireland. Fifty years ago Davies and Evans began to show that there had been a great deal of Neolithic activity in the north-east of Ireland, and forty years ago Séan Ó Ríordáin showed that the limestone land around Lough Gur in Co. Limerick had also been densely settled. These discoveries did not upset the idea that the first entry to Ireland had been across the North Channel, and that Neolithic settlement had been restricted to land of good quality, the infertile west being avoided.

Work now in progress is showing that there was Neolithic activity at at least three sites in south-west Kerry, and that Neolithic people settled and prospered in the valleys and bays of west Connemara, and also on the north Mayo coast. In addition to entry across the North Channel, we may have to picture an entry from Brittany through Cornwall and the Isles of Scilly into the south-east, and even an entry from Brittany direct to the west coast. Our picture of population numbers must also change. While we have no real idea of the population in Neolithic times, it is clear that whatever hazy estimate we may have, it will now have to be substantially increased.

Estimates of population will depend on the number of centres of activity recognized, and we can recognize these centres in three ways, two direct, one indirect. Many Neolithic groups built tombs of large stones, and so we speak of *megalithic* tombs. There were standard patterns for such tombs, and if we identify such a tomb, then we know that there must have been Neolithic people in the area. Again Neolithic pottery falls into clearly recognizable classes, and if we excavate such pottery, again we have evidence of occupation.

The indirect method is botanical. The clearing of woodland had a double effect on local pollen production; as trees were removed, the amount of tree pollen in the air in spring was reduced; new plants, chiefly cereals and their weeds, in the tillage plots added new types of pollen to the Irish air; grasses flourished in the grazing paddocks, and the amount of grass pollen in the local air increased; the hay that the immigrants brought with them to feed their animals *en route* contained weed seeds, possibly from plants hitherto unknown to Ireland. Unfortunately cereals (wheat, barley, oats and rye) only produce pollen in very small quantities, though the grains are large and easily recognizable. This man-produced alteration in the pollen-rain is recorded in lake and bog deposits, and can be noted by the pollen-counter.

About fifty years ago Johannes Iversen in Denmark was the first to put two and two together and recognize that the increase in grass pollen and the appearance of the pollen of herbs that even today are still farming weeds — such as ribwort plantain (*Plantago lanceolata*), dock (*Rumex*) and nettle (*Urtica*) — must indicate forest clearing followed by farming, and he called this process 'landnam', using an old Scandinavian word for 'land taking'. Unfortunately these changes coincided with a massive drop in the amount of elm pollen in the counts, and for Iversen and many workers after him — including myself — this was the clinching point; the drop was due, we thought, to farmers concentrating their clearances on the good soils on which the elm trees grew. Great attention was concentrated on a man-produced 'elm-decline', which we all looked for in our pollen-diagrams.

I now think we are dealing with coincidence. The farmers had arrived and were making small clearances in the woods, particularly the elm-woods, when all of a sudden, to their amazement, the elms they had been struggling to clear away died, and great

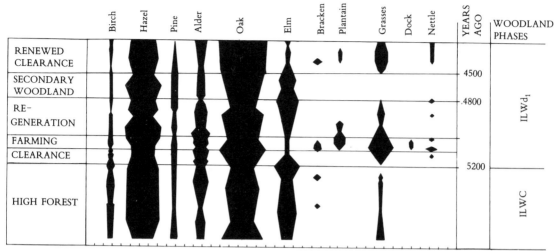

Scale in units of 10%

Fig. 5.1 A schematic pollen-diagram from Fallahogy, Co. Londonderry, to illustrate a cycle of Neolithic land clearance.

areas of unshaded fertile land opened up before them; they must surely have thought the gods were on their side. This welcome offer of more land must have led to more food and more population, and the rate at which Neolithic activity expanded in north-west Europe may owe much to this outbreak of disease.

A 'landnam' cycle has been studied in Ireland in a bog at Fallahogy, Co. Londonderry, where detailed pollen-counts were combined with numerous radiocarbon datings; the results are shown in Fig. 5.1.

In this type of diagram the pollen-values are represented as free-standing columns, which expand or contract in width as values increase or diminish. A scale divided in units representing 10% of all pollen counted is shown along the base of the diagram, and along any horizontal line the total intercepts of the columns should add up to 100%. After the pollen-counts had been made, the recorded values were adjusted to accord with observations that some tree genera produce, area for area, very much more pollen than others. The aim is to make pollen-values relate to the areas occupied by the different trees, and not just report the crude pollen-values. This is the only diagram in this

book in which such an adjustment has been made.

At the base we see the Climax-phase continuing, with hazel, oak, elm and alder providing the bulk of the pollen, and the grasses only able to make a trifling contribution to the pollen-rain. Then forest-clearance begins, at this site simultaneously with the 'elm-decline'. Hazel falls in value, and grasses begin to rise. A period of agriculture lasting about 350 years follows; grass rises to higher values, and some plants, notably plantain, dock and nettle rise to weed status in the cultivation-plots; bracken may have grown more freely. The natural fertility of the surface soil of the patches was quickly reduced, and when the farmers abandoned them, they were invaded first by hazel and then by the forest trees. The grasses and weeds were gradually suppressed, and secondary woodland was established.

During the period of secondary woodland the deep roots of the trees penetrated down to levels where the soil was still rich in nutrients. These substances were drawn up into the leaves and wood of the tree, and when tree-debris was incorporated into the forest humus, the surface layers of the soil regained much of their lost fertility. The farmers could thus return to an area they had earlier abandoned. They did return at Fallahogy after another 350 years had elapsed, and at the top of the diagram we see the opening of the next farming phase.

The dramatic fall in elm pollen is now firmly dated by radiocarbon to about 5100 years ago. We have good radiocarbon dating for a Neolithic settlement 5700 years ago at Ballynagilly, near Cookstown, Co. Tyrone, and a nearby bog recorded contemporaneous pollen fluctuations which indicated woodland clearance. Pre-'elm decline' forest disturbances have been recorded at many sites in the British Isles, and there has been much discussion as to whether Mesolithic man might have carried out some forest clearances; occasional grains of cereal pollen have also been recorded as pre-5100 years ago. These disturbances may well have been brought about by very early Neolithic immigrants.

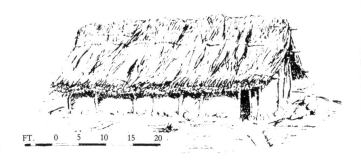

Though relatively high, at 180 m (600 ft), Ballynagilly was a most attractive site, which continued to be occupied by prehistoric man over a long period of time. Here there was a low well-drained hillock of glacial gravel, with a strong spring of clear water nearby. That the first phase of settlement was Neolithic is shown by pits and a hearth with pottery. Settlement continued, and a substantial house was erected. This was almost square, with 6 m sides, and had been built by erecting radially split oak planks in a foundation trench; it had probably burned down, and charred plank remains gave a C-14 date of 5165 years ago. Within the house post-holes indicated how the roof had been supported, and there were also two hearths and a refuse-pit with pottery and other debris.

A much larger rectangular house (13 m by 6 m), dated to 4600 years ago, was found at Ballyglass, near Ballycastle, Co. Mayo. It produced both Neolithic pottery and flint implements. A megalithic tomb of court-cairn type had

later been erected over the ruins of the house, and there were thirty similar tombs in the area; a substantial local population is implied. Later Neolithic houses were discovered at Lough Gur, Co. Limerick, during the extensive series of excavations carried out in that area by the late Seán Ó Ríordáin, whose untimely death was such a blow to archaeological studies in Ireland. Both rectangular and round houses were revealed, and charcoal from the base of a post-hole gave a C-14 date of about 4500 years ago: an artist's impression (Fig. 5.2) suggests what the houses may have looked like. As at Ballynagilly, most had a hearth and a refuse-pit inside them: the pits may have started as store-places, and only been used for refuse later. Besides protecting their stock, the settlers had

Fig. 5.2 Reconstructions of types of Neolithic houses excavated by S. P. Ó Ríordáin at Lough Gur, Co. Limerick.

to protect their seed-corn against damp and weevils, as well as against thieves, and what better place could be found than beside the constantly attended hearth?

When the necessary energy had been expended on house and homestead, patience and resolution were the next qualities needed; in animal husbandry patience extending over years, until the foundation-stock had been built up to a level at which it could be safely cropped, and resolution to ensure that no matter what hardship, what famine, came, the long-term breeding-stock would not be sacrificed to meet a short-term crisis, however severe it might be. In plant husbandry not only had the seed-corn to be guarded, but when sown it had to be defended during daylight hours against pigeons and sparrows. When it appeared above ground new enemies — deer, wild boar and hares — as well as the local farm beasts had to be guarded against night and day, and careful weeding was necessary if the return was to be as high as possible. Children and old folk, of course, could carry out much of this work, but the total amount of labour required in the growing-season must have been very great. If the crop was a light one, resolution was again needed to carry an adequate seed-stock through

to the next season. Taken all in all rare qualities of leadership were needed if the immigrant group was to survive the first few years of transplantation.

We can now move forward to the point where the farming communities are established in Ireland, and ask ourselves, 'What equipment have they got, what do they do with it, and what are they doing to the landscape?'

We can take the polished stone axe (Fig. 5.3c) first because it was with this tool, suitably mounted in a wooden handle — occasionally preserved in bog-finds — that the farmers were enabled to establish mastery over their environment to a degree that was not possible to their Mesolithic predecessors. They were now able not only to eradicate trees on a large scale but were also able to work big pieces of wood, and as we have seen, build substantial houses. If the axe were mounted with the edge at right angles to the shaft, it would serve as a digging-implement or *mattock*, and there are early pictorial representations both in Egypt and in Italy which show the mattock being used in cultivation.

These Neolithic people knew that in addition to flint certain types of fine-grained rock were suitable for the

*Fig. 5.3 Some typical Neolithic objects: **a** decorated round-bottomed bowl, Mound of the Hostages, Tara, Co. Meath; **b** plain-shouldered bowl, Browndod, Co. Antrim; **c** polished axe, stone, Dunloy, Co. Antrim; **d** javelin-head, flint, Bann Valley; **e** hollow scraper, flint, Tamnyrankin, Co. Londonderry; **f** end-scraper, flint, Ballynagard, Co. Antrim.*

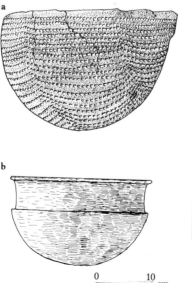

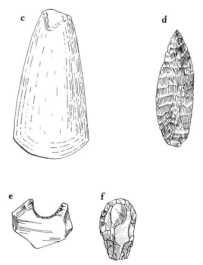

making of axes, and it was not long before 'factories' were established where outcrops of such rocks occurred. We have seen that at one time volcanic lavas in the north of Ireland were weathered under tropical conditions to clayey residues, and when more lava was poured on top, the residue was sometimes baked to a china-like texture, producing a rock known as *porcellanite*, eminently suitable for the manufacture of axes. In Antrim this rock outcrops at Tievebulliagh on the mainland and on Rathlin Island, and at each outcrop

roughed-out axes and debris indicate the former existence of an axe-factory. Axes produced here were of special character, and were distributed widely as the distribution-map (Fig. 5.4) shows. These Irish factories have not been dated by C-14, but factories in the Lake District and in Scotland indicate an age around 4500 years ago, and the Irish ones were probably operating at the same time.

There are several types of flint implement with trimmed edges,

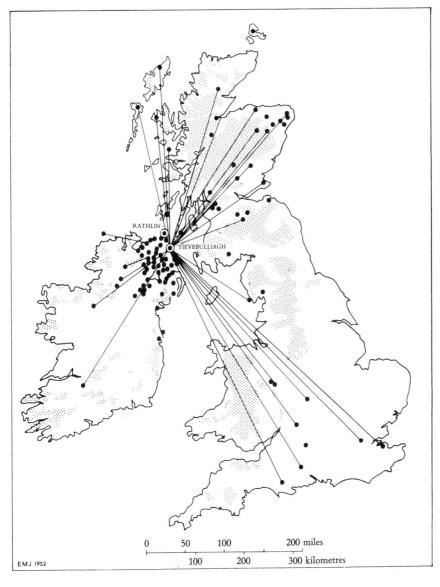

RATHLIN

TIEVEBULLIAGH

0   50   100   200 miles

100   200   300 kilometres

EMJ 1952

Fig. 5.4   The distribution in the British Isles of polished axes of porcellanite originating from the 'axe factories' on Rathlin Island and at Tievebulliagh, Co. Antrim. (After E. M. Jope)

obviously used in scraping and planing, and flakes with a concave working edge — the so-called 'hollow scraper' — useful for stripping bark and buds off slender stems, which could then be used in basket-work or as shafts for arrows. Thin, carefully worked, lozenge-shaped pieces in various sizes were arrow or javelin heads, and though not yet found in Ireland, Neolithic bows of yew wood have been found in bogs in Somerset.

But evidence for agriculture is slight. There are no small flint blades which might have been mounted along an ox-jaw or a curved piece of wood to be used as a sickle, and stones whose shape suggests they might have been used for grinding corn are very rare. This, combined with the abundance of cattle bones on the dwelling-sites, would suggest that in the early stages emphasis was on cattle-grazing rather than on cereal-farming, and that the woodland clearances were designed to give grazing areas rather than tillage plots. Cattle would feed eagerly on the shoots of bushes and regenerating trees, and extensive areas of grass may have been rare. This may be the explanation why grass pollen in the Neolithic — and also the beginning of the Bronze Age — shows only low values in some diagrams (see Fig. 5.1), even though the general movements of the pollen curves make it clear that forest disturbance was taking place.

In what sorts of woodlands did they find themselves? Five thousand three hundred years ago the midden-users living on Dalkey Island, an outcrop of granite, still had access to oakwoods, if we can take the small number of pieces of charcoal identified as representative — oak 11, ash 1, holly 1. But when the houses on the limestone slopes at Lough Gur were occupied, the firewood tended to be drawn from bushes rather than forest trees, as the charcoal list (in order of frequency) indicates hazel, ash, hawthorn (*Crataegus*), holly, oak, whitebeam (*Sorbus*), cherry (*Prunus*) and pine. Here

the dry limestone soil is indicated by the frequency of ash and the absence of alder. Megalithic tombs on slaty soils in Leinster yielded hazel, willow or poplar (*Populus*), oak, whitebeam, hawthorn, birch, alder, ash, ivy, elm, elderberry (*Sambucus*) and cherry. Apart from clearance, the low ranking of ash and elm here probably reflects the non-calcareous nature of the soils, and the elderberry will have been growing around the habitation-sites, where the dumping of refuse had raised the nitrogen content of the soil. It will be noted that in the last two examples hazel is the most common charcoal.

The hazel at all times found conditions in Ireland very favourable, and in its first expansion in the Beginning-phase (ILWB) its contribution to the local pollen-rain seems to have been greater than elsewhere in Europe (p. 77). In the Climax-phase of high forest (ILWC) it was forced back, and its contribution to the pollen-rain falls below 50%. But as soon as a woodland area which had been cleared by farmers was abandoned, hazel immediately expanded into it, in exactly the same way as it had expanded on its first arrival in the country. We had thus an area of hazel scrub, producing abundant pollen. If the scrub remained undisturbed for long enough then it was invaded and overshadowed by the forest trees, just as had happened when the primary climax woodlands were establishing themselves. In these secondary woodlands elm and ash were often important, and if we see their pollens climb to high values in our diagram, we can be sure that there had been a substantial reduction of farming in the vicinity.

But the high forest never re-established itself to the extent that it seriously depressed the output of hazel pollen, and the pollen record shows that at all times from the first woodland disturbance more than 5000 years ago, until the Tudor clearance in the late sixteenth century, there must have been very extensive areas of secondary hazel scrub in Ireland. Today this scrub is largely confined to the limestones of western Ireland, and we think of Ireland as a country of grassland. But this Ireland, the Emerald Isle of the poet, probably only took shape some 350 years ago, and before that it was for long a country of hazel scrub, merging in some places into secondary woodland or remnants of original forest, and opening out in others into patches of agricultural land.

But if the tillage areas in Neolithic times were small, the cattle could have browsed in the hazel scrubs, as we see them do in the Burren today. And beef was the chief element in the Neolithic meat diet. Our first record of domestic animals is from Ringneill Quay in Down, where the sea as it rose to its maximum level washed away a Neolithic site, and scattered flints, bones and charcoal; the charcoal had a C-14 age of 5380 years. Domestic ox, domestic pig and possibly sheep or goat were identified. Dalkey Island, at 5300 years ago, produced domestic ox, domestic sheep (though the possibility of goat cannot be ruled out) and pig (it was not possible to say whether domestic or wild); the absence of red deer should be noted. Other animals certainly eaten were various fish and birds, and possibly eaten were bear and grey seal. Bones of domestic dogs were also recorded.

In a paper published in 1954 Ó Ríordáin described seven sites on Knockadoon, an island in Lough Gur. All the sites were mainly Neolithic, but some had continued in use until the opening of the Bronze Age. All seven sites yielded ox bones in abundance, five yielded some bones of pig (either wild or domestic) and red deer, four yielded sheep (or goat), and two yielded horse. Bear occurred on two sites, and it is thus clear that the bear must have survived at least until this time in Ireland. Dog (or wolf) occurred on three sites.

We can thus picture the beginning of a slow change in the lowland landscape. There would have been some small tillage-patches, but the bulk of the effort went into breaking the forest canopy, and opening up rough meadows through which saplings and bushes were scattered and so provided fodder for the growing herds of cattle. When the tilled area was exhausted, the group would move on, and the forest would relatively quickly re-establish itself in secondary woodland. In the regrowth, all traces of house and stockades would be swallowed up, and the next round of clearance would ensure that nothing was left for the future archaeologist. This I feel is the main reason we know so little of the habitation-sites not only of the Neolithic, but also of the Bronze Age. As long as forest regeneration was capable of swallowing up the houses and stockades that had stood in woodland clearings, then evidence of former habitation had little chance of survival; it is only after AD 300, when woodland had shrunk in extent and timber was no longer so freely available for building, that habitation-sites begin to survive. The natural limestone terraces and light soils around Lough Gur on the one hand attracted continuous settlement, and on the other discouraged regeneration of heavy woodland, and there some record of the Neolithic habitations has survived.

The relative scarcity of remains of red deer is remarkable. Today in many countries venison is prized as a delicacy, and it seems odd that Neolithic man should have turned his back on this animal as a source of meat. Many of the records are of worked antler rather than meat bones. This is all the more curious, because, as we have seen, man's interference with the woodlands must have greatly increased the number of deer.

To obtain adequate food a Mesolithic family would have to wander over a wide area, and so there was an upward limit to the size to which family communities could grow, and there were few operations, other than driving flocks of wildfowl or shoals of fish towards traps or nets, in which more than a limited number of hunters could profitably combine.

Farming produced much more food from a smaller area, and at certain times of the year quite large groups of people could work together with much more efficency than smaller groups. Given adequate natural resources, Neolithic communities could improve their farming techniques. This has been clearly demonstrated by Seamus Caulfield in his excavations at Behy on the north Mayo coast. Here the area of Neolithic occupation had been overgrown by blanket-bog, and by stripping away the peat a remarkably sophisticated farming landscape was revealed (Fig. 5.5).

In an area of about one square kilometre, a series of parallel stone walls, spaced about 150 m apart, were traced up the hillside for a distance of more than 500 m where they disappeared under still uncut bog; cross-walls at about 200 m intervals created large fields, clearly for grazing and not tillage. The walls would have restrained cattle, but not more active sheep or goats. An enclosure in one of the fields was dated to 4500 years ago. The fields had obviously been laid out on an organized plan, and the excavator reckoned that even if beef production had been less than half that of present-day grassland, the square kilometre would have supported four or five families. Thus successful Neolithic communities tended to expand in size. As they did so, two things became apparent, first that at certain times of

Fig. 5.5 Old field-system being revealed as blanket bog is cut away at Behy, Co. Mayo.

▲ *Tomb*   ■ *Enclosure*

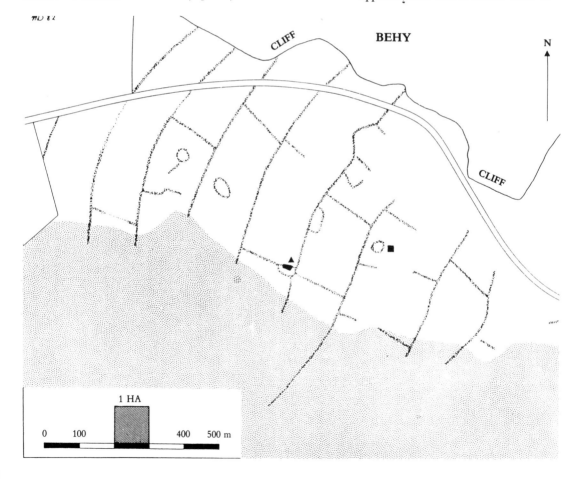

BEHY

N

CLIFF

CLIFF

1 HA

0   100   400   500 m

the year there was a considerable amount of spare adult labour, and second that if this was to be employed in an organized fashion, qualities of leadership had to be still further developed. The heavy work of transforming woodland into tillage-plots and grassy strips, clearing away large stones and building them into walls, building houses and stockades, and butchering, was obviously for adults, but the weeding and bird-scaring of crops, and the milking, butter-making, spinning and weaving, and the guarding of stock could be largely carried out by older people and children.

Like all primitive folk these Neolithic people will have seen their surroundings as peopled, not only by the living community, but also by potentially beneficial deities who had to be propitiated, by hostile demons who had to be avoided or exorcized, and by the spirits of the former members of the community. The first farmers who reached Ireland obviously believed in the continuity of the community after death, and after cremating the body, they would deposit the burned bones in a communal tomb. This belief and practice were common to all the early farming communities along the western seaboard of Europe from Spain to Scandinavia, and must have had its origin further to the east, probably on the shores of the Mediterranean Sea.

The essential element in a communal tomb was an accessible chamber, protected by a mound of earth or stones, and from this basic formula a very great variety of tomb-types developed. The chamber was built of tree trunks or large stones, and as the latter are much more durable, by far the majority of surviving chambers are stone-built, and hence the term *megalithic tomb* (Fig. 5.6).

Radiocarbon dating suggests that the first type to appear in Ireland was the *Court-grave*, dated at Ballymacdermot, Co. Armagh, to 4800 years ago. The

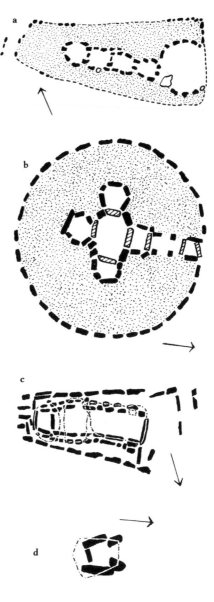

Fig. 5.6 Types of megalithic tomb found in Ireland: **a** *Court-grave, Browndod, Co. Antrim;* **b** *Passage-grave, Carrowkeel, Co. Sligo;* **c** *Gallery-grave, Labbacallee, Co. Cork;* **d** *Dolmen, Kilfeaghan, Co. Down.*

typical Court-grave has an elongated cairn of small stones, delimited by a kerb of upright stones or dry-stone walling; the cairn is about 30 m long. Recessed into the broader end of the cairn there is a court of roughly oval, circular or semi-circular shape, which gives its name to the tomb-type. The burial chamber opens from the inner end of the court, and consists of a gallery of two, three or four chambers.

The gallery walls are of great upright stones, and the roof stones are supported on one or more tiers of slabs, called *corbels*, which are laid overlapping inwards upon the uprights of the chamber walls. The remains of more than thirty individuals in one chamber have been recorded, and unburned as well as cremated burials have been found. In addition to being given a resting-place in a communal grave, the dead were provided with necessities for the afterlife as these tombs yield polished stone axes, arrowheads, scrapers and pottery vessels (see Fig. 5.3).

Over 300 Court-graves are known in Ireland, mainly north of the central lowlands. Their distribution is a scattered one, and suggests that they are the tombs of a rather spread-out ranching community. It was first thought that the builders moved up the Irish Sea to a landfall in eastern Ulster. The next suggestion was that they had come from atlantic France by a western route, by-passed southwest Ireland, and landed on the fertile limestone soils around Sligo and Killala Bays. But we now know that these tombs are common in west Connemara, the north coast of Mayo (there is a splendid tomb apparently associated with the field system at Behy), and south-west Donegal. The entry-routes are still speculative.

In England the closest relative of the Court-grave is the Long-barrow, which centres on the Severn Valley, and the two types are similar in many details of form and content. From the south of England a coastal movement up the east side of the Irish Sea would first reach the Severn basin, and if continued on would ultimately bring Ireland clearly into sight and tempt a crossing into eastern Ulster.

But the Wicklow Mountains can be seen from the top of the Lleyn Peninsula on a clear day, and in summer the cumulus clouds over the mountains could be seen from sea-level, and these early navigators would have been aware of the significance of cumulus clouds over the horizon. In good weather a direct passage could be made to the Leinster coast.

This may have been the route taken by another important group of tomb builders, who favoured a round mound delimited by a circular kerb of horizontal stones, in which they set a passage lined with tall stones and a lintel roof, the *Passage-grave*. Most Passage-graves have the inner end of the passage expanded into a chamber, off which smaller side-chambers may open. But at Townleyhall in the Boyne valley (Fig. 5.7) a small tomb had a simple passage without a chamber, and this type is called an *Undifferentiated Passage-grave*, meaning that the passage had to serve the function of both passage and chamber. The Townleyhall tomb had been erected over the site of a Neolithic house, from which both carbonized wood and cereals were recovered. The charcoal had a radiocarbon age of 4680 years, and the cereals were presumably of like age. At the time of the excavation the field surrounding the tomb was carrying a cereal crop, and it gave one an uncanny sense of continuity in the Irish landscape to realize that the same field had perhaps been performing the same function for some 4500 years.

Undifferentiated Passage-graves also occur in Waterford and in the Scilly Islands, and it may well be that there were crossings from the Scilly Islands to Waterford, across the waters of the Celtic Sea.

In more developed forms the passage at its inner end expanded into a chamber, which could have a variety of shapes, and often had side and end-chambers, thus becoming cruciform. The roof of the chamber was usually formed by a fine corbelled vault. The stones of the passage and chamber, and also the kerb around the mound, are sometimes decorated with incised abstract designs, ultimately derived from Iberia.

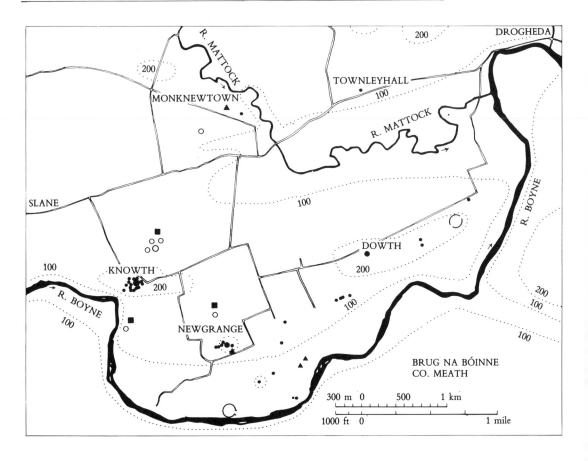

Cremation was the general rule but unburned bones are also present. Some small tombs which had not been opened since Neolithic times were crammed with cremated human bones, sometimes to a depth of 1 m in the chamber and completely filling the passage. Hundreds of burials can be inferred. Unburned bone pins, lying among cremated bone, suggest that the burned bones may have been placed in leather or woven bags, the mouth of the bag closed by the bone pin, and the bag then carried in and deposited in the tomb. Round-bottomed coarse pottery decorated by stabs and incision, hammer shaped pendants, stone balls like children's marbles, and a wide assortment of beads are commonly found in these tombs.

Almost 300 Passage-graves, are known in Ireland, chiefly in groups or cemeteries sited on hills or ridges in eastern Ireland, but sending out limited numbers into Court-grave country in Sligo and Antrim. The cemeteries thus range widely in area, and the individual tombs vary greatly in size. At Townleyhall the enclosing cairn was 13.5 m in diameter; at Fourknocks it was 20 m in diameter, and hardly big enough to accommodate the handsome cruciform tomb within; at Dowth the mound is 84 m in diameter, and rises to a height of 15 m; the main tomb only penetrates the mound for a distance of 12 m.

Even since Edward Lhuyd visited Newgrange in 1699, Passage-graves

Fig. 5.7
● *The great mounds of Brug na Bóinne, the House on the Boyne*
▲ *Early Bronze Age sites*
■ *Early historic sites*
... *Form-lines*
(After O'Kelly)

Photograph 20 The great Passage-grave mound with its surrounding kerb-stones at Knowth, Co. Meath. Smaller satellite tombs with surrounding kerbs lie nearby; these too would have had mounds, and two reconstructed mounds can be seen at top right. A black circle in the lower right-hand sector covers a reconstructed souterrain; from here a passage in which were found coins struck in Winchester about AD 950 leads down the side of the mound. Scattered masonry blocks on the top of the mound come from an Anglo-Norman building.

Photograph 21 Cutting to show the complex construction of the mound at Knowth, Co. Meath. The lowest layer is of field sods, the second is of small stones, and the third is of black shale, the local rock. Similar layering is repeated in the mound.

Photograph 22 Knowth, Co. Meath. The macehead is quite small, about the size of a clenched fist. It was found in dark earth in the righthand side-chamber of the east tomb. It is of flint, and must have been cut and polished using slivers of quartz and sand; its fabrication must have been a very lengthy process. When completed it was precious and important, and was probably paraded on ceremonial occasions. (G. Eogan)

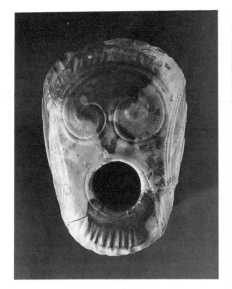

have been a matter of interest and controversy. Hitherto I have always regarded all Passage-graves as repositories for the cremated remains of a community, and not just of its leaders. This would appear to be clearly the case at Tara where in the so-called 'Mound of the Hostages' the inner stone cairn containing a Passage-grave had been sealed in Bronze Age times by the addition of a thick rind of earth. When excavated the Passage-grave was found to be packed with a large quantity of cremated human bone, perhaps derived from as many as 200 bodies. The radiocarbon age was 4050 years ago.

But the three great tombs of the Boyne valley, Dowth, Newgrange and Knowth (Photo 20, Pl. 26) differ from all other Passage-graves by virtue of their very great size; do they also differ in function? Were they once filled with masses of cremated bone? About this we cannot be certain, because all three have long been disturbed. Both Dowth and Knowth were re-occupied in Early Christian time; Newgrange was accessible in Late Roman time, when coins and jewellery were scattered at the entrance. The view that they were communal tombs was supported by the fact that they had not yielded prestige objects, indicative of especially important persons.

But Knowth has now produced two prestige objects, a remarkably carved flint macehead (Photo 22), the finest so far discovered in the British Isles, and a great stone basin (Photo 23), again elaborately carved, much the finest basin of the Passage-graves of the British Isles. Both objects were found in the right-hand side-chamber in the big cruciform tomb, and it appeared that the basin had been inserted before the side-chamber had been completed. At Newgrange also the basin in the same side-chamber could not have been emplaced after the chamber had been built. The macehead and the basin are objects worthy of a pharaoh; are Dowth, Newgrange and Knowth royal pyramids, and not communal tombs?

Photograph 23   Knowth, Co. Meath. This magnificently decorated stone basin, more than 1 m (3 ft) in diameter, lies in the chamber in which the macehead was found. The back stone of the chamber is decorated with typical symbols. (J. Bambury)

*Fig. 5.8   Knowth, Co.
Meath, key to Photo 20:*
a *The megalithic mound
surrounded by a kerb, the
Passage-graves concealed
within it, and the
associated satellite-tombs.*
b *Later activities,
extending perhaps from
AD 300 to AD 1000. The
concentric ditches dug
around the flanks of the
mound and the occupation-
areas with their souterrains
are indicated.*

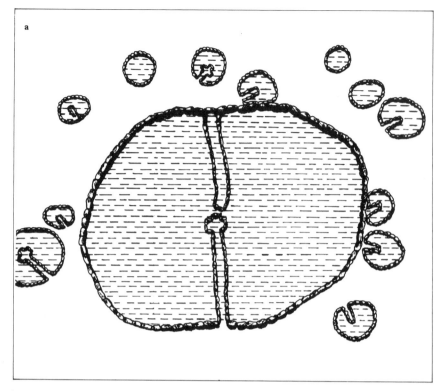

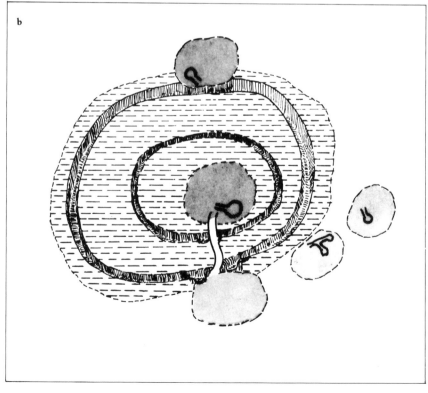

If Knowth (Fig. 5.8) is a royal pyramid, erected as the resting-place of one pharaoh, why has it two chambers, apparently erected simultaneously? The two chambers are very different in style; that in the east sector is cruciform and typically Irish, very similar to Newgrange. But that in the west sector is bottle-shaped, without side-chambers, and set at an angle to the passage. It closely resembles some tombs in Brittany, where Passage-graves go back beyond 5500 years ago. Was it a cenotaph, to recall a Breton ancestry?

Knowth, as we see it today, has had a long history. The site is a splendid vantage-point, looking straight down on the Boyne. There was an early Neolithic settlement here, whose inhabitants began to erect small Passage-graves, and remains of seventeen of these have been revealed by excavation. Four tombs have a cruciform plan, the others are simple. The kerb of one of the tombs was later pushed back a little to allow the kerb of the great mound to run interruptedly past it, and so we may infer that the smaller tombs precede the great mound and are not satellite to it. Other small tombs may lie concealed below the great mound. At Newgrange there is one small tomb to the east, and two to the west: at Dowth there are two on the east. Also at Dowth the cruciform chamber of the large tomb has a curious, awkwardly approached, L-shaped extension to the south; this may be part of an earlier small tomb which became buried below the later large mound.

In the smaller Passage-graves, the tomb sits neatly in its protective cairn. In the great tombs the mound is grossly disproportionate to the tomb it encloses, though the latter is not on a mean scale. Even for the craftsmen who built the tombs, there was an upper limit to the size of corbelled chamber that could be constructed, given nothing but stones of various sizes and strengths as building materials. It would seem that the basins and chambers were emplaced first, and the

cairns were built around them; at Knowth the two chambers were erected simultaneously. But if there was a limit to the size of the chamber, there was no technical limit to the length of the passage, as the type of construction could be extended indefinitely. One would think that below the centre of the cairn would be the most appropriate place for the chamber, but the builders were content with relatively short passages.

In essence the great tombs stand apart from the others in the size of their cairns. Obviously resources of a different magnitude were necessary to build a great tomb instead of a small one. New command structures were necessary to control the increased resources. Did a king, whose status demanded a royal tomb, emerge?

That Newgrange, Knowth and Dowth are large monuments is a matter for simple observation; we are just beginning to realize how complicated they are. If asked a few years ago, 'How were they built?', we would probably have said, 'Well, first of all you laid out the surrounding kerb, and set people to work heaping up the mound inside it with whatever materials came to hand; at the same time others were erecting the passage and chamber, and building ramps of earth — which were subsequently engulfed in the mound — to enable the large stones used to be drawn up into position.'

We now see that the actual work was much more complicated. At Newgrange both the passage and corbelled vault of the chamber were built as free-standing structures, and subsequently buried by mound material; the junction between the lintelled passage and the corbelled chamber is an especially neat point of construction. The roof of the first part of the passage has a second false roof above it, and through the gap between the two roofs, rays of sunlight can shine up the passage and into the chamber at dawn around the time of the winter solstice, and thus the layout of the passage must have been very carefully aligned. The flagstones roofing the passage abut against one another, and had nothing more been done, water could have leaked down into the passage between their ends. Two things were in fact done; soil containing charcoal debris was used to caulk the gaps (and it was this charcoal that gave the radiocarbon date); and to make assurance doubly sure, gutters were cut in the upper surface of the slabs, so that any percolating water was discharged laterally beyond the sides of the passage.

And the mound, both at Newgrange and at Knowth, is not just a heap of randomly dumped material, but a carefully organized structure. Although the bulk of the mound at Newgrange is of water-rolled cobbles, presumably drawn from the glacial outwash gravels of the vicinity, there are also layers of sods, thickest at the perimeter, and thinning out towards the centre. The sods appear to have come from poor pastures, which may have developed on former tillage-plots or fields. The margin of the mound above the kerb was supported by a revetting-wall, which was further embellished in the vicinity of the entrance. Here there were large numbers of oval granite boulders about 25 cm long, of a type of rock that probably occurs in the Mourne Mountains. Such boulders are not common in the local glacial gravels, and must have been carefully collected somewhere, probably between Newgrange and the Mourne Mountains. There were also large quantities of vein quartz, which must also have been specially assembled on the site; there are veins of quartz in the local slaty rocks, and such material could perhaps have been obtained in the vicinity. After very considerable study of the way these materials were lying in their collapsed positions, Professor Brian (M.J.) O'Kelly came to the conclusion that these materials had been decoratively arranged on the wall-face in the vicinity of the entrance. During the restoration

work that was carried out by the Office of Public Works at Newgrange, the granite and the quartz again were put up on a wall-face. While it cannot be claimed that the present arrangement necessarily resembles the original arrangement in any way, it does serve to impress on us still further that for the users of the grave the entrance area had a special significance, a fact already apparent from the splendid quality of the decorative design on the great stone that lies across the entrance.

At Knowth also, though the quantities were trivial compared with Newgrange, there were the same granite boulders and the same pieces of vein quartz in the vicinity of the entrances to both the tombs. The mound structure is even more complicated at Knowth (see Photo 21) than at Newgrange. The knoll on which the mound lies is of black Carboniferous shales, and the mound is built up of layers of shale, layers of water-rolled cobbles and layers of sods. Just as in building procedures for large modern structures, there must have been both architects and quantity surveyors employed, the architects to design the tombs and the mound, and the quantity surveyors to see that the necessary materials were available in the right amounts when they were called for.

What labour force was available to move the necessary materials? If we stand on the top of Newgrange and look about us in every direction, we overlook a basin of about 50 square kilometres before rising ground cuts off our view. If we imagine this basin as completely cleared of trees, everyone working within it could either see the mounds, or feel that he ought to be able to see them, and could perhaps have a sense of devotion or commitment to them. What size of Neolithic population could this area support? I picture the typical farm family as consisting of one grandparent, two parents, and three children aged fourteen, eight and two; there would thus be four able-bodied persons, an eight-year-old child, capable of tending stock and scaring birds, and an infant. I allow each such family a 25-hectare farm, as I reckon the yields would have been far less than those of today, even though the type of farming used was essentially gardening rather than farming. The basin would thus have held some 200 farms with a total population of 1200 persons, a number that is in the same order as today's population. During a two-month spring lull in farm operations, each farm could have spared two able-bodied persons for other duties. Four hundred able-bodied persons could therefore have been called up for a two-month period to build tombs or do other work. Carrying earth and other materials would have been an important task. If I am given a leather sack and the scapula of a cow, and directed to a gravel pit 400 m from the construction-site — as could have been the case at Newgrange — how many sacks will I fill and carry during a day? I should reckon not more than ten, and each day should therefore bring 4000 sacks, and each working-season 240,000 sacks of material to the site. Newgrange must contain about one million such sackfuls, and so four working-seasons would have been spent on assembling the material. When we remember that not all the materials came from near at hand, that stone had to be quarried, dressed, transported, decorated and erected, and that the layering of the mound had to be arranged, we can add at least one more working-season. So we can possibly envisage that 50 square kilometres, if free of trees and all closely farmed, could support the building over a five-year period of such a tomb as Newgrange. What would the cost be today? Twenty-four thousand five-day weeks are involved, and this at current rates for agricultural labours represents a bill for £2,500,000. While I should be the first to agree that all the figures I have chosen are so highly speculative as to be almost worthless, nonetheless the point cannot be avoided that Newgrange represents a very considerable capital investment, and that

a large area of farmland must have been necessary to provide the capital. Michael Herity has discussed this same problem; he reckons that when the great tombs were being built a population of some 4000 people based on 'urban' dwellings were carrying out large-scale farming in the Boyne valley.

Even today some forms of capital investment are imprudent, and it can only have been imprudent in the extreme for sods to be skimmed from fields to construct the mounds. The palaeobotanical examination of the sods tells us that the fields had already passed their prime at the time they were cut. What can they have been like after the valuable humus of the sod layer had been removed?

What sort of social organization lies behind this ability to erect, probably in a relatively short space of time, three enormous and complicated tombs, separated by distances of less than 2 km, and what can have been the landscape that produced the wealth to support the social organization? I think we must reject the concept of simple peasant groups assembling together at such times as the yearly cycle of agricultural activities made it possible to do so, and erecting the tombs by direct labour. There must have been an authority to direct the work of the labour force. In modern industrial nations a great deal of wealth and labour is expended on the manufacture of sophisticated weapons of such terrible power that even those who make them trust that they will never be used. Yet when one is made there is no alternative but to make another one, or else much of the economic structure of the nation would collapse. It has been argued that the pyramids of Egypt reflect a similar position; the whole economy became geared to the construction of such public works, and when one was completed another had to be begun. Could it have been the same in the Boyne valley? Was the driving force the desire to impress or the need for a large mausoleum? Each of the great tombs had the capacity to hold the cremated remains of thousands of individuals. If the community was of such a size as to make three such mausolea necessary, its numbers must have been very large indeed, and the area it farmed must have been enormous.

We can avoid this dilemma if we say that an overlord — call him pharaoh, priest or king as we wish — stood at the head of the organization, with professional men — farm overseers, storage managers, architects, quantity surveyors — to advise him, and in the lower tiers foremen and labourers. But the overlord was mortal, and during his lifetime a mausoleum was erected, where after death his cremated remains accompanied by his symbol of authority, his decorated macehead, would be deposited in the elaborately carved stone basin in the right-hand recess of the chamber. Other members of the caste might be deposited in the other recesses. Perhaps his closest associates were slain to accompany him to the next world. The erection of another mausoleum, for his successor, would then be begun.

I say very little about the abstract art which decorates many Passage-graves as it has little relevance to landscape development. This is not to belittle its importance, or the further evidence of sophistication that it gives. It is especially abundant at Newgrange and Knowth and in the hill-top cemetery at Lough Crew, 40 km west of the Boyne tombs. The art has so far defied all attempts at interpretation, although it has been approached from many angles, alphabetical, anthropological, astronomical, mathematical and pictorial.

For thousands of years man has employed personal identification symbols, and symbols of the pharaohs appear on the pyramids. If the great Boyne mounds are royal tombs, then I would have expected some symbol to be repeated many times on a tomb, just

as the lion and the unicorn still commonly appear in Britain. But while the tombs produce numerous variants of a particular motif, there is little or no identical repetition.

In this discussion I have made many references to the royal pyramids of Egypt. These evolved from simple tombs called *mastabas*, and I believe the larger tombs on the Boyne developed from smaller ones. But when we think of the pyramids we must remember that they are later — more than 1000 years later — than Knowth, Newgrange and Dowth.

Our earliest date for the establishment of Neolithic farming is 5700 years ago, based on charcoal associated with pottery at Ballynagilly, Co. Tyrone. This is the time when the earliest Passage-graves were beginning to be erected in Brittany. In Ireland the Court-grave goes back to 4800 years ago, and simple Passage-graves are appearing at Knowth at the same time. Newgrange itself was built 4500 years ago. What did the Irish landscape look like after 1000 years of farming attacks? The farming communities had come on a long way in that millennium, from the time when the first few family parties struggled ashore, to the position where a wealthy and sophisticated group could expend capital and man-power on the erection of large and complicated monuments.

The ridge of *Brug na Bóinne* lies between the valleys of the Boyne and the Mattock, and on the ridge each mound is set on the top of a knoll (see Fig. 5.7). It may have been ritually necessary to set the mound on a high point, in which case whether one could or could not see it from a distance would be without significance. But the Passage-graves in the Wicklow Mountains are not set on the highest point of the relatively flat dome-like tops, but rather a little way down the slope at the level at which they were most widely visible, always provided that the view was not blocked by lowland forest. I think we may take it that the Boyne tombs were placed on their knolls in order to make them more visible from a distance, and this must imply a very considerable forest clearance in the surrounding area and therefore there must have been a pretty substantial output of grass pollen. Yet as already noted some pollen-diagrams suggest only a very small output of grass pollen as compared with that of the trees. Area for area, trees produce more pollen then grass, but it may be that only limited areas in the vicinity of Passage-grave cemeteries had been so cleared of trees, or alternatively that the areas had still a considerable amount of woodland, and that the community must have been more widely dispersed in area than I have envisaged.

The Neolithic communities certainly had an appreciation of the agricultural potential of different soil types, as has been demonstrated for Co. Leitrim by Gabriel Cooney. Most of Leitrim is covered by wet gley soils developed on glacial deposits. But some rock islands rise through the wet soils, and here there are well-drained soils with a good structure. The megalithic monuments of the county cluster on the good soils, and avoid the gleys.

We have also very simple megalithic tombs, the *Dolmens* (see Fig. 5.6d), consisting today of no more than some erect stones supporting a capstone. Originally the whole structure was probably protected by a mound or cairn, but these have disappeared, as have also any contents of the grave, by which we might hope to date it. Some Dolmens are probably early in the megalithic tradition; others may be quite late.

A record of woodland interference from Neolithic times to the present day

Some thirty years ago Hilda Parkes and I made a boring 8 m deep in a raised-bog near Littleton in Co. Tipperary, and she made detailed pollen-counts from the samples taken. The pollen-diagram showed that the bog held a continuous record from the Woodgrange Interstadial 12,000 years ago until almost the present day, and the bog was subsequently chosen as the type-site for the current warm stage, which is thus in Ireland called the Littletonian Warm Stage. The bog lies in a fertile area, and its *Sphagnum*-peats provided a splendid record of the waxing and waning of agricultural activities in the vicinity of the bog.

With the coming of C-14 dating, we were anxious to give more precision to the agricultural events recorded at Littleton, and to see to what extent they could not only be traced throughout Ireland, but also be shown to be contemporaneous. A research programme was organized, and among the raised-bogs investigated was Red Bog, Co. Louth, at an altitude of 60 m, 15 km west of Dundalk. The bog had been very much cut away, but this was all the better for our purpose, because it made it possible for us to collect vertical columns of *Sphagnum*-peat and bring them back to the laboratory. Detailed pollen-counts were made, and the horizons at which significant changes took place were identified. Slices were then cut from the column at the critical points, and these were dated in the Trinity College C-14 dating laboratory.

The end of the Climax-phase (ILWC) is seen at the base of the diagram (Fig. 5.9), where pollen of elm falls dramatically in value at 5200 years ago. Neolithic farming started in the vicinity at about the same time, and pollen of grass and of plantain is recorded.

At the beginning of the Damage-phase (ILWd₁) grass and plantain continue for

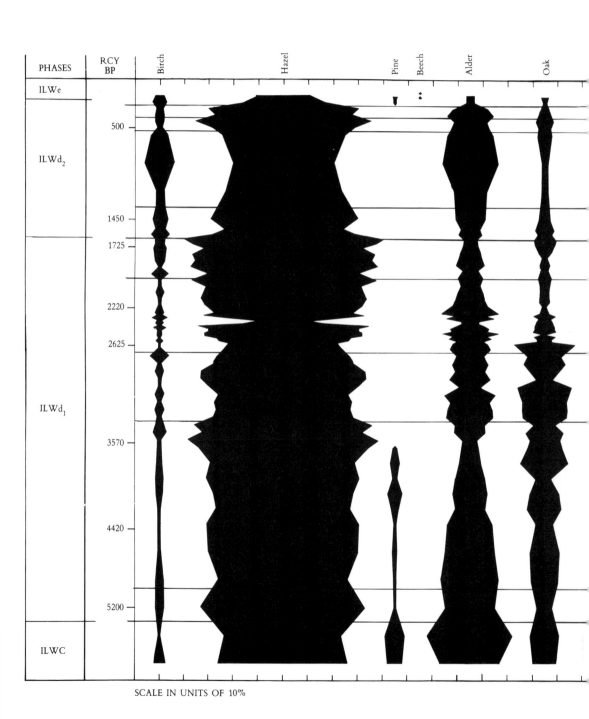

SCALE IN UNITS OF 10%

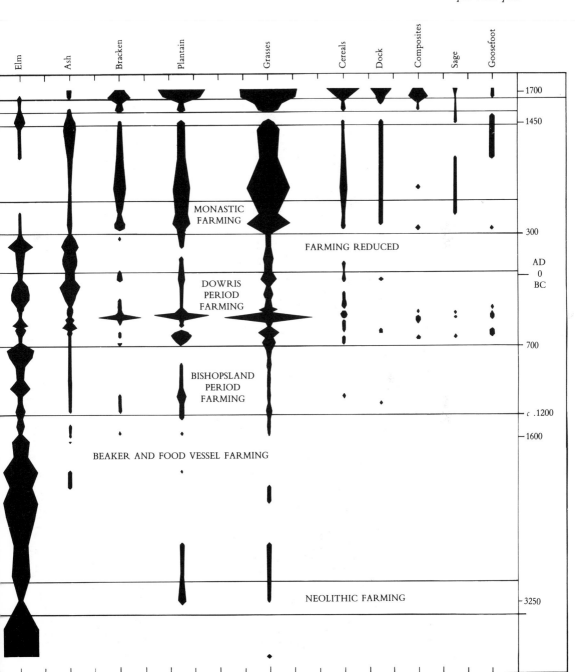

Fig. 5.9 A pollen-diagram from Red Bog, Co. Louth, with a record of vegetational developments through the past 5000 years.

a while, but then elm rises again and they disappear. Farming in the vicinity has diminished or ceased, and elm again contributes substantial amounts of pollen. About 4000 years ago it begins to decline again, and grass and plantain reappear, accompanied by bracken and ash. Bracken suggests open ground, and ash is an 'opportunist' tree, quickly springing up where trees have been cleared or fields have been abandoned. This woodland disturbance is probably due to farming by the first users of metal to appear in Ireland. Some workers think that there was a major reduction in tree cover at this time, but I think this impact on woodland was less severe.

About 3150 years ago the Irish Bronze Age became more prosperous and farming extended in the Bishopsland Period of the Bronze Age. In the diagram, grasses and plantains are almost continuously present, and cereals and docks are recorded. More severe forest disturbance and clearance is indicated. Ash is continuously present, and it is almost certain that if the pollen-samples were re-counted today, yew pollen, perhaps in substantial amounts, would be recorded here. In the early days of pollen-counting it was thought that the thin-walled grains of yew did not survive when buried, but in recent years better microscopy has shown that in many fossil environments yew pollen does survive, and it is now regularly counted. Like ash, yew is well equipped to exploit major perturbations in the woodlands. A lull in farming follows; plantain and bracken die away, and elm rises.

Next the diagram shows clearly that about 2650 years ago the picture of the countryside changes dramatically, with an obvious intensification of agriculture in the Dowris Period (see p.139). Here we enter the Deterioration-phase (ILWd$_2$). As we shall see later, in my opinion this is the time at whch the plough — or at least a primitive type of it, the ard (see Fig. 5.16) — was introduced into Ireland, and much more

efficient tillage became possible.

Agriculture centres on grassland on the one hand, and tillage on the other; can these be separated in the pollen records? High values for grass, plantain and bracken are thought to indicate grassland; high values for cereals and for weeds associated with arable land in Ireland such as docks (*Rumex*), thistles (*Compositae*), sage (*Artemisia*) and goosefoot (*Chenopodiaceae*) are thought to indicate tillage. Thus in the diagram do the sharp but short-lived rises in grass, plantain and bracken at about 2400 years ago indicate a sudden swing to grassland? Or does it merely mean that a new meadow was established quite close to and upwind from the point on the bog where the samples were taken? Similar sudden rises in these pollen types can be seen in other Irish pollen-diagrams, but efforts to interpret the pollen record in agricultural terms can easily be carried too far.

Two thousand two hundred years ago (about 300 BC) the pollen-picture obtained from raised-bogs changes dramatically. Pollen which may indicate arable land virtually disappears, and grass and its associates fall back to low levels. Hazel, elm and ash (and doubtless yew also, had the counts been made today) increase. It is not easy to interpret the picture, but an expansion of secondary woodland would seem to be indicated. This is the time, the Pagan Iron Age (see p.144), when iron was beginning to displace bronze as the metal in most common use, and it has recently been described as 'one of the more obscure periods in Irish prehistory'. Large forts, usually on hills or promontories appear. It seems to have been a time of upset, and over wide areas on the central lowlands farming may have been disrupted. The disruption came to an end about AD 300.

This generalization is based on studies made in raised-bogs now a number of years ago. Since then many workers have switched their attention to lake-muds, which record rather a different picture. If farmers used fire as part of their clearance rotation, very little charcoal will have blown onto the surface of the bogs. But a great deal of it may be washed by rain into rivers, and so into lakes, or be carried by soil erosion directly into lakes. We can see that soil erosion took place, because often at a level where the pollen-record shows that there has been woodland clearance, the rate at which sediment accumulates in the lake shows an increase due to washed-in debris. At the same time pollen of the heather, *Calluna* or ling, rises in quantity, while that of the trees falls away. These features are interpreted as indicating that man's activities are disturbing the local vegetation.

Many such disturbances are recorded in the period 300 BC to AD 300, though these do not appear in the raised-bog diagrams. At Killarney there was attack on woodland between 2000 and 1800 years ago, and on Valencia Island field-banks were being built on the surface of blanket-bog 1700 years ago. It ought to be possible to reconcile the contrasting pictures that we get from raised-bog peat and lake muds, but we can continue to accept that the period in question, the Pagan Iron Age in Ireland, was one of unrest.

A new phase opens about AD 300, when the raised-bog diagrams show a devastating clearing-away of elm and ash, and an attack on hazel-scrub also. Tillage is resumed, and grasslands expand. Here the Destruction-phase (ILWd₃) begins. Though the Romans never invaded Ireland, knowledge of their way of life and of their agricultural techniques certainly penetrated the country. I picture that it was at this time that ploughs armed with iron coulters (see Photo 29) came into Ireland, and that tillage became both easier and more rewarding. The spread of Christianity in Ireland, and the establishment of large monasteries with their own farmlands will have hastened the rise in agricultural efficiency.

Pollen of sage (*Artemisia*) appears about AD 500, and the increase of this weed may be associated with different agricultural practices. It made a similar appearance in the Burren area about AD 800. The first pictorial representation of a plough fitted with a mouldboard is in a manuscript dated to about AD 650. Use of this type of plough may have favoured mugwort.

A feeble return of elm and a weakening of agriculture can be seen about AD 1450, and it is tempting to correlate this with the fall of temperature that is thought to have taken place at this time (see Fig. 6.5). At the very end of the phase we see the final clearance of the Irish woodlands, which set in in Tudor times, and see how even the hazel scrub that had for so long dominated the Irish countryside was swept away at this time.

The top sample, with its traces of pine and beech, probably marks the start of the Expansion-phase (ILWE) when exotic trees began to be planted on large estates.

Further bog-development: after 5500 years ago

On the lowlands reed-swamp and fen continued to invade and to obliterate open-water, and where raised-bogs had been established, they continued their slow growth both upwards and outwards, building up a *Sphagnum*-peat that was in general highly humified. Hammond's radiocarbon dates from the bogs of the Central Plain enable us to follow the lateral expansion (see Fig. 4.13a). On the right-hand side of the figure we can see that 5000 years ago the *Sphagnum*-community was beginning to develop on top of wood-fen-peat which, as water-logging increased, had been creeping up the sloping surface of the underlying glacial deposit. At the left-hand side of the diagram we see wood-fen-peat beginning to form at a still higher level about the same time. Here after 1000 years had gone by, and about 50 cm of this type of peat had been built up, its surface had become too poor in nutrients to allow this kind of vegetation to continue to grow, and the *Sphagnum*-community moved in, and started to form highly humified peat. Thus throughout the Neolithic period raised-bogs surrounded by a rim of waterlogged fen-woods were invading and engulfing areas of low-lying forest.

When about 4000 years ago we move on into the Bronze Age, such bog-growth was continuing. The raised-bogs were now creating an obstacle to man's wanderings in the countryside, and trackways were constructed across them at strategic points. Unfortunately the study and particularly the radiocarbon dating of early trackways is much less advanced in Ireland than it is in England, where Godwin and others have done detailed work in the Somerset Levels and elsewhere. A trackway in a raised-bog at Corlona in Leitrim was examined by Dr van Zeist, and one of its timbers was dated to 3390 years ago, which places it early in the Bronze Age. It lay in peat of varying composition and humification,

but it was not possible to find positive evidence that the bog surface had got wetter (and softer) at the time it was constructed.

At Ballyscullion Bog (see Fig. 4.13b) at about 4200 years ago peat of varying humification, such as that in which the Corlona trackway lay, began to form instead of the peat of uniformly high humification that had preceded it, and a similar change at Fallahogy Bog was dated to about 4450 years ago. Corresponding changes can be seen in other raised-bogs, and it is not impossible that this more rapid growth was due to a climatic deterioration — an increase in wetness or a decrease in temperature, or both.

At about the same time profound changes were taking place on the uplands, which had the end-result that over thousands and thousands of hectares that had originally had a relatively well-drained soil with woodland, and had in many areas been extensively cultivated by early farmers, the soils first degraded to peaty podzols, and then became buried below thick layers of peat. Upland peat had certainly started to form before 4000 years ago, and its invasion of new areas appears to have continued into the present millennium.

This changeover from mineral soil to peat can be well demonstrated at Goodland, Co. Antrim (Fig. 5.10), where at an altitude of about 250 m the bedrock is chalk. About 1 m of sandy glacial material rested on the chalk, and when first deposited this material must have had some content of calcium carbonate; today all trace of calcium carbonate has been removed by long-continued leaching. Early Littletonian woodlands developed in the area, and as the soil formed under forest there was some modest movement of iron downwards, so that a layer about 50 cm below the surface became enriched in iron, giving rise to a brown podzolic soil. About 5000 years ago Neolithic farmers arrived in

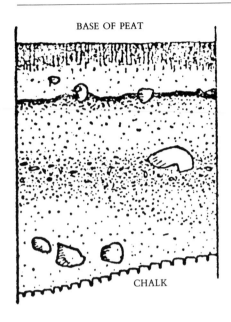

Fig. 5.10 Double soil-profile below peat at Goodland, Co. Antrim: the graph on the right shows modest accumulation of iron in the enriched B-horizon of the primary forest soil, and also the much greater quantity of iron in the 'iron-pan' B-horizon of the podzol soil that formed later. (After Proudfoot)

the area, cleared away the trees, and proceeded to scratch the surface of the ground, initiating as they did so a new cycle of soil formation; Early Bronze Age folk continued the farming activities. Then, either because of continued disturbance of the ground encouraging leaching or deterioration in climate, podzolization took place, and a layer of iron pan formed about 30 cm below the surface. Waterlogging of the soil followed, as the pan blocked the downward movement of water, and by 4150 years ago the wetter parts of the area had been smothered by invading rushes (*Juncus*). The sward of rushes gradually built up a thin layer of amorphous vegetable debris or peat, crowded with *Juncus* seeds, and the soil became a peaty podzol.

The surface of this peat was very low in inorganic nutrients, and it was invaded, just as the lowland fen-peats had been earlier invaded, by the *Sphagnum*-community, which started to form a highly humified peat. As water-logging enabled the rushes to spread, so the formation of peaty podzol could expand also, and gradually the ground became buried beneath a layer of peat which covered it like a blanket, initiating the formation of the so-called

blanket-bog, which is now so widespread in Ireland (see Fig. 4.14, Pl. 22).

The locations at which the ground first became sufficiently waterlogged to enable peaty podzol and then peat to start to form will have depended on the local topography, and so, just as with the raised-bogs, peat formation will have expanded outwards from initial foci. There was no moment in time at which peat started to form everywhere, and at different points the basal peaty podzols may be of very different ages. There is no reason why basal layers younger than AD 1000 should not be found, because if the blanket-bogs had not been interfered with by man, it is quite possible that they might still be thickening and expanding at the present day. But for thousands of years man has grazed his animals on them, has burned the vegetation to stimulate young growth, and has cut the peat for fuel, or dug it away to reclaim agricultural land. We can show that some of them have built their thickness up by 10 cm during the last 250 years, but we have no record of how their margins have behaved.

We can say 'thousands of years' because of the work that is being done in north-west Mayo, where blanket-bog has a very wide extent at the present day. In early Littletonian time forest development in this area seems to have paralleled that in the rest of the country, except that elm was rarer. A pine-stump at Bellonaboy, rooted in mineral soil, and with a radiocarbon age of 7100 years, goes back to the time when the climax woodlands were developing.

Neolithic man appears to have been established 4500 years ago in the Behy area, where he built tombs (Pl. 23) and field-walls. Similar walls, also sitting on mineral soil, appear in the Belderg valley, and here Seamus Caulfield has revealed a very complex series of features, all again buried by blanket-bog. Neolithic pottery and flint implements are found on the mineral soil, and there must have been some forest clearance. Blanket-bog peat then started to form, but after no more than a thin layer had been laid down, its surface was invaded by secondary woodland, with large trees of both oak and pine. A pine-stump, whose roots were clearly separated from the mineral soil by a thin layer of peat, had an age of 4300 years, and a similar oak had an age of 3850 years. At Bellonaboy (already referred to) a pine-stump sitting on 20 cm of basal peat had an age of 4350 years. These tree-datings add to the amazement of the modern visitor to this now bleak and treeless area, who has to recognize that not only was it clothed in high virgin forests 7000 years ago, but that after those woods had been damaged by Neolithic man, climate was still good enough 4000 years ago for secondary woodland of tall well-grown pines and oaks to re-establish itself. If man's influence was removed, trees would return again to the areas where mineral soil is exposed, but they would be slow to invade the bog surface.

Three thousand two hundred years ago, when Ireland had moved on into the Bronze Age, man returned to Belderg, where blanket-bog had now developed

on an extensive scale, though the peat perhaps was not as yet very thick. There is a vein of copper ore in a nearby cliff, and this may have been the lure that brought man back to a site that was by now much less attractive from the agricultural point of view. A house, 10 m in diameter with a drystone wall and post-holes, produced saddle querns and rubbers; a charred block of wood within the house had an age of 3150 years. Nearby there were further stone walls; these started on mineral soil but continued on out into the blanket-bog which surrounded the site; here the wall rested on peat. Oak stakes built into the wall extended down into the peat, and when the wall ended a line of stakes continued into the bog; the stakes had a radiocarbon age of 3200 years.

The whole site had been subsequently deeply buried by peat, and this had protected some remarkable features of the site, criss-crossing dark marks in the subsoil, interpreted as plough-marks, or marks of an ard, the more primitive fore-runner of the true plough (see Fig. 5.16), and cultivation-ridges of the type still used in western Ireland today, and generally known as 'lazy-beds'. If the modern title is taken to imply lack of energy and enterprise on the part of the farmer who employs this system, it is a complete misnomer, because the building up of drier ridges separated by trenches to drain off the surface water gives an efficient method of cultivating soils with poor natural drainage.

The field-evidence suggests that the house is younger than the cultivation-ridges, and therefore the age of the latter may lie between the Neolithic occupation of the site, starting perhaps at 4500 years ago, and the building of the house about 3200 years ago. Whichever end of the range we favour it is clear that this cultivation method is of high antiquity in Ireland. What of the plough-marks?

Ard-marks on chalk-soils in Wiltshire

are more than 4750 years old, and there is also evidence of early use of the ard in northern Europe. There is therefore no chronological reason why the ard should not have been in use in Mayo at an early date, but the very stony nature of the soils there, with consequent constant damage to the share of the ard, would seem to make its use hardly worthwhile.

Nearby at Ballyglass a Court-grave had been built on the site of a large rectangular wooden house, dated to 4600 years ago, and there can be no doubt that this area which today is so desolate and so lacking in human inhabitants, had considerable settlement in Neolithic time.

At Bunnyconnellon, also in Co. Mayo, on the north-west slopes of the Ox Mountains, at an altitude of about 100 m, Michael Herity has revealed extensive lazy-beds by digging away the blanket-peat. At this point the base of the peat was dated to 3600 years ago, although on the coast nearby bog-formation had started much earlier. There was a concentration of lazy-beds on a nearby knoll, and a pollen-diagram suggested that these were in use 2750 years ago. The primary soil on the knoll gave clear indications of strong podzolization, which means that it cannot have had a high fertility. What compelled Bronze Age people to occupy an area of poor climate and poor soils requires some explanation. The date is 100 years earlier than that taken for the general expansion of agriculture that accompanied the Dowris Period of Bronze Age prosperity, but population pressures may have been building up. Agricultural pollen then falls back in value in the pollen-diagram, but it rises strongly again at several higher levels. Looking at the barren blanket-bog landscape today, it is hard to imagine why earlier people could have chosen to live there.

If we picture that the 'climatic optimum' was a time of relatively continental climate with warmer summers and fewer rain-days, then we can envisage any subsequent 'deterioration' as involving falling temperatures, more rain-days, and lower evaporation-rates generally. Where raised-bogs already existed their rate of upward growth will have been speeded up, and the soils generally will have become loaded with an increased content of water; raised-bogs will have expanded still further laterally, and the formation of blanket-bogs will have been encouraged.

There is some evidence, as we have seen, that between 4500 and 4200 years ago the type of peat being formed in the raised-bogs began to change, a peat that was of uniformly high humification giving way to a peat of varying humification. In south-west Ireland a pine-stump rooted in mineral soil and buried by blanket-bog on the slopes of Carrantoohill at 250 m had an age of 4600 years; in eastern Ireland a pine-stump in like position on the slopes of Kippure at 730 m had an age of 4200 years; in the west of Ireland tree-stumps on thin blanket-peat at Belderg had an age of 4300 years. All this evidence adds up to suggest that climate did alter in the centuries preceding 4000 years ago, and that the change enabled the raised-bogs to grow more quickly, and blanket-bogs to start to form throughout the country. As these bogs spread, they gradually covered great areas of country that had been farmed by prehistoric peoples. There is circumstantial evidence that some blanket-bogs may have been established in Mayo before Neolithic man arrived there. We have tombs on the north coast between Downpatrick Head and Belderg, and again on the east shores of Broad Haven, but in between there is a blank. Was this area already covered by bog?

It is tempting to think that there was a deterioration of climate which led inevitably to the development of blanket-bog wherever a critical threshold was passed, and that the part that man played was only a secondary one, in that his agricultural activities had made the soil particularly susceptible to podzolization and waterlogging. It would be nice to know whether man had abandoned the former farm areas after exhausting the soil before peat had started to form, or whether he was as it were forcibly driven out, when the soil became waterlogged to the point that it was impossible to cultivate it. Whatever happened, the upland soils changed drastically as agricultural areas gave way to blanket-bog, and we have to recognize that when work still to be done enables us to draw a map of the soils of Neolithic Ireland, it will differ very substantially both from the sketch-map of the first Irish soils (see Fig. 4.2), and from the map of Irish soils today (see Fig. 6.6). As far as prehistoric man was concerned, great areas of agricultural land on the uplands in the east and at low levels in the west must have been abandoned, while farming continued in other areas. If we take two limestone areas both intensively occupied in Neolithic and Early Bronze Age times and lying in the same longitude but at different elevations, we can see this exemplified. The low hills (alt. 120 m) around Lough Gur in Limerick were not buried by peat; the outlines of the Neolithic houses there can still be seen above ground, the sod layer is full of prehistoric pottery, and agriculture still goes on: the higher hills (alt. 250 m) at Carrowkeel in Sligo are covered by peat which has built up to a depth of 250 cm, and partly buries the cairns of the Passage-grave cemetery. Today men cut the peat for fuel, and sheep graze on the blanket-bog, but that is all. People must have moved from the higher land to the lowlands, but the archaeological story is not yet able to tell us whether the refugees endeavoured to take farmland by force from those already occupying the better land, or whether they contented themselves by clearing further woodland and scrub.

Today blanket-bog is extensively developed wherever annual rainfall in excess of 1250 mm per annum waterlogs the grounds (see Fig. 4.14). Thus in much of the west of Ireland the blanket-bog runs down to sea-level, and even below it, giving great stretches of country buried by peat, which is interrupted only where slopes are steep; below much of the peat there is, as we have seen, a layer of tree-stumps to indicate the former extent of forest (Photo 24). Away from the west coast rainfall only rises to 1250 mm on higher ground, and the blanket-bog is confined to hill-tops and upper slopes.

The blanket-bog areas (Pl. 22) give an impression of dreary uniformity, covered by a sheet of bog vegetation, pierced only by occasional rocky outcrops or lakes. But the underlying substratum has its own minor relief, rising into elevations and sinking into hollows. In many of the hollows sediment had accumulated since the opening of the Littletonian Warm Stage, and this was the case at Emlaghlea, Co. Kerry, which was examined by Professor Jessen during his programme of work in Ireland. Part of Jessen's section is reproduced as Fig. 5.10c, and the early peat, which was a wood-fen-peat, can be seen at the base of the right-hand end of the section.

The fen surface in its final stages seems to have become relatively dry, because pine and birch were able to grow freely on it. Up to this point the formation of the peat had been controlled by surface water and by groundwater, and the ridge of higher ground to the left had been bare of peat and perhaps under cultivation. Then some change took place and the oligotrophic plants of the bog community which need to be nourished only by rainwater invaded the whole area, and began to bury it below blanket-bog. At Slieve Gallion, Co. Tyrone, a similar change was dated to 4165 years ago.

Today we tend to draw an arbitrary distinction between raised-bog on the one hand and blanket-bog on the other,

but the plants of which both are composed are essentially the same, though the proportions they occupy in the various communities are rather different. Typical raised-bog is found where the topography of the ground can bring about waterlogging, even though the rainfall is below 1250 mm per annum (and can be as low as 750 mm p.a.) The additional water is provided, either by groundwater filling a closed basin, or by drainage water being concentrated by a slope. Fen vegetation flourishes, and the raised-bog plants come in as soon as the fen-peat has blanketed off the soil nutrients. The raised-bog is thus always surrounded by a rim of fen where the necessary waterlogging of the ground is taking place. If the lateral advance of the fen is slow, then lateral growth of the raised-bog must be slow. But there is no corresponding limitation on upward growth, and the bog centre thus grows upwards into a domed form, with its plant cover dominated by *Sphagnum*.

In the blanket-bog regions with rainfall above 1250 mm, the ground is of necessity waterlogged, except on steep rocky slopes, and the ombrogenous vegetation can establish itself everywhere. Neither lateral nor upward growth is restricted, and peat forms a layer of relatively uniform thickness. There are some *Sphagnum* hummocks, and there can also be pools, but on the whole the low-growing *Sphagna* are largely concealed by the taller cotton-grass (*Eriophorum vaginatum*), purple moor-grass (*Molinia caerulea*), bog-rush (*Schoenus nigricans*) and white beak-sedge (*Rhynchospora alba*). Among the heathers *Calluna vulgaris* and *Erica tetralix* are widely distributed, while in the west of the country some of the rarer heathers find their last refuge on the blanket-peat.

Peat formed in this way is seen at

Photograph 24 Lough Mask, Co. Mayo. Stumps and trunks of pine, perhaps about 4000 years old, have been exposed by peat-cutting. Such 'bog-deal' was formerly valued both for fuel and for building.

Emlaghlea (see Fig. 5.10c), where the top of the bog is formed of almost 2 m of blanket-bog peat. The peat was dominated by remains of *Molinia* and fibres of both species of cotton-grass, *angustifolium* as well as *vaginatum*, and twigs of *Calluna* and *Myrica gale* were also common. The bog-myrtle, *Myrica*, is widely distributed on the western blanket-bogs, and it alone of the bog plants can supplement its nitrogen intake by means of symbiotic nitrogen-capturing bacteria living in nodules on its roots, in just the way that clovers and other legumes do in grassland; it has a rather less fortunate distinction in that its pollen is very like that of hazel, and must often be confused with it in pollen-counts from such peats.

Where the surface of the ground below the blanket-bog is undulating, and there are some relatively level areas, there will be little lateral run-off. Here the peat may thicken, and the bog-surface will rise into a dome, mimicking the dome of the raised-bog.

The human population was not the only population to be affected by the expansion of blanket-bog; plants and animals had also to adjust themselves. Today the country between Roundstone and Clifden in Co. Galway carries a lake-studded area of blanket-bog with relict stations for rare heathers, *Erica mackaiana* and *E. erigena*, with St Dabeoc's heath (*Daboecia cantabrica*) growing on rocky outcrops protruding through the bog. At the end of the Ice Age this was an area of ice-scoured rock with innumerable ponds in the hollows. In the early Littletonian the area was wooded, and the ponds gradually filled with mud and fen-peat, containing seeds and pollen from the surrounding area. Professor Jessen did a lot of work here, and was able to show that when the mud was forming the surrounding countryside was wooded, and that *E. mackaiana* was growing in the woods in the same way that it grows in its main centre, north-west Spain, today. It seems almost incredible that this plant, which was presumably already struggling for existence at the limit of its ecological tolerance, should have been able to make the drastic change in habitat from shaded forest floor to open blanket-bog, and still survive as it does — just — in Ireland today.

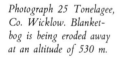

Photograph 25 Tonelagee, Co. Wicklow. Blanket-bog is being eroded away at an altitude of 530 m.

In many upland areas the blanket-bog — for reasons which nobody understands — is being stripped away by erosion, and a complicated mosaic presents itself. In one place deep channels are beginning to dissect a still continuous peat cover, in a second strips of mineral soil are separated by islands or 'haggs' of peat, while in a third, mineral soil is dominant, its surface broken only by a few isolated mounds of surviving peat. Various reasons have been put forward to explain the erosion, which presumably stems from a breaking of the continuous vegetation-cover. A climatic change, overgrazing by sheep, burning of the surface-vegetation to encourage young growth — all have been suggested (Photo 25).

It seems unlikely that peat would continue to form after the bog surface has been broken. We have seen that around AD 1700 pine was reintroduced, and exotic trees were brought in for plantations. We find the pollen of these trees in the top layers of some blanket-bogs, which must have continued to grow after that date. Traces of industrial soot also indicate late growth. It is thus possible that the erosion only started relatively recently, possibly due to over-grazing by larger sheep-stocks. It is proceeding actively, and if it had been going on for a long time, presumably very much more peat would have disappeared, and left the summits in a barer state than we find them today.

The Bronze Age

Beaker prospectors and settlers:
4000 to 3250 years ago (2050-1300 BC)
Recent years have seen a tremendous upsurge in the intensive prospecting of the Irish countryside for economic deposits of metallic ores, and in several areas the search was rewarded by massive discoveries of lead and zinc. Massive alterations of the landscape have followed. The discoveries were brought about by the use of sophisticated geochemical and geophysical techniques, whose application in the field has been made all the more easy by the fact that Ireland today is virtually treeless, which is a considerable aid to the transport of equipment and the carrying out of precision surveying.

Today's surveyors are the lineal descendants of the first prospectors who were at work in the Irish countryside about 4000 years ago, operating on behalf of a new group of people who had entered Ireland, bringing with them knowledge of metal and of metal smelting and fabricating. They needed still more metal.

The Neolithic people can claim to have been Ireland's first geologists, because not only did they collect attractive stones to decorate their monuments, but they also groped their way through dense woodland to find the all too rare exposures of rock suitable for the mass manufacture of axes. It was in the same woodlands that the metal prospectors had to search, and even though the copper compounds in the superficial layers of the deposits would have occurred as brightly coloured carbonates, green *malachite* and blue *azurite*, nevertheless, they required some finding. The prospectors did have success, finding gold in Co. Wicklow and copper in Co. Cork and elsewhere. Today gold is again being sought for in Wicklow, and also in the Sperrins in Co. Tyrone. Tin eluded the prospectors but for this they cannot be blamed as even to the present day Ireland has not produced any significant quantities of

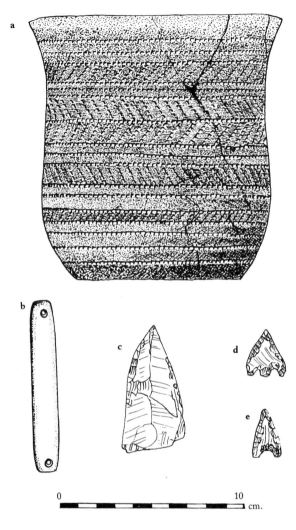

Fig. 5.11 Some typical Beaker objects: **a** *beaker, Dalkey Island, Co. Dublin;* **b** *wrist-bracer, stone, Carrowkeel, Co. Sligo (found below 2.5m of blanket-bog peat);* **c** *pointed knife, flint, Dalkey Island, Co. Dublin;* **d** *barbed and tanged arrowhead, flint, Dalkey Islnd, Co. Dublin;* **e** *hollow-based arrowhead, flint, Dalkey Island, Co. Dublin.*

tin. Four thousand years ago tin was a very strategic metal, as copper needed to be blended with it to produce the harder alloy, bronze. But when we think of the isolated successes the prospectors had, we must also think of the thousands of barren hectares that they prospected in order to make those finds.

Who were these people who first brought metal to Ireland? We know them principally from their sophisticated pottery vessels (Fig. 5.11) which had thin walls and were frequently elaborately decorated; we picture these as used for drinking and call them

beakers; their owners are the Beaker folk. These Beaker people seem to have had a wave-like expansion throughout north-west Europe, just as their Neolithic predecessors had had.

The Beaker folk must have arrived in Ireland in force, as our first view of them is a dramatic one. We have seen that we have at Newgrange in the Boyne valley a large and magnificent monument, built about 4500 years ago. Cheek by jowl with it, separated by no more than 10 m, are the remains of an equally magnificent monument of Beaker age, with radiocarbon dates centring on 4000 years ago, only 500 years after the building of Newgrange (Photo 26).

Like the Neolithic mound at Newgrange, the lay-out is circular, and the diameter of 90 m is greater than the diameter of the mound, but unlike the mound, nothing can be seen above ground. When excavated, the monument was revealed as a circular band of pits; the band was about 9 m wide, and as many as six pits lay radially across the band. The pits held either the remains of posts or cremated animal bones; many of the posts were large.

The great mound at Newgrange is defined by horizontal kerb-stones; in the Beaker monument the essential features are vertical. The circle was defined by large upright wooden posts. The world-famous Stonehenge is a monument of this type, also built by Beaker people; it has survived because the uprights were made of stone; many others, where the uprights were of wood — in what is sometimes described as wood-henge — have long since vanished from view. As well as the uprights the henge monument usually has associated pits with neat pockets of cremated bone. At Newgrange the scraps of cremated bone came from animals, not from human beings; does some curious ritual lie behind these depositions?

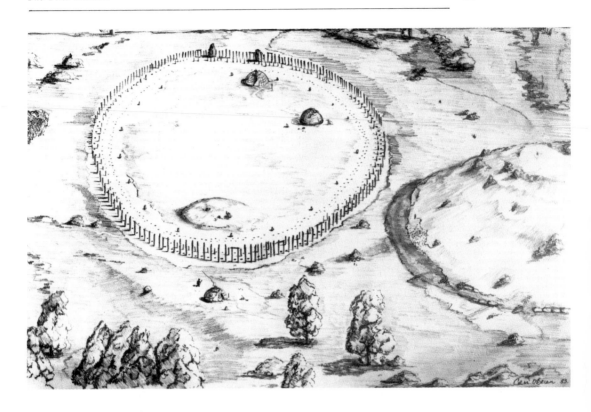

At one point immediately inside the circle, the remains of a Beaker hut was found; just to the west of the great Neolithic mound there was more Beaker material, including part of a unique stone vessel, decorated with typical Beaker designs. Beside the great mound at Knowth a spread of Beaker debris was found, but there were no signs of elaborate structures. At Monknewtown, 3 km to the north, there are the remains of a circular bank, 100 m in diameter, and other monuments of this type are known in Ireland. Inside the bank at Monknewtown there were cremated bones (some human) and Beaker pottery in pits, and the remains of a house dated to 3800 years ago. The north of Ireland has also produced Beaker material dated between 4000 and 3800 years ago.

What are we to make of these Beaker people? We know that outside Ireland they had knowledge of metal, but very little metal has been found with their

pottery in Ireland. I used to picture a few bedraggled prospectors struggling ashore in Ireland, finding metal deposits and working them, building up an export trade in ornaments and weapons of gold and bronze, and so achieving prosperity. But the copper mines we know are dated to about 3500 years ago, much later than the Newgrange henge monument. How was the latter financed?

Did the Beaker people arrive in force in the Boyne valley, dislodge the Neolithic Passage-grave builders, seize their wealth, and proceed defiantly to erect their own monument under the shadow of the older mound? Did they from there send out prospectors and miners to win them further wealth?

In the west of Ireland the Beaker people seem to have maintained the tradition of megalithic tombs and communal burial as their pottery is found in *Gallery-graves*, which seem to have originated in Brittany. These

Photograph 26 An artist's impression of the great henge monument at Newgrange, Co. Meath. The Neolithic mound is in the foreground on the right.

tombs are essentially a narrow lintelled gallery, often with a double enclosing wall, set in a short oval or circular cairn; the gallery often lies along an east-west axis (see Fig. 5.6c). Also south-west in their distribution in Ireland, and also pointing towards Brittany and beyond, are abstract designs inscribed on outcrops of living rock, which seem to have their home in Galicia in Spain.

Methods of mining changed little from the first prehistoric winning of ore until the Industrial Revolution, and to find a primitive mine-working is no proof that it must be of high antiquity. Mount Gabriel, near Skibbereen in Co. Cork, is irregularly impregnated with copper ores, and its flanks have many small holes quarried into them, and lying across the mouths of the holes are heaps of broken stone and charcoal; the charcoal has been given a C-14 age of 3450 years ago, and these mines could well have been operated by Beaker folk. In the holes, on the tip-heaps and trailing up the slope of the hill there can be found rounded beach cobbles, both broken and intact, often with abraded ends showing that they had been used in pounding. We can thus picture the early miners, after they had located a suitable outcrop of ore, first lighting a fire against it to expand the rock, and then throwing on water to shrink and shatter it. The stone mauls, some of which were grooved to give a better purchase for a wicker handle, were then used both to free the shattered rock, and to pound the fragments still further, so that the ore-rich pieces could be collected for smelting. If the richness of the ore made it worth following back into the rock, gradually a tunnel was developed. The diameters of the tunnels or holes in the hillside suggest that elaborate staging was not used, as they are about the size that could be excavated by a man standing on the ground, and using a handled hammer. The miners could only go a limited distance into the hillside, because beyond a certain point ventilation would become poor, and

seepage of water from the tunnel walls would make it difficult to apply heat effectively to them. Since the mines were abandoned, peat has formed both on the hillside and on the tip-heads.

Mining of copper and gold made it possible to produce bronze, with tin imported from Cornwall. Soon smiths were fabricating and exporting collars and ear-rings of gold, and were casting daggers, axes and halberds in flat stone moulds, both for use at home and for export. But beyond their beakers, their jewellery and their weapons, we know very little about their way of life. It is thought that they were accomplished archers, because barbed and tanged flint arrowheads and wrist-guards are commonly associated with them.

NEWGRANGE ANIMAL BONES

	Bone-fragments %	Minimum number of individuals
DOMESTIC ANIMALS		
Cattle	57	37
Pig	31	30
Sheep/goat	5	12
Horse	2	6
Dog	4	12
WILD ANIMALS		
Red deer	1	1
	100	

At Ballynagilly, a site with a well-marked Beaker phase, there was evidence of forest clearance around 3850 years ago. It is not impossible that it was Beaker folk who set up the cultivation-ridges at Belderg, although their characteristic pottery has not been found on the site. Deposits of copper are available, there is a Gallery-grave on a nearby hillside, and the ridges were probably in use more than 3250 years ago. But the pollen-diagrams in general give little indication of their presence, and the scale of disturbance that they created in the woodlands must have been of the same order as that produced by their Neolithic predecessors. Louise van Wijngaarden-Bakker has produced a very interesting analysis of the animal bones at the Newgrange Beaker site, and the table opposite is based on her work. Hare, wild cat, goshawk and water-rail were also identified. We see, as always, the dominance of cattle, with the pig in second place. We also see the first appearance of the horse.

The individual grave and the Food Vessel 3750 to 3150 years ago (1800-1200 BC) Rather later than the first finds of Beaker material, and perhaps about 3750 years ago, we begin to find skeletons which had been inhumed, usually in a crouched position, in a simple box or cist of stone slabs, sunk into the ground, often into glacial sands and gravels. Here we see the rejection of communal burial, and a different

Fig. 5.12 Some typical Food Vessel objects and one Cinerary Urn: **a** *bowl-form vessel, Mount Stewart, Co. Down;* **b** *Cinerary Urn, Burgage Mor, Co. Wicklow;* **c** *vase-form vessel, Ballon Co. Carlow;* **d** *battle-axe, stone, Bann Valley;* **e** *flat decorated axe, bronze, Scrabo Hill, Co. Down;* **f** *flanged axe, bronze, no locality.*

0   5   10   15 cm

concept of afterlife, because the remains are often accompanied by a pottery vessel, and sometimes by a weapon as well. Thus we all too easily leap to the conclusion that the vessel must have contained provisions for the next world, and call it a Food Vessel.

So-called Food Vessels are generally of heavier texture and rougher ornamentation than the lightly walled and delicately ornamented Beakers. They have two main forms, one with a rounded base or bowl-form, and the other with a more flower-pot form and flat base, the vase-form (Fig. 5.12). The bowl-form may represent a native development from an amalgamation of earlier Irish pottery forms, but the vase-form is thought to have affinities with Britain.

The call for cremation seems to have been very strong in the prehistoric world, and this rite gradually re-established itself in Ireland, though the remains continued to be deposited individually. To protect the cremated debris a larger pottery vessel, the Cinerary Urn, decorated with cordons, rosettes and zig-zags in bands of applied

clay, was evolved, probably with its origins in the vase-form Food Vessel. The cremated remains were placed in the urn, which was then buried in an inverted position in a cist or pit. Sometimes a mound was then thrown up over the burial, or the burial was inserted in a pre-existing mound.

There is no doubt that the abandoned megalithic tombs must have been a source of fascination to Bronze Age people, just as they are to us today. They have been used over and over again, either as burial places, or as convenient fireplaces, or, as in the case of Professor de Valéra's excavations at Behy, as a site for an illicit still. As a result they may contain charcoal of different ages, and often produce bizarre results when efforts are made to date them by the C-14 method. Sometimes they were substantially altered before being used again as a burial site.

The Mound of the Hostages at Tara (Photo 27) started its career as a Passage-grave, built of stone about 4000 years ago, and parts of the chamber still contained the original cremated debris. Other parts had been cleaned out by

Photograph 27 The Mound of the Hostages, Hill of Tara, Co. Meath. The partly exposed mound of stones contained an undisturbed Passage-grave, built about 4000 years ago. A rind of earth was later laid over the original mound, and burials in Cinerary Urns were inserted in this about 3500 years ago. The hostages would be of a much later date.

Food Vessel people, who had deposited uncremated bodies in crouched positions, accompanied by food vessels, a bronze awl and conical V-perforated buttons of jet and stone. Users of Cinerary Urns then laid down a rind of clay about 1 m thick on top of the cairn of stone, and inserted their burials into the clay. Most were single cremations in inverted urns, sometimes accompanied by food vessels and weapons. One burial was accompanied by a magnificent stone battle-axe and a bronze dagger, both severely burned, probably in the funeral pyre. One unburned body, that of a youth of about 14-15 years of age, had been inhumed in a flexed position with an elaborate and very valuable necklace around the neck. He was perhaps the son of a chieftain, or a boy-king. The beads were of bronze, possibly of Irish origin, of amber, probably from Scandinavia, of jet, probably from the south of England, and of *faience*. Faience is made by fusing blue glass and quartz grains, and moulding them into the required form; its production is a considerable technological achievement, and many people think that its manufacture was carried out in the eastern Mediterranean; some think it was made in Britain also. But wherever it was made it was at all times prized, and its occurrence at Tara adds emphasis to the value of the necklace, which demonstrates by its varied elements the wide range of Ireland's trading connections at this time.

While on the whole we know very little of the way of life of the times, we do have some glimpses. Cooking by throwing heated stones into water held in a wooden trough in the ground, or in an animal skin supported by sticks, is one of the oldest methods of cooking; it survived into medieval times in Ireland, and is still practised in New Guinea. In Ireland the method was widely used during the Iron Age, and the heaps of burned stones that still mark the former sites are called *fulachta fian*, the cooking-places of the wandering warriors. Professor O'Kelly

investigated some sites in west Cork, and revealed not only the trough and its associated mound of burned stone, but also hearths, huts and various fittings; in his usual thorough manner he rounded his excavation off by cooking and eating meat processed in this way, and was amazed at the efficiency of the method and the tastiness of the result. Wood from one trough was dated to 3710 years ago, and so the method of cooking goes back to this stage of the Bronze Age (Photo 28).

Some of the wood bore the marks of small axes, and a *fulacht fian* at Millstreet, Co. Cork, produced a flanged bronze axe of this period. At Ballyvourney O'Kelly reassembled planks into the oak trees from which they had been cut, and showed that the carpenters were able to deal with trunks 50 cm in diameter from trees over 100 years old. The woods used for construction, the charcoal from the fires, and the pollen in the associated peat, all combined to show that the area was still wooded when the sites were in use. This is an acid area, with

Photograph 28 The reconstructed cooking-site (fulacht fian) at Ballyvourney, Co. Cork, showing the water-filled pit in which heated stones were placed; within the hut a bench-like structure perhaps supported a butcher's block.

Old Red Sandstone as the underlying rock, and peaty podzols as the modern soils, and the Bronze Age woods were dominated by oak, pine and birch, with only small amounts of elm and hazel.

Three rather younger *fulachta fian* were found in blanket-bog in the Imlagh basin in Valencia Island, Co. Kerry. The fuel used was stems of *Calluna*, collected from the neighbouring bog-surface. One example was well constructed with a large stone trough, the others were much smaller; the dates ranged from 3150 to 3400 years ago.

This type of site is nearly always in a damp situation, where the water-table is almost at surface level, so that if a hole is dug it quickly fills with water, which is immediately available for cooking. But one of Professor O'Kelly's sites was on what is today the dry alluvium of the flood plain of a river, 50 m back from the water's edge, and Professor O'Kelly pictured that water would have had to have been carried from the river to fill the trough. Another site at Curraghtrasna, Co. Tipperary, was on the bank of a dried-up stream (with six other sites nearby). The trough had been made by re-using part of a boat hollowed out of an oak-trunk, whose outer wood had an age of 3140 years.

These apparent lowerings of the local water-table raise another question, which has so far been entirely neglected in Irish geomorphological studies, namely — What is the age of the flood-plains of the Irish rivers? We look idly at these features today, and imagine they have always been there — but have they? Man has been interfering with rivers for centuries, by building roads and bridges across them, by erecting weirs and mill-races for water-power, and by deepening and narrowing their channels in an effort to drain the surrounding agricultural land.

Perhaps at the time that the Ballyvourney cooking-site was in use the local river was still building up

its flood-plain, and the water-table may have been higher, high enough to fill the cooking-pit on the flood-plain. At the southern tip of the Blackstairs Mountain range near Ballinvegga in Wexford a shallow basin is drained by a stream which runs north-westwards to join the Barrow. The stream has an extensive flood-plain which is now being drained artificially, and the walls of the drainage-cut show about 150 cm of sands, gravels and silts resting on glacial deposits. The deposits of the terrace are crowded with drifted vegetable material, ranging from oak trunks to hazelnuts. An oak trunk at the base of the deposit was given a radiocarbon age of 3825 years, or in other words it *could* have been growing at the time that people were cutting down oaks to construct *fulachta fian* — and *fulachta fian* are quite common in Wexford. Could it be that there was extensive forest clearance in the valley by Bronze Age farmers, that the run-off regime of the stream was changed when there were no longer trees to retard water flow, and that the flood-plain as we see it today is the result of forest clearance 4000 years ago?

A very extensive drainage scheme is going on over the whole catchment-area of the River Boyne at present. Scariff Bridge, about four miles south-west of Trim, was built across the flood-plain in medieval times. There was a drainage-scheme in the nineteenth century, a channel was cut down into the flood-plain, and a big arch was inserted into the old bridge. Now with modern earth-moving machinery a much more ambitious scheme is under way, and the channel is being further deepened. Again about 2 m of terrace material rests on glacial deposits, and muds, bones and driftwood lie in what were former channels across the accumulating terrace. A piece of driftwood at the base of the terrace w given a radiocarbon age of 1680 years (AD 280). This was a time at which the clearance of woodland was being resumed in Ireland, and it is not impossible that the Boyne flood-plain, though its date is very different from that at Ballinvegga, may also owe its origin to a change in river regime consequent on forest clearance. The bones include those of red deer and cat. Discussing the history of the cat in Ireland Louise van Wijngaarden-Bakker considers that the domestic cat, which reached England in Roman times, probably was introduced into Ireland during the first centuries AD. The cat remains at Scariff Bridge may therefore be either from a domesticated animal, or from a wild cat.

The increased prosperity of the Bishopsland Period:
3150 to 2650 years ago (1200 - 700 BC)
Around 1200 BC immense economic changes were taking place in Europe, and it was not long before these changes affected Ireland. Rich ore deposits were now being worked in central Europe, and this area was beginning to outstrip the eastern Mediterranean in wealth and in technical achievement. Gold ornaments of advanced workmanship, found both singly and in hoards, indicate corresponding prosperity in Ireland. But

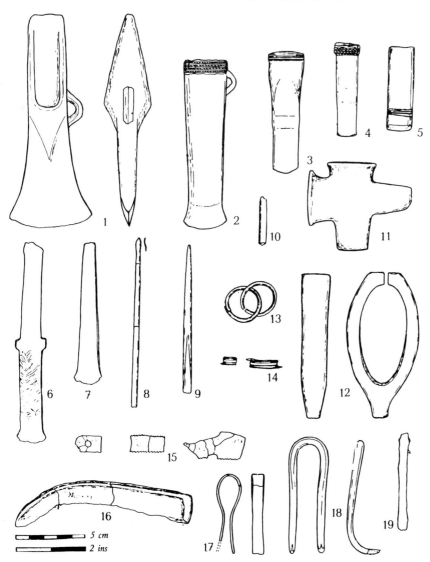

Fig. 5.13 Bishopsland hoard, mainly of bronze tools: **1** *palstave;* **2** *socketed axehead;* **3, 4** *socketed hammerheads;* **5** *light hammer or punch;* **6, 7** *chisels;* **8, 9, 10** *gravers;* **11** *anvil;* **12** *slotted anvil;* **13** *rings;* **14** *bracelet fragment;* **15** *saw;* **16** *sickle;* **17** *tweezers;* **18** *flesh-hook;* **19** *hollow bar.*

5 cm

2 ins

the most interesting, though not the most opulent, evidence of these new influences is the hoard of bronze tools and implements that was discovered at Bishopsland, Co. Kildare (Fig. 5.13). When the rock-walls of the Poulaphuca meltwater channel were being scraped down to remove loose debris, so that the end of a dam for a hydroelectric scheme could be bonded firmly to solid rock, a shower of bronze implements was released from some cache where they had been hidden for about 3000 years.

The hoard obviously belonged to a travelling smith. He had socketed hammers, two anvils, a punch, a graver, chisels and a saw; one of the anvils (12) was slotted so that sheet metal could be held in it, while it was being embossed or engraved. One old-fashioned item is the *palstave,* or axe with flanges and a stop-ridge for hafting (1), which could have been cast in a simple two-piece stone mould. In sharp contrast is the socketed axe (2), a type which first appeared in northern Germany, and from there overflowed into England and Ireland; the axe has a basal loop, and when the axe was being secured to its handle, string would be passed through the loop, and then wound round the base of the axe and the end of the haft, to bind the two firmly together. If we look closely at the base of the axe, we seem to see a decorated rim, but this is in fact a replica in bronze of remains of such binding string. This shows that the axe was manufactured by copying a pre-existing axe by a complicated process. Two blocks of soft clay approximating in size to the object to be copied were taken; one side of the object was pressed down into one block and the other side into the second block; grooves and ridges were made in the blocks to ensure that they would fit accurately together. The clay blocks, with the impressions facing one another across the central hollow, were then hardened by baking, and made ready to receive poured-in molten metal. When the axe was being pressed into the clay

of the moulds, it still had remnants of string around the socket. One of the hammers (4) shows the same feature.

The flesh-hook (18) and the sickle (16) have a special interest for us. The flesh-hook exemplifies the importance of meat in the Irish diet, and the sickle, which stems from Europe, is the oldest example of this implement so far found in Ireland.

Contrasting the period of the Bishopsland hoard with the earlier periods of the Bronze Age in Ireland George Eogan says, 'the difference is glaring, so much so that hand-in-hand with the development noticeable in the ornaments and implements must go a development in society, a society not only rich in artistic and technological talents, but, indeed, a society with altered attitudes and habits'. Professor Eogan considers that increased exploitation of the country's natural resources was to a great extent responsible for the new wealth in Ireland, which was thus able to keep pace with the general European advances of the times.

Unfortunately except for the ornaments and the implements, which are widely distributed in the northern two-thirds of the country, we have very little other evidence of these developments. The gold was presumably won from the river gravels of Co. Wicklow, but as these rivers are flash-flood streams, rising rapidly in level when there are rainstorms in the hills, and dropping again equally quickly, simple gravel workings would have been quickly obliterated by later floods. The copper continued to come from surface exposures, but these early workings will have largely vanished also. The development of steam power made the draining and pumping of water from mines immeasurably easier, and the bigger and deeper working of mineral deposits in the nineteenth century has removed most of the evidence for working in prehistoric times.

But a society, like an army, marches on its stomach, and the rise in the standard of living, and presumably in population numbers also, must have brought a greatly increased demand for agricultural products. The Red Bog pollen-diagram (see Fig. 5.9) has a radiocarbon date of 3570 years ago (say 1600 BC), and a little higher we see clear indications of extended agriculture. Elm remains at a low level, ash pollen becomes uninterruptedly present — though at a low level — as field margins now offered an ecological niche not previously available, hazel shows a substantial fall as secondary scrub is cleared away, and bracken and plantain join the grasses in the record. It is not unreasonable to think that here we see the more intensive agriculture of the Bishopsland Period. At Ballynagilly extensive woodland clearance was recorded at 1200 BC and at Gortcorbies agricultural activity was greatly intensified at 1075 BC.

Jon Pilcher has made a detailed study of the peat at an altitude of 430 m on the slopes of Slieve Gallion, Co. Tyrone. As at Emlaghlea, the lower peat was a reedswamp peat, rich in wood in its upper part. About 4165 years ago (2250 BC) this type of peat was supplanted by blanket-bog peat, and at three levels in the blanket-bog peat there are signs of increased agricultural activity. The first is around 1500 BC, when cereal pollen is present and oak shows a fall; this may indicate some Food Vessel activity in the region. The second is around 1300 BC, where plantain rises to a maximum and oak is again reduced; the third is around 900 BC, where plantain again reaches a higher level. The second and third episodes could be associated with the Bishopsland Period.

At Rathgall, a hill-top site in Co. Wicklow, complicated structures and numerous finds indicate a long story of occupation on the hill. A large V-shaped ditch seems to be one of the earliest features, and some of its fill was given a radiocarbon date of 1000 BC, which would place it in the Bishopsland

Period, a date which is also hinted at by the discovery of clay mould fragments for socketed implements with rope mouldings round the sockets. We have seen that such implements are present in the Bishopsland hoard.

Still greater wealth in the Dowris Period: 2650 to 2250 years ago (700-300 BC)
In the diagram from Red Bog (Fig. 5.9) a C-14 date of 2625 years ago (say 675 BC) corresponds with a marked increase in agricultural activity, but we cannot be positive that this increase was widespread throughout Ireland. At Red Bog, above this level grasses and plantain expand substantially, and bracken is almost continuously present. Cereal pollen is present, and pollens of weeds appear intermittently. Elm woods and hazel thickets were cleared away, and a little later the attack spread into the oakwoods.

This date approximates closely with 700 BC, the date that George Eogan has reckoned for the opening of his Dowris Period of the Bronze Age in Ireland, when there were still wider contacts with northern Europe, west-central Europe, Iberia and the eastern Mediterranean, and a further marked increase in wealth, indicated by the numerous finds of gold ornaments and of caches or hoards of bronze implements. In the later Bronze Age northern Europe relied principally on two areas for its supplies of copper, the Carpathians and the Alps. In the eighth century BC the Carpathian area was thrown into chaos by barbarian invaders from the east, and in consequence its output of copper was drastically reduced. Northern Europe then turned to Ireland as an alternative source, and this trade brought not only further prosperity, but still more innovations to Ireland. Some of them could perhaps have been done without; the whole style of warfare was changed; hitherto the warriors had poked at one another with rapiers or halberds; now they cut at one another with slashing swords, while protecting themselves with shields, made of bronze, leather or wood, depending on social or economic status. Feasts were provided with buckets and cauldrons, and musical interludes were given by trumpets. Gold ornaments became still more numerous, and were accompanied by ornaments of imported Scandinavian amber. The horse was utilized, and provided with elaborate trappings. Wheeled carts appear. Hoards of bronze and gold were deposited, perhaps for safety, perhaps as sacrificial offerings: such hoards are widely distributed throughout Ireland.

Our interest is more particularly with the impact these Dowris folk had on the landscape. What tools did they use, where did they live, how did they farm? The chief tools of the Dowris Period (Fig. 5.14) are the knives, both socketed and tanged, with straight and curved blades, the chisels, both socketed and tanged, and the socketed gouges, all of which made a very much higher standard of wood-working possible. Socketed sickles also appear, and these, combined with the saddle-querns and the steady presence of cereal pollen in the diagram, indicate a more intensive

Fig. 5.14 Bronze tools of the Dowris Period of the Bronze Age:
1, 2, 3, 4 *socketed and tanged knives;* **5** *curved socketed knife;*
6, 7 *socketed sickles;* **8, 9** *socketed gouges;*
10, 11, 12 *socketed chisels;*
13, 14, 15 *tanged chisels;* **16** *socketed hammerhead;* **17** *razor.*

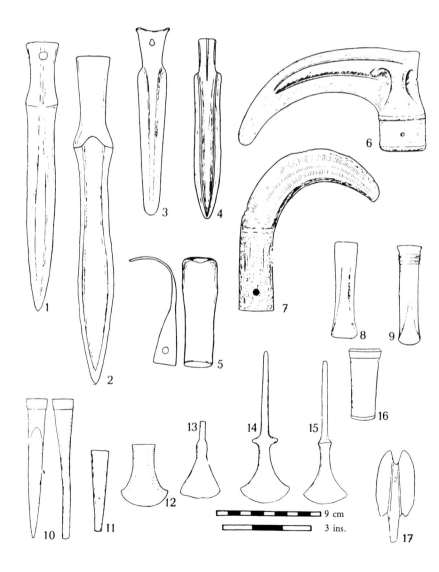

system of agriculture. Pottery, of which there is no record in the Bishopsland Period, reappears as flat-bottomed bucket-shaped vessels of poor quality.

Four settlement sites are known, the hill-top site at Rathgall, which continued in use, and three crannogs (see Photo 32), or man-made structures in lakes, where the lake waters had a twofold effect — they not only gave protection to the site when it was occupied, but if wet conditions persisted after the site had been abandoned then there was a good possibility that the organic debris left behind by the crannog-dwellers would be preserved.

At Rathgall a socketed bronze gouge, coarse pottery, clay moulds for casting swords and several radiocarbon dates ranging from 600 to 250 BC make it clear that the occupation continued on into the Dowris Period. A wooden structure appeared to be a bronze-smith's workshop; a black layer in and around the building yielded many fragments of clay moulds, bronze ingots and lumps of waste bronze; there were hearths outside the building.

In addition to saddle-querns a small mass of carbonized crushed cereal grains was found; the mass must represent either a loaf, or porridge, or brewer's grains; the first probability is perhaps the most likely; the radiocarbon age was 540 BC, which would place the material firmly in the Dowris Period.

Knocknalappa, Co. Clare, is the simplest of the crannogs. In a shallow part of Rossroe Lake an oval area, 40 m long and 20 m across, was surrounded by a ring of hazel stakes. Peat and stones were then laid inside the ring of stakes, and charcoal and archaeological objects were apparently carried in from some other site with the peat, as there was no evidence that the crannog itself had ever been occupied for any significant length of time. A count of 43 pieces of charcoal gave the following result — hawthorn 18, hazel 15, oak 4, alder 2, willow (or

poplar) 2, ash 1, holly 1 — and this count strongly suggests that the gatherers of firewood had immediate access to secondary scrub which had not been long established, and was still rich in hawthorn and hazel. Carpenters could get other material because a wooden structure showed a rather different count — oak 5, willow (or poplar) 4, ash 2, hazel 1, alder 1. Animal bones were dominated by ox, and sheep (or goat), pig and horse were also found. A layer of lake-mud rested on the crannog, and the excavator, Dr Raftery, thought that this had been artificially deposited, but as lake level appears to have risen after the crannog had been abandoned at the second site, Ballinderry, Co. Offaly, and a layer of mud had been deposited naturally on top of the crannog, it is not impossible that the same thing happened at Knocknalappa.

At Ballinderry the settlement seems to have been on a low gravel island in a lake, and in places brushwood and rings of piles extended the occupation-site out into the lake waters. The lake subsequently rose in level and deposited muds on the former settlement; later in Early Christian times a much larger crannog was built at the same spot on top of the earlier site.

On the site there were a number of circular wicker huts between 1 and 2 m in diameter, and it is possible that these were used as granaries. There was also an elaborate wooden foundation about 12 m square of parallel rows of oak planks about 1.5 m apart joined at the ends by cross beams; each plank had a row of squarish holes to carry an upright post about 6 cm in diameter. It suggests an aisled hall of some type, though the aisles might have been inconveniently narrow. One saddle-quern and some rubbing-stones were found. An unusual feature was the abundance of red deer bones, but some of them may be the remains of animals which had died naturally in and around the lake, and were not necessarily killed by the crannog-dwellers. Of the other bones about three-quarters were of ox, one-tenth were pig, and the remainder sheep and horse. The bulk of the charcoal was of alder, ash, hazel and willow, and hawthorn and yew were represented in the pieces of worked wood found. Again secondary woodland is indicated.

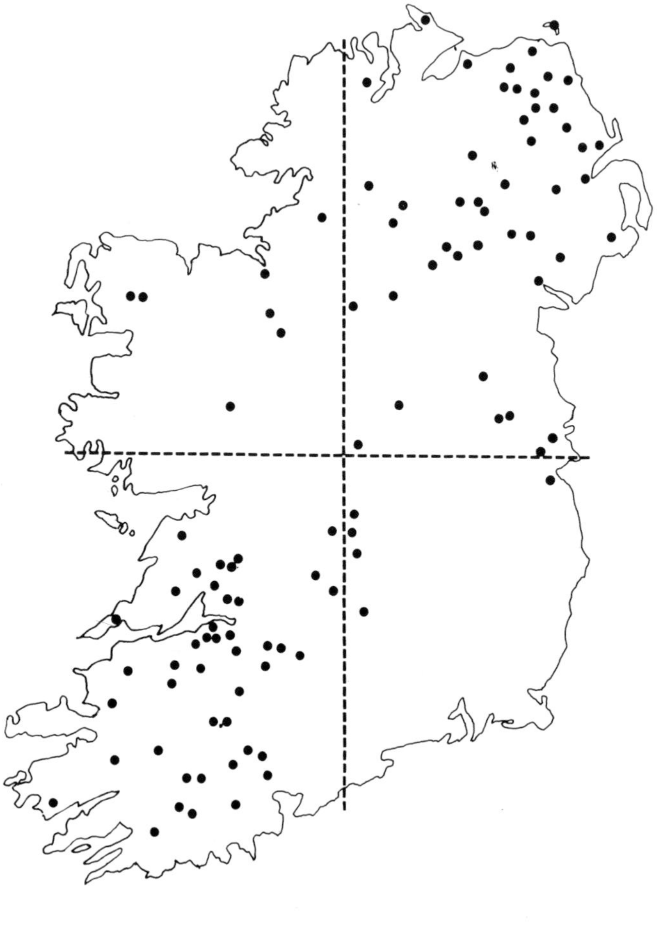

Fig. 5.15 In the Dowris Period the north-east of Ireland has many finds of new implements of British origin; the north-west has fewer similar finds; the south-west is rich in finds of new implements from a variety of sources; the south-east has very few finds of this age.

At Rathtinaun in Lough Gara a small settlement site had been constructed in the shallow water of a swamp, by laying down a ring of wooden piles, and building up the enclosed area with brushwood and peat. Evidence of occupation was scanty, but there were a number of hearths surrounded by clay-plastered wicker-baskets; pieces of the baskets were dated by radiocarbon to about 150 BC. There must have been a

kiln for drying grain which became overheated on at least one occasion, with the result that the contents became completely carbonized, and were dumped over the edge of the crannog into the lake. Naked barley provided the bulk of the material, but Hans Helbaek also identified small amounts of hulled barley and of wheat; other food plants were various species of *Polygonum* (knotgrass) and *Chenopodium* (goosefoot), blackberries and raspberries (*Rubus* spp.) with in addition flax (*Linum usitatissimum*) and a large variety of weeds.

In the Dowris Period we have the curious situation that, while we know only a handful of occupation-sites, we have a very large number of well-localized artefacts, and these can be plotted on distribution-maps. These maps show marked regional differences in Ireland at this time. If we imagine the country cut into quarters (Fig. 5.15), we find in the two northern quarters several types of implement not previously known in Ireland, though the north-east quarter is much richer than the north-west; these new types appear to come from Britain. The south-west quarter also has new types of implement, but these stand quite apart from those in the north. This south-west quarter is the richest, and even within it the Shannon valley is notably more productive than the rest of the area.

There we find magnificent gold ornaments, bronze trumpets, perhaps for use in battle, and bronze cauldrons, perhaps for important feasts, and these we do not find elsewhere in Ireland. They seem to be imported; but from where? Wide ranges of territory, from Scandinavia to the Mediterranean, have been suggested. How were they paid for? The area has no deposits of gold, nor any significant amounts of copper. Yet the famous gold hoard from Mooghaun, Co. Clare, discovered when a railway line was being constructed, had more than 150 objects, and is the largest single find of gold ornaments from northern or western Europe. At Dowris itself, in Co. Offaly, the hoard consisted of more than 200 bronze objects. Concentrated in this restricted region there must have been wealthy local chieftains controlling large areas of land and large numbers of people; did they also control the export of copper? Was this the source of their wealth?

This rich south-west quarter is in marked contrast to the south-east quarter. Although this quarter had good sources of both gold and copper, it does not show any signs of wealth at this time.

How did the Dowris people farm? As we have seen, the Red Bog diagram (see Fig. 5.9) shows a dramatic upward spurt of agricultural activity about 700 BC. It is very probable that this expansion is due to the introduction of some form of plough. At this time ox-drawn ard-ploughs were being used in Scandinavia, and finds of amber beads in Ireland prove that there must have been trading connections with the north. Similar ards found in Danish bogs range in radiocarbon age from 900 to 350 BC, and an ard in Scotland was dated to 400 BC. If the ard-plough was being used in Scotland at this time it will certainly have been in use in Ireland also (Photo 29, top).

The type of plough or *ard* (Fig. 5.16 top) used was, of course, very simple compared with the modern plough. It had neither a *coulter*, a vertical knife-like blade to cut the roots in the soil, nor a *mouldboard* to turn the surface layer over, and so create ridges and furrows. It was a device for drawing a pointed oak rod, the *share*, across a field immediately below the surface of the ground. As it moved across the field the share would push the soil it was penetrating upwards and forwards, while at the same time some of the upper soil was falling down into the cavity left by the share as it moved along. In this way not only was the soil loosened, but some lower material, richer in nutrients than the already cultivated earth above it, was brought

nearer the surface, where it was more accessible to plant roots. The wear on the share was, of course, very heavy, and in modern experiments the share had to be replaced, or resharpened, six times in the course of ploughing one acre. In the experiments the ard, because it had not got a coulter, was

Photograph 29 Above: Bronze Age ard-plough. Centre: Medieval coulter-plough. Below: Medieval mouldboard-plough. The boy should be walking backwards in front of the team, the man sowing has nothing to do with the plough.

*Fig. 5.16 Plough-types
Top: The frame of the
ard supports a basal
projecting point, the share,
which is either of wood or
stone. Middle: A
downward projecting metal
knife, the coulter, is
mounted on the frame in
front of the share to cut
plant roots. A curved
board, the mouldboard,
follows the share, and
inverts the cut sod.
Bottom: Twisting by the
mouldboard inverts the
severed sod. (After H.C.
Bowen)*

not able to break up old grassland, and
the sod had to be chopped up with
spades or hoes before the ard could be
used. A second ploughing at right
angles was necessary to break up the
whole of the ground, and the fields
would thus tend to have a square
outline.

It seems quite legitimate to picture that
cereal-growing in ploughed fields made
a substantial contribution to the rise in
wealth that took place during the
Dowris Period in Ireland. However,
such a standard depended on the
fertility of the soil, and could not be
maintained unless the fertility remained
high also.

The enigma of the Pagan Iron Age: 2250 to 1650 years ago (300 BC - AD 300)

If we look at the section of the Red
Bog diagram (see Fig. 5.9) that follows
after the burst of agricultural activity
that marked the Dowris Period, we see
a gradual fading away of evidence of
agriculture. The weeds of cultivation
disappear first, followed by cereals and
bracken, while grass and plantain fall in
value. On the other side hazel rises
first, followed by rises in ash, elm and
oak. And then, with dramatic
suddenness, the situation is reversed. At
1725 radiocarbon years ago (AD 225)
grass, plantain and bracken rise sharply,
accompanied by the reappearance of
cereals and the weeds of cultivation.
Elm and ash fall back from relatively
high values, and hazel falls markedly.

And this is not a phenomenon unique
to Co. Louth. It can also be seen in
other raised-bog diagrams from
Limerick, Tipperary, Meath, Antrim
and Tyrone. The renewal of agriculture
has been dated at several points, and in
general the dates centre around AD 300.
Unfortunately we have as yet no date
for the point at which the previous
decline becomes clearly apparent, and,
rightly or wrongly, for our present
purposes I have taken it to occur at
about the time Iron Age influences
began to reach the country about 300
BC (2250 years ago). It cannot be
claimed that there was a complete
cessation of agricultural activity during
this 600-year period. Other pollen-
diagrams can be cited which do indicate
at least local farming.

We must therefore ask ourselves 'What
was going on in Ireland at 300 BC ,
and what was happening to the
landscape?' First, iron objects and a
knowledge of ironworking were
beginning to spread. We are not
concerned here with fashion. We do
not want to know when it was that
designs fashionable in Iron Age Europe
first began to be copied in bronze in
Ireland, or when it was that glass beads
began to be imported, in addition to

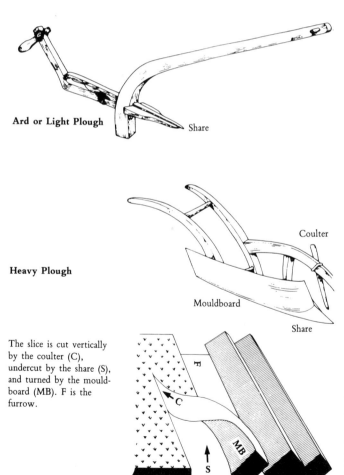

Ard or Light Plough   Share

Heavy Plough

Coulter

Mouldboard

Share

The slice is cut vertically
by the coulter (C),
undercut by the share (S),
and turned by the mould-
board (MB). F is the
furrow.

F

C

MB

S

Pl. 26 *Newgrange and the Plains of Meath. Low in the picture we see the great mound of the megalithic tomb, with its reconstructed facade; the tomb was built about 2500 BC. Below the mound we see what appear to be some figures on a giant clock-face; these are the openings that revealed a large Bronze Age monument, built about 2000 BC. (Aerofilms)*

Pl. 27 Tara, Co. Meath (looking north). In the foreground we see the great enclosure, Ráth na Ríogh, with its bank outside the ditch; inside, centre, we see two conjoined raths, and, top right, the Mound of the Hostages. The mound holds an inner Passage-grave, and an outer rind of Bronze Age date. North of the mound, and outside the Ráth, we see the Rath of the Synods, which produced objects from the Roman world. North of the Rath, we see the so-called Banqueting Hall; it is more probably a ceremonial approach avenue. In the top left-hand corner we see further raths. (Aerofilms)

Pl. 28 Looking south-west to Scariff and Deenish Island, Co. Kerry. The offshore islands lost their population a long time ago. The small holdings on the mainland slope are difficult of access, and will find it hard to remain viable. (Liam Blake)

Pl. 29 Clonmacnoise, Co. Offaly. Here we have an impression of what the great monastery looked like around the year AD 1200. We see the enclosing wall lined by houses and workshops. The churches and the graveyard occupy the centre, and there are also two round towers and several high crosses. (James Gardner)

31

32

Pl. 30 Caherconnell,
Co. Clare. Again in the
Burren we see on the left
a farmstead of the early
centuries of the Christian
era, where the dwellings
were protected by a round,
drystone cashel. Further
left we see early fields
bounded by curved stone
walls. On the right is a
modern small farm, whose
buildings occupy about the
same area as the cashel.
Curved field walls survive
beside it. (Aerofilms)

Pl. 31 Ballyduagh, Co.
Tipperary. Here the
remains of a 'deserted
village' (see Photo 39)
have been reclothed to
suggest what an Anglo-
Norman village looked
like in the thirteenth
century AD. We see the
moated manor and its
farm buildings at the
bottom right. In the centre
we have houses with
gardens; at the top there
are roadside cottages. At
the top left we have the
parish church, and on the
left margin we see the
ploughman breaking up
the stubble. (V. Bell)

Pl. 32 Valencia Island,
Co. Kerry. On the
horizon we see the ridge
of the Great Blasket
Island, shaped by
Hercynide mountain-
building forces many
millions of years ago. On
the right we see Slea
Head, and on the
mainland we have
blanket-bog which has
been heavily cut away. A
discarded motor-car ruins
the view. (G.F. Mitchell)

Pl. 33 Bellacorick, Co. Mayo. The whole of this expanse was formerly covered by blanket-bog. A considerable area is now being harvested mechanically to provide peat to fuel the small electricity generating station. (Aerofilms)

amber beads. What we want to know is when did the properties that for many purposes make iron superior to bronze come to be widely recognized in Ireland, and when was the first iron object fabricated here.

We must retrace our steps to the crannog site at Rathtinaun in Lough Gara. Here as at Ballinderry there were two stages of occupation separated by a period of desertion, caused, in the opinion of Dr Raftery, 'by a sudden and unexpected rise in the level of the water'. For the earlier stage there is a cluster of radiocarbon dates ranging from 300 to 200 BC; for the later stage there are two dates, 150 BC and AD 320. The earlier stage produced typical Dowris material in bronze, gold and pottery; the later stage produced similar bronze and pottery, with in addition an iron pin, an iron fork and an iron axe-head with a shaft-hole, clumsily forged out of three pieces of metal; here surely we have the arrival of iron in Ireland.

In a ditch buried beneath a rath at Feerwore, Co. Galway, Dr Raftery found another forged iron socketed axe-head. Dr Raftery had been attracted to the site because it was in its immediate vicinity that the famous Turoe Stone, decorated in abstract curvilinear style, originally stood. This impressive monument is fashioned from a glacial erratic of Galway granite, and must weigh several tonnes; it cannot therefore have been carried into Ireland by boat from distant parts, but must have been smoothed and decorated nearby, perhaps in the first century BC. Its designs, in *La Tène* style, stem from Celtic Europe, and such designs also occur in Ireland on numerous portable objects — sword-scabbards, spear-butts, horse-trappings, gold ornaments — which again have prototypes in Europe.

Should we picture bands of invading warriors, displaced by the Roman conquest from Britain and Gaul, plundering their way through the Irish countryside, and bringing about a collapse of an organized society and its pattern of agriculture? But there would be little point in capturing Ireland, if the assets of the country were destroyed in the process. The Romans clearly recognized that if an area was to be worth conquering it had to be capable, not only of maintaining a Roman garrison, but also of providing a surplus for the imperial exchequer. It is perhaps relevant at this point to recall that the Romans dismissed Ireland as not worthy of conquest.

It may be that invading Celtic warriors reorganized the social structure, placing themselves at the top of an aristocratic élite, with the native population forming subject tribes. The tribal chief and his entourage would install themselves in a hill-fort, which they would occupy as a palace in times of peace, but all the tribesmen and their cattle could be accommodated within its defences in times of danger. This is the picture that Richard Warner would draw of the hill-fort at Clogher, Co. Tyrone, probably built not long before the opening of the Christian Era. Here a roughly rectangular area less than 2 hectares in extent was protected by a bank, created from the upcast from a ditch immediately outside and downhill from it.

The fort at Clogher is a relatively small structure. In England the disturbed times of the Iron Age brought about the erection of very large hill-top and promontory forts; did the same happen in Ireland?

We do have hill-forts with more than one line of defence and a central citadel in western Ireland, and some of these, such as the well-known Dún Aengusa in the Aran Islands, are extremely impressive. Strategically they are equally mysterious. Were they built by native folk for protection against invaders, or were they built by newcomers trying to establish a foothold on the Atlantic coast? They have allied forms in south-west England, and may ultimately stem from Iberia. They do not resemble the multi-vallate hill-forts of southern

England, such as Maiden Castle. The promontory forts, whose distribution is chiefly along the southern and western seaboard, may also have roots in south-west Europe.

There has been considerable confusion between these defensive enclosures and another type of enclosure, often large, with a single bank and ditch, the ditch being *inside* the bank, the opposite of what one would expect in a defence line. These enclosures usually occupy the summits of low, rounded hills that overlook good fertile agricultural land. Sometimes the site had been occupied in earlier times.

The Hill of Tara (Pl. 27) has a large enclosure of this type, *Ráth na Ríogh*, and within it lies the Mound of the Hostages, which, as we have seen, was first built as a Neolithic Passage-grave and was later used in the Bronze Age. On the hill but outside the enclosure there is the Rath of the Synods — first excavated a hundred years ago by British Israelites looking for the Ark of the Covenant. Re-examination by Sean Ó Ríordáin revealed concentric ditches and post-holes for wooden structures; the inhabitants were in touch with the Roman world in Britain and Gaul, and finds of a seal, a lock, glass and pottery showed that the occupation of the site extended from the first to the third centuries AD. In addition to enamelling, iron-smelting was being carried on, and here we must be firmly in the Iron Age. The site threw no light on contemporary agriculture. There are also later conjoined raths (*Teach Cormaic* and *Forradh*).

Not far from Armagh is the similar Navan Fort (*Emain Macha*), enclosed by a bank and inner ditch (Photo 30a). The hill-top was first occupied in the Dowris Period, when a circular wooden house and attached stockade were built inside a round ditch with a bank outside it. The house was rebuilt many times, and gradually Iron Age objects replaced those of the Bronze Age. Among the finds was the skull of a Barbary ape from Spain or North Africa, which suggests that some of the occupants were of high social status, who indulged in the exchange of expensive gifts.

About 100 BC the house was replaced by a huge circular structure 40 m in diameter, with a massive double row of posts around its circumference; it appears to have been roofed, and was probably a place of assembly. In the centre the trunk of an oak tree at least 200 years old was erected as a massive centre piece or totem pole, perhaps 12 m high; a detailed count of its annual rings showed that it had been still growing at 100 BC.

Thirty kilometres south of the Navan Fort there is a large sub-rectangular enclosure, the Dorsey, which was protected by banks, ditches and palisades. The tree-rings of an oak post in the palisade exactly matched those of the great post in the fort, and the two structures must be of the same age. From the Dorsey an intermittent series of banks and ditches, the Black Pig's Dyke, runs west to the Atlantic coast; it takes its name from a legendary pig which is supposed to have thrown up a furrow from coast to coast in the course of one night.

Later in the first century BC the people of the fort decided to destroy their arena. They first filled the interior with large stones, and then set fire to the wooden parts that still protruded; earth and sods were then piled on top, and so the great mound we see today was created. Today, alas, we also see the quarrying that has grossly interfered with the ambience of the fort (Photo 30b).

What are we to make of all this? Did the people of the fort feel themselves menaced around 100 BC? First they built the Dorsey and its dyke to protect their territory; when that was overrun, did they realize their defeat was inevitable, and burn their headquarters to stop it falling into enemy hands?

Photograph 31 Derryadd raised-bog, near Lanesborough, Co. Longford, now being developed mechanically. Here the intact bog-surface formerly showed many open pools. The ribbon of fen that once separated the dome of the bog from the mineral soil of the drumlin island has been damaged by local peat-cutting, but the broad band of pale vegetation between the fields and the bog indicates its former position. The island is now treeless, but the prefix Derry in the name of the bog, shows that the region was once covered by oakwoods. Corlea can be seen in the top right-hand corner. A wooden trackway runs from Corlea to the drumlin island (see Pl. 25).

At Dún Ailinne, Co. Kildare, a bank with a ditch inside it outlines a hill-top area of almost 20 hectares; excavation produced glass beads, coarse pottery, and a sword of La Tène type that would have been at home in the second century BC.

In addition to these great enclosures, we can get more modest indications of activity in the two centuries preceding the birth of Christ. At Derryadd, 13 km south of Longford town, a drumlin had become completely surrounded by raised-bog, which served as a protective moat for the island (Photo 31). The bog is now being developed by Bord na Móna, and in the course of peat-removal a trackway, 1 km long, of massive oak-stems from the mainland out to the island at Corlea came to light. Detailed study of the tree-ring pattern of some of the oaks in the dendrochronology laboratory in Queen's University, Belfast, showed that the trees had been growing about 150 BC. Many of the stems had been split, and show cuts

from axes and adzes, probably made of iron. Some smaller pieces of dressed wood had been incorporated in the track, which in some places rested on baulks of wood, including ash and alder, which had been thrown down as a foundation. A second trackway at a lower level in the peat has since been discovered.

Toghers, tracks across wet ground and bogs made by throwing down timber and brushwood, go back to the Bronze Age (see p. 122). The Corlea 'road' was capable of carrying wheeled vehicles. The sagas tell us that heroes were driven to battle in light carriages, extravagantly described as chariots. There were also unsurfaced droving-roads, cattle-tracks and pathways. *Slige*, a general word for road, implies 'felling' or 'cutting-down', and suggests the cutting of a way through forest.

Moving past the birth of Christ, the same indications continue. In Kerry on Valencia Island earthen field-banks were

laid out about AD 240. At Carrownaglogh in Mayo there was a burst of agricultural activity about AD 300. Animal husbandry was indicated at Freestone Hill, Co. Kilkenny. Here there was a hill-fort, where a bank with an external ditch enclosed an area of about 2 hectares. No structures were found, and it was thought that the site had perhaps only been occupied for about one hundred years; a find of a Roman copper coin of Constantine struck about AD 340, and in mint condition, suggested a mid-fourth-century date for the occupation; some iron objects were found. There was no evidence of agriculture; the report says, 'Neither quernstones, plough-shares, coulters, billhooks, sickles or any other implement for tilling the soil came to light.' By far the majority of the animal bones were ox; pig was frequent and next in quantity; sheep were in small quantity, and there was one goat horn-core; horse was present in small numbers; there were a few remains of dog. Antlers of red deer had been turned into simple pick-axes. Freestone Hill is one of the very few Irish sites where molluscs have been studied, and as a result we have a useful landscape picture. The earth at the base of the ditch contained snail-shells, and here Arthur Stelfox identified seventeen different forms. He considered that they were types characteristic of a fairly dry woodland. 'I do not mean trees, but what we call scrub. I would suggest that the sides of the hill (below the ditch at any rate) were covered with patches of hazel (*Corylus*) scrub, giving plenty of shade under the bushes, but with open areas between patches of scrub.' Freestone Hill is an outlying limestone hill on the slopes of Castlecomer Plateau; today these slopes are in many places still carrying hazel scrub of the type envisaged by Stelfox.

This evidence of forts and enclosures, scrappy as it is, does suggest that social organization changed at least in some parts of the country in the centuries preceding the birth of Christ, and that there were contacts with the Roman world both in Gaul and in Britain. Why then should some pollen-diagrams tell us that in the area that they represent there was a marked falling-off in agricultural activity? I believe they reflect the culmination of a long-continuing and widespread exhaustion of soil, rather than drastic social upheaval brought about by military conquest. Areas of primary fertility, i.e. where the parent materials of the soils were rich in basic nutrients and had a texture that meant that soil drainage was good, had by this time had that fertility progressively depleted by cropping which had been in operation for some 3000 years.

For the first 2000 years the net loss of fertility where soils were deep was probably small. The Neolithic farmers scratched the surface of the soil, and quickly drew down the nutrient supplies available; but they then moved on, and secondary woodland reoccupied the site. Tree growth restored the fertility of the upper layers. In the Burren in Clare where soils were shallow fertility loss was high. As population grew during the Bronze Age the agricultural pressure on the good soils increased, and the intervening periods when the soil lay fallow under secondary woodland shortened, and the rate of loss of fertility must have steepened.

When 'welfare states' became established in the western world after World War II, poverty was very widely reduced, and the average *per capita* consumption of staple foods increased. We can be sure that much the same happened when the wider European contacts that marked the opening of the Bishopsland Period about 1200 BC materially increased the wealth of Ireland, and more and more nutrients must have been drawn from the soil. Increasingly sophisticated technical skills were largely responsible for the increase in wealth, and as technique becomes more complicated it also becomes less mobile. For an increasing proportion of the population the practice of changing one's residence, as the local soils became exhausted, will have become more and more difficult.

And we must remember that until the opening of the Dowris Period about 700 BC when — in my opinion, though I may well be wrong — the ard first came into use in Ireland, all cultivation was done with a mattock, a spade or a digging-stick, and that these implements could not reach down deeply into the soil. Only a very thin superficial layer was turned over, but this happened again and again, and in Ireland's wet climate, leaching of nutrients from this loose layer will have been severe, and it will have grown progressively sour and acid. This still happens even with the modern deep plough, but today's farmer rectifies the acid condition by adding calcium carbonate, in the form of ground limestone, to the soil.

At first sight the introduction of the ard might have seemed the panacea for all soil evils. On average the share of the ard did penetrate more deeply — else we should have no 'plough-marks' to discover — and it did lift some lower soil materials, still relatively rich in nutrients, nearer to the surface where crop-roots could draw on them. But the all-wooden ard must have been very vulnerable to collision with stones, and children and old folk will have been kept busy collecting stones from what we can now call fields, and depositing them in heaps or building them into walls. Heaps of field-stones, buried by peat, have been found both in Antrim and in Mayo. This further factor, that the ard was more successful in stone-free fields than in rough open ground, will have tended to 'fix' farming operations still more firmly in certain localities, and restrict them from wandering in search of less exhausted soils. As population rose, 'empty' land to move on to must have become increasingly difficult to find.

It may well be that the ard, which in the short term appeared to be such a

boon, turned out in the long run to be a disaster. In the beginning the ard did bring new nutrient material to the surface, but only from the still very limited depth to which it could reach; it probably created a good 'tilth' more easily than the spade, and for a time all went well. But the more finely divided the tilth became, the more easily nutrients could be lost from it by leaching, and a very acid surface layer created.

Today between Newbridge and Kildare we have the Curragh, a great expanse of gravelly glacial deposits, chiefly occupied by a racecourse and a military barracks. The modern soil is a grey-brown podzolic and, as its name implies, leaching is carrying surface materials down to lower levels. Where the modern farmer owns his fields, he counteracts this by adding farmyard manure and other fertilizers to the fields, and the grey-brown podzolic then gives him one of the best soils in Ireland. But in recent times much of the Curragh was held in common and used as a sheep-walk; as it belonged to everyone, no one fertilized it. Thus in certain areas the soil went undisturbed and neglected for long periods, with the result that although the parent material was calcareous, continued leaching combined with over-grazing removed all the calcium carbonate from the surface layers, which became acid and low in nutrients. As a result, ling (*Calluna vulgaris*), a member of the heather family, which can survive on a low supply of nutrient, invaded the area, and covered parts of it with a heath vegetation. We have already seen *Calluna* growing on bog-surfaces, where the nutrient supply is also low.

It may well be that as the Dowris Period progressed large areas of agricultural land, through over-cultivation with the ard, and increased leaching due to climatic deterioration, became depleted of nutrients. Grasses could no longer thrive, and the fields degenerated into heath. This certainly was the case on sandy soils in Bronze

Age Denmark. If this happened the output of pollen of grass and its associated weeds into the air would be reduced, and the output of pollen of the heather family (ericaceous pollen) would be increased. Unfortunately, as I have already explained, most of the pollen-diagrams in this book are based on samples from bogs, and as their purpose is to illustrate changes in the vegetation of the surrounding countryside, and not the development of the bog, the pollens arising from plants growing on the bog-surface itself have been omitted from them. Thus if heaths surrounding the bog started to produce ericaceous pollen in addition to that developed by the bog vegetation, this is not revealed by the diagrams. This further illustrates the weakness of the 'relative' type of pollen-count. Suppose we are making counts of 'trees' on the one hand, and 'grasses' on the other; if the supply of grass pollen to the air is reduced by heath taking over former grassland (and we do not take into consideration the extra ericaceous pollen produced), then the quantity of 'tree' pollen in our counts will rise, even though the tree cover may not have expanded significantly.

But this does not vitiate our argument that if pollen and spores of grasses and its associated weeds, plaintain and bracken, fall drastically in value, agriculture must have been reduced, and that if they bound up again, agriculture has returned in force.

Let us see what a pollen-diagram from a lake, as opposed to one from a bog, can tell us (Fig. 5.17). Near Dunshaughlin in Co. Meath there is an extensive lake-basin surrounded by calcareous glacial deposits; today the local soil is a grey-brown podzolic. A large crannog in the basin, Lagore Crannog, was excavated by Hugh Hencken, and shown to have been built not later than AD 650. The crannog was built on lake-mud, and there was a further thin deposit of mud on top of the margins of the crannog. The muds below the crannog produced a piece of Neolithic pottery and a bronze spearhead, and their contained pollen indicated long-continued farming activity in the country around the lake. We cannot put absolute dates on the diagram, but it begins in the later part of the Bronze Age.

Fig. 5.17 Schematic pollen-diagram to show development of heath vegetation at Lagore, Co. Meath.

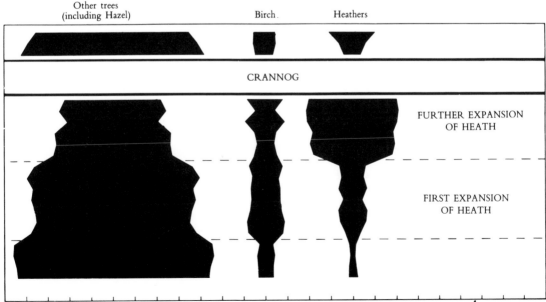

Other trees (including Hazel)

Birch

Heathers

CRANNOG

FURTHER EXPANSION OF HEATH

FIRST EXPANSION OF HEATH

SCALE IN UNITS OF 10%

At the base we see low values for birch, and very low values for heathers. A townland about one mile away carries the name 'Red Bog', and the name suggests that a raised-bog, now completely cut away, may have formerly existed there, and the bog-surface may have been the source for the very few heather pollens that were then reaching the lake. A little higher in the diagram, values for both birch and heather rise. Birch, like heather, is a plant of dry acid soils, and here we see the heath community invade the exhausted fields as their surface layers become increasingly acid. Higher again the ericaceous pollen rises still further in value, and by now there must have been extensive heaths growing on the acid surface of the over-leached soils around the lake.

If such developments were widespread in Ireland, agriculture will have been very much reduced. In the primitive cultivation-plots of earlier times the soil fertility had never been so seriously reduced; the forest-trees could regenerate in the plots, and their deep roots could draw fertility to the surface once more. But the soil of the heaths had become too infertile for forest-trees to re-establish themselves, and the heaths, once established, tended to be self-perpetuating. The farming of the Dowris Period that had opened with a bang with the introduction of the ard, may have ended with a whimper as infertile heaths extended widely.

The crannog, which served as a palace for the local kings, was then built in the lake; in the course of excavation it produced many iron tools and implements, including a share and a coulter for a true plough (see Fig. 6.1), and these finds make it clear that the crannog-dwellers had moved on into a new agricultural world. With their new ploughs they were able to rip up the heaths and bring up subsoil from a deeper level, and so restore fertility to the area. Thus we are not surprised that in the mud which rests on the crannog, values for heathers have shrunk drastically, and birch has also fallen in value. In Britain we have evidence of heathland during the Roman Iron Age. Sods were incorporated in the structure of a Roman fort near Glasgow which had been built about AD 150. Plant fossils in the sods showed that the vegetation in the vicinity of the fort was rough heath and grassland pasture.

6
THE RISE
AND FALL
OF POPULATION:
AD 300 to 1900

Farming with the coulter-plough: AD 300 to 600

As we have seen, at a date that radiocarbon tells us must lie at about AD 300, there was a dramatic expansion in agriculture (see Fig. 5.9). Grasses, plantain and bracken increase in value, and pollen of cereals and docks are continually present. Part of these rises may depend on the bringing back into agricultural production once more of land that had degenerated to heath, but the final disappearance at this level in the diagrams of pollen of elm and ash suggests that extensive areas of secondary woodland were being cleared away. Here the Destruction-phase (ILWd₃) of the woodlands opens. It seems reasonable to assume that new farming practices are being introduced, that agricultural output is rising, and that the population is increasing. Agricultural land is still more in demand.

By AD 300 the principle of mounting a vertical iron knife or *coulter* in the frame of the plough (see Fig. 5.16, Photo 29) so that it would cut through matted roots as it was drawn along, and so open up the way for the *share* (which was itself fitted with an iron shoe to protect it), was well known in Roman Britain, and from there must have spread into Ireland, because we now know that there were contacts between the two areas. The simple ard could not deal with matted roots, which had to be given a preliminary cutting with a spade blade. The coulter speeded up the rate of ploughing, but as the plough had as yet no *mouldboard* to turn the cut sod upside down, cross-ploughing must still have been necessary.

But we must not think that the day the first Irish farmer saw a coulter-plough at work, all Irish farmers immediately adopted its use. Shortage of capital and innate conservatism probably combined to make the spread of the use of the new plough a very slow one. History repeated itself at the beginning of the nineteenth century when all-metal ploughs, which were more efficient and required fewer animals to draw them, were beginning to become available; many contemporary writers deplored the way farmers clung to their locally built wooden ploughs, and could not be persuaded to change.

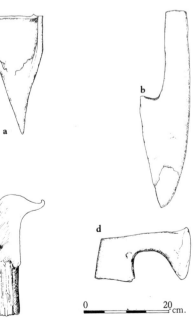

Fig. 6.1 Iron implements from Lagore Crannog, Co. Meath: **a** *plough-share;* **b** *plough-coulter;* **c** *billhook;* **d** *axe.*

a

b

c

d

0   20 cm.

Perhaps as important as the appearance of the plough was the coming into general use of iron implements for a wide range of operations. In addition to the plough share and coulter, the crannog at Lagore produced axes, billhooks, a hammer, an adze, a spokeshave, saws, chisels, gouges and awls (Fig. 6.1). As befitted a royal seat, the Lagore crannog was a very big one, about 40 m in diameter, and surrounded by three wooden palisades. Oak was the principal wood, hazel was second and ash third, with small quantities of poplar, yew, elm, holly, hawthorn, birch, cherry and dogwood. Not a single piece of pine was found, and alder was only used in small pieces of carpentry. The brushwood fill also contained sods from the surrounding fields, straw and — in harmony with what we have seen from the pollen-diagram (see Fig. 5.17) — pieces of peat and twigs of heathers. Most of the timber came from secondary woodland and scrub, but there were occasional large oak timbers, including part of a dug-out boat, that must have come from a tree not less than 1 m in diameter.

The concept of the *crannog* (Photo 32), an artificial island protected by a natural moat of lake-water, is a simple one, and some small crannogs may go back to the Bronze Age, but the large crannog seems only to have developed when iron tools became generally available. The crannog continued in use until the seventeenth century AD. About 250 are known, but this number pales into insignificance when compared with the number of the other types of simply fortified circular site, the *rath* and the *cashel*, which is estimated to lie between 30,000 and 40,000.

The rath seems to be an innovation of in Early Christian times, and some continued in use until the seventeenth century. Radiocarbon datings of raths are still all too few, but they seem mainly to lie between the fourth and the eighth centuries AD.

The rath (Photo 33, Pl. 24) is the main structure of this early period of advanced farming, and if we could understand its organization, we would understand much of the social life and the landscape of the time. The word *rath* is cognate with 'digging', and the simplest type is a circular bank of earth about 20 m in diameter, the earth being obtained from a ditch which encircles the bank on the outside. When in use the bank was supported by timber palisades or stone revetments. More important raths may have up to three banks and ditches, and an overall diameter of 125 m. In regions where suitable stone is available the earthen bank becomes a stone wall, and the structure is known as a *cashel* (Pl. 30). If the walls are impressive and the structure is large, it is often called a *dun* or a *caher* (Photo 34).

In an earlier chapter I deduced that the paucity of remains of Bronze Age occupation-sites implied that they and their surrounding stockades had been constructed of wood, and that the sites had been completely obliterated when the area in which they lay had first been reclothed by secondary woodland, and later recleared for further agricultural use. The corollary of this is twofold: first, after the secondary woodlands had melted away in the face of advanced agricultural practice, there was no longer an unlimited supply of heavy timber for the building of stockades, and banks of earth and stone had to take their places, and second, if the banks were overgrown by secondary woodland, their stout construction meant they could survive further clearance.

We can perhaps picture the simple type of rath as the homestead of the lowest rank of 'free' farmer, who might have had (as we shall see later — p. 167) about 70 statute acres (30 hectares) of good land, or 'home farm', together with rights elsewhere to pasture, timber and peat. How does this match up with the density of raths in the countryside? Not all the raths whose

banks have survived will have been in use at the same time, and we may thus arrive at too dense a spacing; once built, many will have an extended occupation; others will be abandoned and will be ploughed out. If we go to Co. Cavan, where raths are common, though not unusually so, and take 6″ Ordnance Survey map No. 21 we can count 59 raths in the 15,000 acres (over 6000 ha) covered by the map, or about 1 rath to 250 acres (100 ha). We can pick out 1 square mile (260 ha) which holds 6 raths, or about 1 rath to 100 acres (40 ha). In south Antrim (map No. 55) there are five raths to 1 square kilometre. Such a density is compatible with the size of farm we have envisaged, and more important it signifies that if the land is well cleared of trees the raths will be intervisible from one another, and this was absolutely vital in a countryside where cattle-raiding was a constant occupation. We can almost picture a

Photograph 34 Near Shrule, Co. Mayo. This hill-top caher, with a drystone wall, lies almost on limestone bedrock. Part of its interior was cleared relatively recently, but bushes are re-invading it. The clearance revealed older cultivation-ridges; some are still buried by heavy scrub.

group of raths as forming a type of extended village. It was probably possible to shout from one rath to another, and quickly raise an alarm.

Raths are sometimes called *ring-forts*, but they are not forts, if we mean by that a strong-point capable of resisting siege for some time. Raths almost never have a well, and the bank and ditch would have offered little difficulty to a determined attack. But they could offer short-term protection to livestock, and they were intervisible. I picture that all the raths of a vicinity would belong to the same clan. If cattle-raiders from other groups came into the locality, each clansman would drive his stock into his own rath, and then hurry off to assist in the defence of whatever rath was first attacked, and if possible drive off the raiders. Modern strategists would call it defence in depth; it was almost inevitable that the first rath to be attacked would be pillaged, but then

the counter-attack would come, and it would have a good chance of success.

That the defenders of the raths did not expect the attacks to be prolonged is shown by the presence of underground passages and chambers, known as *souterrains*; radiocarbon dates range from AD 700 to 1000. The passages often have constrictions and obstacles to compel slow movement, and so place an intruder who forced an entry at the mercy of a defender already inside. Presumably the women and children, taking the family valuables with them, will have hidden in the souterrain at the first threat of attack, but they could not have remained there for long, even if smoke was not used to force them out. Such a type of refuge can only have been devised on the assumption that the raider, if he did temporarily overrun the rath, would only be there briefly before he was forced out by a counter-attack. The temperature of the souterrain would have been below that of the outside air, and would also have been relatively constant, and in time of peace it would have provided a useful storehouse for dairy products and other foods.

Within the rath there was an open green space, the *lis*, where livestock could be penned in time of emergency, and there were also houses and small farm buildings. Who lived in the houses? Perhaps only the farmer and the members of his immediate family, while the servants lived in huts propped against the inside of the bank, or squatted in the ditch outside the rath. Unfortunately in early Irish society the lower orders, who probably formed the largest part of the population, had no legal status, and therefore no legal existence, and the laws are silent about them. But there were serfs who were tied to their masters and owned neither land nor stock, there were slaves and there were prisoners of war, and it is as yet quite impossible to say what part they played in the social structure.

Most raths lie below an altitude of

150 m OD, which is about the limit of cultivation today. Above 150 m modern disturbance has been less, and though raths are fewer in number, surrounding field systems have had better opportunity to survive. These have been studied at altitudes between 200 m and 300 m on the hills north-west of Belfast in an area of enclosed pasture and mountain land. At Ballyutoag (Fig. 6.2) an area of good soil provides grass for mountain grazing on the top of a small ridge. Here there is a rath with an old field-bank around it. Inside the rath a circular wall-footing, 7 m across, is perhaps the foundation for a house; two low platforms could be bases for lesser buildings. Eight hundred metres to the south-west there are curvilinear field-banks enclosing an area

Fig. 6.2 Ballyutoag, Antrim. At 200 m (625 ft) on the Antrim Plateau north of Belfast there are fields and habitations of the Early Christian period. At top right there is a rath with the ruins of a round house and smaller structures. Lower centre is a 'village' with two round enclosures each containing foundations for numerous huts. There are small irregular fields nearby. (After B.B. Williams)

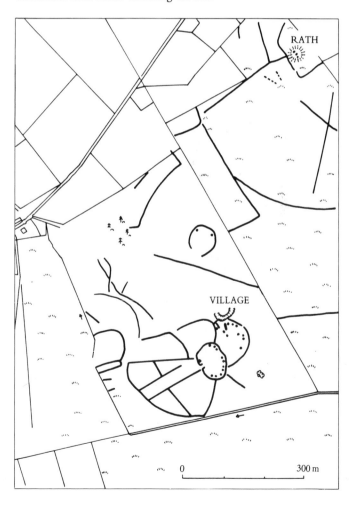

of 10 hectares (25 acres); associated with these are three small rounded enclosures containing low, circular, flat-topped mounds which are house-platforms. There are twenty such structures, which might have housed one hundred people. One house, 5 m across, was excavated, and finds and radiocarbon dates suggest an extended occupation centring on AD 650.

Here we clearly have a village, the type of settlement to which Estyn Evans has given the name of *clachan*. The excavator regarded it as a *booley* village, occupied only in the summer by a people who practised *transhumance*, that is to say they migrated following a seasonal pattern. Such a practice was well known in early Ireland, and there are documentary records of women going to the herds in the mountains, to youths herding cattle in the mountains, and to the *macha samraid*, the summer milking place in the hills. But the site seems to me to be too substantial for temporary use, and it may be an out-village, under the patronage of the nearby rath.

Not far away at Killylane there was another site with banks, souterrains and a series of dams for a horizontal water-mill. Here the mill-site did not yield any datable timbers, but such mills are well dated by dendrochronology to the period AD 630 to 930. I feel that the combination of raths, souterrains and mill means that there was permanent settlement, and not transhumance, at this relatively high level.

Several workers have pointed out that it is possible to find elaborate systems of souterrains without any associated rath, and have suggested that such souterrains may be a refuge point for a hut village which has completely vanished. About 5 km south of Ardee, Co. Louth, a small cemetery of slab-lined graves was associated with a group of souterrains in a rock-knoll; here there must have been a village.

The farmer himself was a member of a clan group, and as such was linked to the head of the clan in a relationship of mutual obligation; the chieftain gave legal decisions and organized military forces; the clansmen submitted to his adjudication, did service in his army, and provided food and hospitality at regulated times. The chieftain had surplus land, stock and equipment. The farmer could rent land, paying with stock and services, and he could get stock and equipment on a hire-purchase system. While the chieftain enjoyed special lands that went with his office, essentially the land was held in common by the full members of the clan, and no individual could alienate land from the clan.

The rath and the lands surrounding it at first sight suggest an independent farm on today's pattern, but there was the important difference that today when the farmer dies the whole farm generally passes to a single chosen heir, usually in *primogeniture* to the eldest son, but in early Ireland the use of the land had to be apportioned in *severalty* over all the immediate kin, with the result that there was extensive sub-division and constant rearrangement of holdings. Neighbouring raths of the same clan group probably co-operated with one another, and there may well have been interlocking holdings.

The advanced agriculture made possible by the coulter-plough must have increased output, and caused the population to grow. This in turn created a demand for still more farmland, and the ability 'to clear plains', and thus provide more land, became an attribute of heroes. Place-names containing the words *rath*, *lis*, *dun*, *caher* and *cashel* are both common and widespread in Ireland, and probably in quite a short time all the land from which a living could be wrested was occupied.

It is not easy to understand why western Britain, with its much closer contacts with the Roman world, should not have had a similar growth in population, taking up all the empty land, but emigrants from Ireland were able to cross the Irish Sea and establish themselves. Writing had now reached Ireland, but with a clumsy cipher version of the Latin alphabet, and standing-stones with simple *ogham* inscriptions became common in the south of the country. From here in the later part of the fourth century Irish emigrants carried this type of monument into Wales and Cornwall, and perhaps the rath and the souterrain also, the latter reappearing as the *fogou* of Cornwall. There was also a movement from the north of Ireland into Scotland and the Isle of Man.

In turn, at the opening of the fifth century Christianity began to reach Ireland from western Britain and from Gaul, and when the Irish church later began to be moulded in monastic rather than diocesan form, the Irish students went to St David's in Wales and to Whithorn in Scotland. Already by the opening of the sixth century there was trading contact with the Continent, and oil and wine in Mediterranean jars were being exchanged for wolfhounds. By contemporary standards Ireland was probably a fairly prosperous and well-

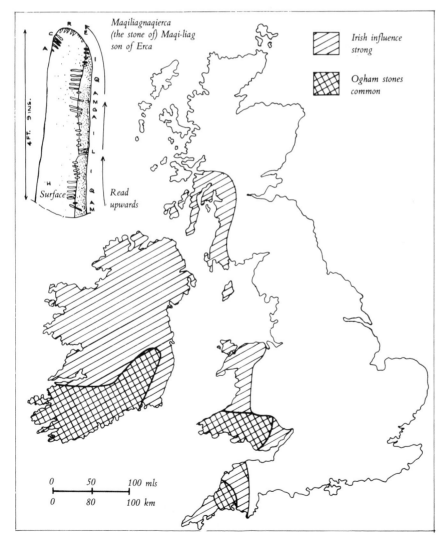

Fig. 6.3 Typical ogham-stone, and distribution-map to show areas where such stones are common, and also areas in western Britain into which there was migration from Ireland in the fourth century AD.

Maqiliagnaqierca (the stone of) Maqi-liag son of Erca

Irish influence strong

Ogham stones common

Read upwards

Surface

0   50   100 mls

0   80   100 km

inhabited country, even though she still lacked towns and an established coinage.

The kin-group rather than the individual was dominant, authority was diffused rather than centralized, and occasional hostings of clans served the purpose of cities, parliaments and law-courts. The larger monasteries, such as Derry and Clonmacnoise (Pl. 29), may have served as local centres of population, but the figures of the Annals, which number the inhabitants of these 'monastic cities' in thousands, are probably greatly exaggerated. Finances were catered for by loans in kind, barter, services and an elaborate hire-purchase system, and the lack of coinage did not give rise to special difficulties.

Farming with the mouldboard-plough:
AD 600 to 1150

The next advance in agriculture was the addition of a sloping board, the *mouldboard* (see Fig. 5.16, Photo 29), to the plough. The leading edge of the board inserted itself into the vertical cut made by the coulter, and as the plough moved forward the wedge-like action of the sloping board turned the sod over, so that it fell upside down into the gutter or furrow that had been created by the plough in its previous trip along the field. Once the plough was on the move it was desirable to keep it going as long as possible, so as to reduce the number of times the clumsy plough-team would have to be turned around. This was the origin of the *furlong*, the length along which the team of oxen or horses could be made to cut a furrow, without having to stop for a rest. Cross-ploughing was no longer necessary, and long narrow fields replaced the earlier small square ones.

Such fields appear in Anglo-Saxon England, and it must be from this source that the mouldboard-plough reached Ireland. The earliest picture of a mouldboard plough is in a manuscript, probably dating to about AD 650. The pagan Anglo-Saxons had arrived in England about AD 450, and their conversion to Christianity, in which missionaries from Ireland played an important part, took place around AD 600. From then on the church in Ireland was in close contact with the church in Britain, and groups of churchmen kept coming and going between the two countries. The monasteries, with their emphasis on vegetable diets, will have exchanged farming information.

Although study of the origin of fields and field-systems is still in its infancy in Ireland, the field cannot be ignored in any examination of the Irish landscape. In proportion to its length, the circumference of the circle encloses the largest area, and hence all primitive enclosures are circular (Photo 35).

Fig. 6.4 Pollen-diagram from blanket-bog at Goodland, Co. Antrim, to illustrate change in land-use on the drier soils in the immediate vicinity of the bog.

Photograph 37 Goodland, Co. Antrm. Uncut blanket-bog lies in the bottom left, and there are smaller outlying patches of bog. At the bottom the bog buries Neolithic and Beaker material. Slightly right of centre a field bank can be seen where the peat has been cut away, and it runs north, occasionally still buried by peat. At lower right, right of the bank, fields with plough furrows made after AD 600 by a mouldboard-plough can be seen. The cut-away area shows the foundations of many huts, some of which sit on abandoned field-banks; they probably belong to the fifteenth and sixteenth centuries, when the area was under grass, and was used for summer-grazing in the practice of booleying.

But for dividing and enclosing an area, the square is the most practical, and at Brideswell, Co. Roscommon, we can see both modern and ancient enclosed fields of this shape (Photo 36). For spade cultivation the size of the field is immaterial, and may be dictated by the number of stones encountered, for the easiest way to get rid of these is to build them into long rows, which automatically become walls. With the ard, where cross-ploughing is necessary, the square is a convenient shape, and its size will again depend on the distance the team can draw the ard without pausing for a rest. In general these fields will be small, and will probably be held in single ownership. Small enclosed fields of this type go back at least to the Bronze Age in Ireland.

The mouldboard-plough gives rise to elongated plots, and it requires a much greater length of fence to enclose a rectangle rather than a square of equal area. In a district of limited size where the soil is essentially uniform, and the weather is the same, all vegetative processes will proceed simultaneously, and all crops will ripen at the same time. Under such circumstances communal operations in a single large enclosure, or *common-field*, will make much more sense than individual operations in narrow fields with uneconomic fences. In many cases different farmers will have contributed one or more beasts to the plough-team, and the width of the strip that the team could plough in one day became the fundamental land-unit.

But though the operations will have been conducted in common, the various land-units in the common-field will have been private property. Inheritance in severalty meant constant further sub-division of land-holdings, and plots were frequently exchanged so as to maintain a fair distribution of the better and the poorer land. A complex mosaic of differently owned small plots must have developed. This problem of recurring sub-division will not have affected the big land-holdings of the

larger monasteries, which will probably have been much more efficient than the lay holdings around them.

Beyond the common-field was the permanent pasture, probably held in common but with varying rights, not defined by area, but by the number of head of stock that different members were entitled to put on it. If the group flourished, more of the pasture would be taken into the common-field; in adverse times, the common-field would shrink. At higher levels were the hill-grazings, 'the unenclosed above all', to which the booleying herds would be driven in the summer.

Weeds have always been a problem for agriculture, and it is well known that different agricultural practices all bring their own suite of weeds in train. The inversion of the sod by the mouldboard-plough buried the weed seeds that were lying on the surface deeper in the soil, and in this position some of them found it impossible to germinate. As a result some weeds were greatly reduced by this practice; at the same time the changed practice may not have affected other weeds, and sage (*Artemisia*) may have been enabled to become relatively more common by the introduction of the mouldboard-plough. This plant puts down a deep vertical branching rootstock, and as long as parts of the rootstock could survive, it was a very serious weed of cultivation. In Ireland pollen of *Artemisia* first becomes common in the diagrams at about AD 600, and it is tempting to see in this rise a reflection of the introduction of the mouldboard-plough. At Red Bog (see Fig. 5.9) the appearance of sage was dated to AD 500. In the Burren its appearance was rather later, and it only became established about AD 800.

We have already referred to the site at Goodland, Co. Antrim, where blanket-bog expanded into areas that had been cultivated in Neolithic and Beaker time. Though many pollen-counts have been made in the peat here, and there has been considerable archaeological

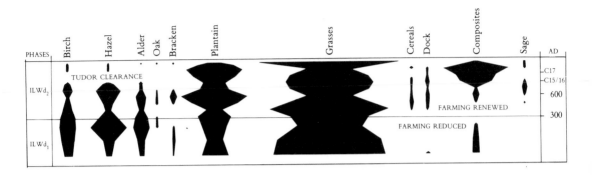

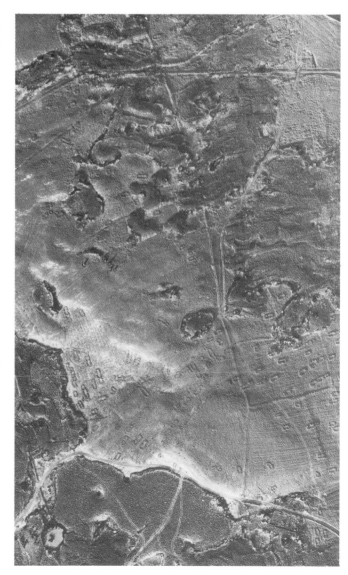

investigation, what follows contains a considerable element of speculation. Peat growth was at first extremely slow, but in the diagram (Fig. 6.4) a feeble expansion in hazel, and a reduction in the amount of grass pollen, can be seen to indicate the reduction in agricultural activity that took place at the end of the Deterioration-phase (ILWd$_2$). The opening of the Destruction-phase of advanced agriculture (Phase ILWd$_3$) at AD 300 is then seen as the tree pollens fall away, while grasses expand, and cereals and dock make their appearance. A little higher grasses fall back, plantain rises and bracken, sage and other composites appear about AD 600. Though they were not seen at the point from which the pollen samples were taken, at other points at about this level in the peat stones occurred in irregular layers and heaps, and these were interpreted as stones collected from the neighbouring fields and thrown out on the bog-surface to lessen the risk of damage to the plough. Some pottery sherds and a wooden knife-handle were associated with the stones, and these would have been at home in an Early Christian or Early Medieval context. The fields themselves can be seen nearby, and they still carry furrows characteristic of those produced by mouldboard-ploughs. That these fields are early is certified by the fact that in the fifteenth and sixteenth centuries huts were built in the area, and these were placed indiscriminately on the now abandoned fields, and the banks which separated them (Photo 37).

It seems not unreasonable to assume that about AD 600 farmers, equipped with mouldboard-ploughs, and practising a system of tillage that encouraged sage, occupied the Goodland area. This land-use gave way to very different operations in the fifteenth and sixteenth centuries; fragments of a jug of this age were thrown out on the bog-surface, and this level is also indicated in the diagram, which is now dominated by pollen of grass and composites. Calcareous grassland infested by thistles is indicated, and the area was probably used for the summer pasturing of cattle, whose booleying attendants built and occupied the flimsy huts whose remains are dotted over the area. There is then the final clearing away of all tree growth following on the Plantation of Ulster in the early seventeenth century, and perhaps a minor phase of tillage, before the uppermost sample shows the establishment of the modern grasslands.

We have seen that the earth bank of the rath might be replaced by a wall of drystone masonry to form a cashel. Cashels of larger than average size and strength, often surrounded by concentric walls, called cahers, also occur, and one of these at Cahercommaun in Co. Clare was excavated by Hugh Hencken. The central space was about 30 m in diameter, and protected by a wall about 7 m thick and still standing to a height of 3 m, though doubtless originally considerably higher. The central space showed the remains of several small structures and several souterrains, but there was no sign of any important residence. The caher stood on the cliffed edge of a ravine, and so the surrounding walls were D-shaped; there was a middle wall 70 m in diameter, and an outer wall 100 m in diameter. Radial walls divided up the space between the walls, and there were also minor structures here, but some of these were probably not of any great antiquity. The entrance passage led through all three walls, but there were no defensive structures associated with

it. Finds of weapons were few; there were some querns, and evidence of iron-working. Over 95% of the bones were of ox, with small quantities of sheep, goat, pig, horse and red deer. Though the sea is 15 km away, shells of edible molluscs were found. The charcoals in order of frequency were hazel, yew, ash, hawthorn, blackthorn, willow and elm. These obviously come from secondary woodland and scrub; the limestones of Clare today provide the refuge of the last native Irish elms, and it is of interest that even in Clare the elm was almost extinct 1000 years ago. The frequency of yew and the absence of oak on the limestone should be noted. The occupation of the site was thought to centre on AD 800; there was little evidence of domestic structures, and it may have served chiefly as a cattle compound for the stocks of a wealthy king.

Much the same type of structure appears to have been adopted by the larger monasteries, because the monastic site at Nendrum in Strangford Lough was essentially similar in layout. It may be, of course, that the monastery took over a pre-existing structure, but when the site was excavated it provided no evidence for occupation earlier than the beginning of the eighth century. At Nendrum the inner cashel had been largely destroyed by later alterations, and the space between the outer walls was occupied by the workshops and scriptorium of the monastery.

Literary reflection of the eighth-century landscape

Some years ago Kenneth Jackson published a short book entitled *The oldest Irish tradition; a window on the Iron Age*, in which he tried to glimpse the heroic society of the Pagan Iron Age through the sagas which were perhaps first committed to writing in the eighth century AD. The same material and the early Irish laws also contain a wealth of information about the countryside and the farmers of Early Christian Ireland. Unfortunately the early law-makers had a taste for detail and for symmetry, and very often the picture is what we would get from a distorting-mirror, rather than from a window. Nevertheless an attempt to peer back into the past is well worth making.

Trees, bushes and other plants
One legal tract codifies all the penalties for unlawfully interfering with trees and bushes, and the fines range from the forfeit of two milch-cows for cutting down a valuable tree to the loss of a sheep for destroying a bush. The severity of the fines indicates the value that timber had reached through scarcity. There are four categories of importance:

Noble trees	Commoner trees
Oak	Alder
Hazel	Willow
Holly	Hawthorn
Yew	Rowan
Ash	Birch
Pine	Elm
Apple	Cherry (?)
Lower ranks	*Bushes*
Blackthorn	Bracken
Elder	Bog-myrtle
Spindle	Gorse
Whitebeam	Blackberry
Arbutus	Heather
Poplar	Broom
Juniper (?)	Rose (?)

Some of the rankings seem odd to our modern eyes, and Fergus Kelly, who has been working on the lists, thinks that the compiler took into account (a) size of tree, (b) quality of its timber

and (c) other uses, particularly of the fruit. If we look at the lists, it is curious to see pine in the first rank, while elm and alder are relegated to the second. The disappearance of pine — for today it is thought that all the pines we have in Ireland have been reintroduced from Scotland, after the native stock had become extinct — seems to have been a gradual one. It had disappeared from north-east Ireland by 2000 BC, but seems to have survived in the south-west till about AD 200. Whenever bog-surfaces became relatively dry, pine could invade them, and some stunted trees were still growing on midland raised-bogs at AD 300. But it is not easy to see that well-grown pine trees could have been common enough at the time the law was codified for them to merit such a high place on the list. Fossil pine-wood, or *bog-deal* (see Photo 24), was available in large quantities in many bogs, and was used as timber in later times, but the fines clearly envisage living trees. Yew wood, though difficult to work, was prized for high-grade carpentry, and masters in yew-carving had a special social rank.

Elm can only be put down to the second rank because of the extent to which it had been cleared away. As we have seen it made a considerable recovery in the centuries preceding AD 300, but with the vigorous renewal of agriculture at that time it was largely swept away. Elm leaves, bark and wood were all valued by early people, and if it had been still common in the countryside, it would have had a higher place in the list. Alder on the other hand was probably still fairly common, but its wood was not used in timber structures; it was used for small objects, shields, containers and dishes.

Oak and hazel head the list, and we have seen how wood and charcoal of these trees occur over and over again on archaeological sites. Oak wins out on all three of Kelly's criteria. It could be a very large tree, its wood was used in carpentry and its bark in tanning, and its acorns were a valuable food for pigs. Hazel, though smaller, and in one sense a pest because of the ease with which it invaded abandoned fields, was valued for its coppiced stems for wattle-work, and for its nuts.

We can perhaps form some impression of a countryside in which woods of alder and willow were still common on wetter ground. There were some oakwoods, but large and well-grown trees were beginning to command a premium; well-grown hollies (especially valuable for cart-shafts) were also becoming rare. Ash, though probably well-distributed in hedgerows and secondary woodland, was in demand for general carpentry and for handles. Secondary hazel scrub would have been widespread. Pine was rare but much sought for, while elm had become so uncommon that it had rather dropped out of sight.

Elder would have been growing around houses and on ruined sites, and any neglected fences would have had hawthorn and blackthorn, and probably many of the other bushes as well. Just as today, the birch and the rowan, the heather, the gorse and the broom would have been growing on rocky hillsides.

Classification of land

There were three grades of land, and if land was to rate as first class, it had to be level, capable of growing a wide range of crops, and free from weeds. Madder (*Rubia tinctorum*) is among the crops listed, but there may be some error in translation here, because madder, an important plant in dyeing, is not known in Ireland today, and only survives in Britain as a casual. In Ireland this plant would have been on the limit of its range, and is not likely to have produced much dye. Weediness was measured by turning a horse onto the land, and if it collected briars, thorns, burdocks or thistles on its legs the land was lowered in value. Land that was potentially first class might be

partly or wholly encumbered with trees.

Uncultivable land also had three grades — which probably indicates a love for tripartite divisions, as much as an eye for soil quality. Rough land is 'land of ferny plants and untouched land', and this may well be badly drained land in valley bottoms, land that is still largely uncultivated today. Very rough land is the upland, 'heathery mountain with furze on it'. This type of land is still abundant today, but nowadays in the absence of the wolf it carries flocks of unattended hill sheep: in Iron Age Ireland a shepherd would have had to stay with the sheep at all times to protect them, and this was work for slaves, as we know from St Patrick's account of his life. 'Black land' is probably the modern peaty gley or peaty podzol, with a thin layer of decomposing humus, not deep enough to be described as bog, resting on waterlogged mineral soil.

If the land had development value, its worth — just as today — was raised accordingly. The bonus points might be accessibility by road or track, access to mountain-grazing, the sea-shore or water, a site for a water-mill, mining-rights, or woodland.

Fields and fences

The old Irish law tracts contain a lot of information on walls and fences, and these have been examined by Donnchadh Ó Corráin.

Where wood was scarce and the soil was clayey, a bank and ditch (*clas*) surrounded the field; the bank was 1 m high and the ditch was 1 m deep. Where stone was common, a wall (*cora*) was built, 1 m wide at the base and twelve fists (say four and a half feet, 1.5 m) high; the stones had to interlock with one another. The post and wattle fence (*nochtaile*) was of the same height, with a gap of 'a foot to the joint of the big toe' (20-23 centimetres) between the posts. Three strands of wickerwork linked the posts, and the top of the fence received a band of blackthorn twigs, which served the purpose of modern barbed wire, or 'thorny wire' as it is still known in the Irish countryside. Erecting such fences was regarded as menial and heavy work, and it was below the dignity of a nobleman to use a hammer, bill-hook or maul, all of which were necessary in such fencing.

After the corn had been harvested temporary fences were put up around the plots, and the stock of several farmers might be turned onto the plots; this practice was probably primarily intended to manure the land for the next year's crop, rather than to provide grazing on the stubble. There were elaborate rules for the maintenance of common fences, and if stock trespassed, appropriate damages had to be paid.

Farming practices
Some farmers had to render food to their chieftains, and the food-lists give some indication of the farm produce of the day; but the lists only show the aristocratic foods that had to be offered to the chieftain and his retinue, and give no indication of what common folk ate; they name calves, sheep, pigs, pork, milk, cream, butter, other dairy products, kiln-dried wheat loaves, malt and herbs.

It is very difficult to attempt to assess the size of the farms. This is because the basic standard of the measurement of wealth was a female slave — a *cumal* — and this measure, like many modern currencies, apparently 'floated', so that it is hard to define its value at any time.

If we put various hints together, it would seem reasonable to say that a *cumal* was about 35 statute acres (14 hectares), and two such units or about 70 acres (28 ha) were the minimum required if one was to establish a position as an independent farmer. According to the figures in the laws, a 'strong' farmer would have ten times as much, say 700 acres (280 ha), and these figures are not impossible if we remember that both stock and yields would be less than today's equivalent. In the first English 'plantation', farm sizes (in acres larger than statute acres) ranged from 25 to 500 acres.

The 'strong' farmer was fully equipped. His house was 30 feet (10 m) long, with an annexe 20 feet (7 m) long, and he had a sheep-fold, a calf-pen, and a pig-sty. For tillage he had a complete ploughing outfit with all its accessories, a barn, a drying-kiln and a share in a mill. He sowed sixteen sacks of grain each year, and if we say that this was at the rate of two sacks per acre, he would only have 8 acres (2.4 ha) under grain each year, which seems a very small proportion of 700 acres. On the other hand excavation results, with their overwhelming quantities of animal bones, and only a very occasional plough-share or quern, do suggest that stock-raising rather than tillage was the main occupation. A law tract says that his minimum cattle stock should be twenty cows, two bulls and six oxen (for ploughing).

Where the land was level, it would be tilled with a plough drawn by four oxen, but we do not know at what rate the plough would work, nor how many times the land was tilled in the course of a season. Grasses were allowed to flower and wither in the meadows, which were subsequently grazed by stock, as the scythe and the practice of hay-making were unknown. Some land will have been lying fallow. There will have been fenced pasture, and on the 'strong farmer's land this was big enough to maintain his flock of sheep without the necessity of moving them on elsewhere. He would also have had grazing-rights on the uncultivable land, which was held in common by the clan to which he was affiliated. He brewed his own beer from his own barley, and the making of malt was a very important task. If there was a bog in the vicinity, he would have a peat-bank, from which to draw fuel.

The small farmer on 70 acres (28 ha) was not so fully equipped. He only expected to plough 3 acres (1.2 ha), and for this it would have been extravagant to maintain full ploughing equipment; he presumably combined with three neighbours, as he was required to provide a quarter part, namely an ox, a plough-share, a goad and a halter. This rule, combined with other references, shows that the plough-team was made up of four oxen.

Cereal grains were used as units of measurement, and in particular for measuring the size of wounds. Binchy and O'Loan have endeavoured to identify the various grains referred to in medical tracts, and suggest that two varieties of wheat, barley, rye, oats, peas and beans are all referred to. For the word *ruadan* which Kuno Meyer translated as 'buckwheat' — still eaten in central Europe today — Binchy and O'Loan prefer 'red wheat'. Buckwheat (*Fagopyrum esculentum*) is a member of the Polygonaceae, which also includes the knotgrasses (various species of *Polygonum*); knotgrass seeds are brown. As knotgrass (or meld) formed part of the diet of the famous Danish Iron Age Tollund Man (whose remarkably well-preserved body was found in a bog), and was also much eaten in medieval Dublin, I think it very likely that *ruadan* refers to Polygonaceae in general, and that these were grown as a deliberate crop, and not just gleaned off the fallows. Flax was grown for its oil and its fibres, and woad (*Isatis tinctorum*) was a source of blue dye.

For animal husbandry the laws provide us with lists of the stock possessed by farmers of different grades, but the law-makers were so anxious to get everything neat and tidy that each farmer is credited with equal numbers of cattle, sheep and pigs, and there never has been a system of farming that carried stock in such proportions. Today we have perhaps 60% cattle, 40% sheep, while the pig has been

condemned to the horrors of factory farming.

Figures based on bone counts by Finbar McCormick at excavated sites show that with cattle in pre-urban Ireland the emphasis was on dairying, with the meat and hides a by-line. Young stock were slaughtered in their second autumn, and only the bulls and the milch-cows were retained.

Young male stock were castrated, and carcass quality, based on the proportion of fat to lean meat, was taken into account. Calving took place in the spring, and when the early summer flush of milk was on, the cows were driven up to mountain pastures, accompanied by herdsmen and women who lived in temporary huts, in the practice known as *booleying*. What to do with the summer flood of milk must always have been a problem. Milk itself was drunk in various forms, was solidified into curds, and was churned into butter. The technique of fermenting milk to make cheese — in the strict sense of the word — does not seem to have been known, and to this day Irish people are not great cheese eaters. Some of the surplus butter was buried in bogs, where cool, anaerobic and relatively sterile conditions slowed up the developments by which it became rancid.

Compared with modern herds the cattle were small, and so were the sheep, which were valued chiefly for their wool. Most sites showed about 15% to 25% sheep, a few, where the land was perhaps especially favourable for sheep had 35% to 40%, a very few had no sheep at all.

At most sites pigs provided about one-third of the bones; some specialized in pigs, with over half of the bones coming from pigs; others had only very small numbers.

The pigs were much leaner and more rangy than the modern pig, in keeping with their more active lives in which ranging for acorns (*mast*) was important (see Fig. 6.9). There are many references in the Annals to years in which mast was plentiful, and to years in which mast was lacking. Bacon was graded as to fat and lean, and a sow was expected to rear a litter of nine, a standard with which the modern farmer would be well satisfied.

The varying proportions of cattle, sheep and pigs recorded at the various sites probably reflect differences in the quality of the land being farmed and in the countryside of the location.

Gardening
Many monastic rules laid emphasis on vegetables rather than meat in the communal diet, and gardens were a feature of the monasteries rather than the lay farms. Cabbages, onions, leeks and celery were principally grown, and there were orchards with apples and damsons.

As I have said our mirror is sometimes clearly distorting, but from it we can form an impression of a countryside in which all the good land is parcelled out in an orderly fashion, and is being worked to a standard of which no modern farmer would need to feel ashamed. There may be battles and raidings, but the basic pattern of life will be resumed when these die away. Beyond the good land there is poorer land, and there the members of the clan will have commonage rights. Expansion can only come either from extension of the good land by the further clearance of trees and bushes, which once gone will have little opportunity to return, or by improved tillage practices which will increase the yield of the land.

The Viking introduction of towns
AD 800 saw the arrival of yet another series of influences in Ireland, those from the Viking world of northern Europe. For the first fifty years the Vikings contented themselves with raiding, especially monasteries that were within easy reach of the sea-coast. The larger monasteries were the nearest thing to a town that Ireland could offer, and were certainly worth plundering; a monastery that could command a work of art like the Book of Kells or the Ardagh Chalice was obviously generally wealthy in its own right, while its strongly built church provided not only a place of sanctuary, but also a safe-deposit for the store-chests of the local population. At times the Viking raiders would be in need of food supplies, and also weapons and tools to replace what had been used or lost on their marauding cruises, just as much as gold and jewels, and the church with its stores of weapons, tools, clothes and food was the obvious source of supply.

After AD 850 the Vikings began to set up trading-ports in suitable harbours, and to settle into the country in the vicinity of these first towns in Ireland. The Viking nature was as turbulent and quarrelsome as that of the Irish themselves, and before long different groups were engaged in internecine struggles and in fluctuating alliances with warring Irish groups. By the tenth century Dublin city was the focal point, with an area of settlement — Fingal — to the north and west, and outlying dependencies in Carlingford and Strangford Loughs, and there were the trading-towns of Wexford, Limerick, Waterford and Cork. Coinage was introduced to facilitate the import-export trade. In addition to everyday dealings, luxury goods were also handled, as an account of the pillaging of Limerick refers to special saddles and silk cloths, as well as gold, silver and jewellery. Such accounts became realities in the Dublin excavation at Wood Quay, where gold-embroidered cloths from Byzantium, and amber and walrus ivory from Scandinavia were found. Viking knowledge of ships and shipping spread to the Irish, and soon there were fleets, both legitimate and piratical, on the coastal and inland waters. There must have been a trading-post at Lough Owel in Co. Westmeath, because an island in the lake has produced several hoards of Viking silver and also coins from the Middle East.

A thirteenth-century account speaks of wealthy Norse farmers owning large numbers of cattle in Wexford, but by and large the impact of the Vikings on the landscape was probably small, and the modest native farmsteads, protected by a bank and ditch and provided with souterrains, continued in operation. This is well exemplified at Lough Gur, where a typical cashel, with associated houses both inside and outside it, on a rocky knoll known as *Carrig Aille*, produced a hoard of Viking silver of tenth-century date. Cattle provided 90% of the bones, sheep and pig accounted for the rest, except for trifling amounts of horse and red deer; there were also bones of dogs, cats and domestic fowl. Hunting on the lake was indicated by fish-bones, and bones of ducks, geese and swans. There were numerous rotary querns, and carbonized seeds of flax and its associated weed, corn spurrey (*Spergula arvensis*) were also found. The abundant presence of flax is perhaps a further indication of Viking contacts. There was also evidence of the working of iron and of bronze.

There was renewed activity in the Boyne valley at this time. A large rath was built about 300 m north of Newgrange, and about 400 m west of Knowth there is another large rath, perched over the river, almost in the position of a promontory fort. At Knowth the mound itself had been re-occupied rather earlier, about AD 300 (see Fig. 5.8). Two large ditches were dug, one around the base of the mound, and the other around the top, and some inhumed burials date from this phase of activity. The ditches were later allowed to silt up, and about 500 years later houses with souterrains were built on and in the fill. The entrances to the large tombs were discovered, and the intruders entered the tombs, and scratched their Irish names on its stones. The passages were incorporated into the souterrain system, doubtless accompanied by the belief that magical giant souterrains had been provided by propitiated gods. These giant souterrains may well have served as local storehouses, just as the churches did, and as such attracted the attention of the Vikings. The Vikings certainly took their boats up the Boyne, and the Annals tell us that in AD 860 the 'cave' of Knowth was searched by the Vikings, who returned again in AD 934, when they attacked and plundered it. The general finds suggested an occupation until at least AD 1000, and this was confirmed by the discovery in one of the souterrains of two Anglo-Saxon pennies of late tenth-century date. Bones of ox, horse, pig and sheep were found, and there were several stones from rotary querns. There was also some iron slag.

At some country sites the Vikings halted long enough to set up monuments. There is a cross with runic inscriptions in the twelfth-century cathedral in Killaloe, and even on Beginish Island in the far south-west a rune-stone was discovered reused in a simple stone house.

By the year AD 1000 the feudal system was well established in western Europe, and the Norman victory at Hastings in AD 1066 established it in England. By AD 1100 an embryonic feudal system was beginning to develop in Ireland also. Chieftains were becoming more powerful, and the kingship of all-Ireland was beginning to be established, although the complicated system of succession in severalty resulted in constant instability. European ideas of strategy began to be appreciated, and strong-points or castles, intercommunicating by roads and bridges on land, and by fleets of boats on the water, began to develop. Although all owed allegiance to a chieftain or king, some farmers were independent and self-sufficient, while others, though independent, borrowed stock, seeds and implements from their overlord. Below this level were the landless tenants, who though they had some stock and equipment, had to rent their land for goods or services rendered to their lord. There was also a large understratum (still with slaves among them) without either land or property, without any security and subject to constant exploitation.

The markets of medieval Dublin

In the same way as we formed some impression of eighth-century farming from the law texts relating to agriculture, we may get some sidelight on medieval farming from the refuse that accumulated in and around Dublin city, and which has been brought to light by recent excavations. The refuse, dung and other litter, was largely derived from the agricultural produce that reached the city markets. A narrow ridge of higher ground lies parallel with the River Liffey on its south side, and the city was first founded on the eastern tip of the ridge. To the west a route led away along the crest of the ridge, and a market sprang up outside the west gate; the site is still known as the Cornmarket.

As the name implies corn was certainly sold there. There would have been winter wheat for the production of fine white flour; there was also spring wheat, but this was probably heavily contaminated with the black seeds of the corn cockle (*Agrostemma githago*), which are much the same size as the cereal grains. The corn cockle seed was also farinaceous, and for a long time it was quite happily accepted as part of the crop, was ground up along with the wheat, and speckled the flour with fragments of its dark seed coat. But the seed has a high content of saponin, and can be injurious to health; modern seed-cleaning methods separate the grain and the weed, with the result that the corn cockle, formerly very common in Irish fields, has now almost totally disappeared. Barley was sold for baking and for brewing, and oats and rye would probably have been on offer also.

In the city refuse there are large quantities of crushed seeds of *Chenopodium album* (goosefoot), and of various species of *Polygonum* (knotgrass or meld). Though these seeds are not eaten as human food in western Europe today, in prehistoric and in medieval times they formed a large part of the diet of the poorer classes either as bread or gruel, and were almost certainly grown as crops in their own right, and not just gleaned as weeds from the fallow. Buckwheat (*Fagopyrum esculentum*), sometimes known as sarrasin because of its eastern origin, is closely allied to *Polygonum*, and is still widely eaten in eastern Europe. A German traveller in Ireland in 1828 records that buckwheat, potatoes and oats were the crops he saw most frequently, and it is possible that it was still grown in the nineteenth century. Peas and beans would also have been for sale, as well as cabbages and onions.

As in later times dung-carts would have carried their loads out to the surroundings of the city, where they would have been utilized in vegetable-gardens and in orchards. At the right season of the year there would have been stalls offering pears and apples, plums, damsons and sloes, cherries, raspberries and strawberries. Some fruits came from farther afield — blackberries from fieldbanks, and bilberries or fraughans (*Vaccinium myrtillus*) from the slopes of the Dublin hills. Imported luxuries, figs, raisins and walnuts, would also have been on sale.

There were large numbers of dairies and piggeries in the city, and these were a constant source of nuisance. But they were tolerated, and hay and straw, together with bracken for bedding, would also have been on sale. Goats were kept for their milk. Other stalls would offer rushes and sedges to strew on house floors. Moss served as toilet-paper for the fastidious, and bundles of moss collected on trees around the city were on sale. Butchers' stalls were probably confined to a special area, the Shambles, while the fishmongers would have been found, as the name makes clear, in Fishamble Street, which still runs down to the river.

Conditions arising out of the meat trade and its associated offal were particularly noisome, and the city ordinances are full of directions as to where guts should, and should not, be deposited. By studying both the refuse

dumped behind the houses, and the age of the animals that were slaughtered, we can see that urban demand had a strong influence on the type of cattle raised in the lands around the city. The older self-contained traditional dairy farm now found itself with a market for beef. The response seems to have been to slaughter male calves, and to retain females until they were more than three years old. These older animals would then have been driven to the city markets. There many of them seem to have been bought by individual householders and held alive in the small plot behind the house, until a group of people could be organized to share the carcass. The beast would then be slaughtered on the spot, and the offal dumped.

The large quantity of meat debris that must have been strewn around attracted carrion-eating birds, and the raven was very common. One site at Lough Gur was a farmyard of the thirteenth and fourteenth centuries, and there raven bones were so common that the excavator thought they might have been exposed on gamekeepers' gibbets, to discourage other birds. There were also bones of buzzard, eagle and red kite. Crop debris included wheat, barley, oats and peas.

Anglo-Norman farming and its decay: AD 1150-1550

The feudal world wanted wealth and military power, and the land had to be the main source of wealth. Subsistence farming on indifferent land was no longer good enough, intensive farming of high quality land had to produce a handsome cash surplus. The great monastic orders were the first to bring this world to Ireland, and of these the Cistercians, with their emphasis on agriculture, had the greatest impact on the Irish countryside. The Cistercians depended wholly on the land for their income, and developed a system for selling their farm produce — cattle, horses and wool — which did much to promote commerce in western Europe. Mellifont was consecrated in 1157, and within a few years daughter houses had sprung up in many parts of Ireland.

The second impact, the military one, began in 1169, and soon great areas of the best agricultural land had been won, a task that was made the easier by the internecine strife that had been raging on a scale that was high, even by Irish standards. 'There has been fighting in all provinces, endless campaigns, cattle-raids, burnings, atrocities — Ireland lies like a trembling sod.'

What did Ireland look like to the invaders? We are fortunate that a Welsh travel correspondent, Giraldus Cambrensis, came to Ireland about 1185, and if we try to see Ireland through his twelfth-century eyes, and not through our twentieth-century ones, we can get some vivid impressions. To adjust our vision we must remember first that he was a cleric, accustomed to the sermonizing of his day, and apt to burst into theological excursions at any time; second, that with his contemporaries he believed all too literally in hell and its torments, and saw the world as populated with monstrous beasts, lying in wait both for the just and the unjust; and third that he was a propagandist, always ready to flatter his betters, and to exalt the Welsh and denigrate the Irish.

Giraldus certainly was an acute observer; he gives a word-picture of an illuminated manuscript that has never been bettered; in natural history he gives a clear description of a dipper, which he thought to be a variety of kingfisher. He refers to raths and cahers, and reports that the Irish 'have no use for castles. Woods are their forts and swamps their ditches' — a comment that was to reappear in many subsequent dispatches from Ireland.

His report tells us that 'Ireland is the most temperate of all countries. Snow is seldom, and lasts only for a short time. There is such plentiful supply of rain, such an ever-present overhanging of clouds and fog, that summer scarcely gives three consecutive days of really fine weather. Winds are moderate and not too strong. The winds from the west-north-west, north and east bring cold. The north-west and west winds are prevalent, and are more frequent and stronger than other winds. They bend (in the opposite direction) almost all the trees in the west that are placed in an elevated position, or uproot them.

Ireland is a country of uneven surface and rather mountainous. The soil is soft and watery, and even at the tops of high and steep mountains there are pools and swamps. The land is sandy rather than rocky. There are many woods and marshes; here and there are some fine plains but in comparison with the woods they are indeed small. The country enjoys the freshness and mildness of spring almost all the year round. The grass is green in the fields in winter just the same as in summer. Consequently, the meadows are not cut for fodder, and stalls are never built for the beasts.

The land is fruitful and rich in its fertile soil and plentiful harvests. Crops abound in the fields, flocks on the mountains, wild animals in the woods, it is rich in honey and milk. Ireland

*Photograph 38
Kilshannig, Co. Kerry.
Old glacial deposits,
smoothed out by more
recent frost-action, lie on
solid rock (compare with
Photo 8). Man has spread
sea-sand over the area to
replace a poor soil with a
fertile one. On the right
we see cultivation in
unfenced strips.*

*Photograph 38
Kilshannig, Co. Kerry.
Old glacial deposits,
smoothed out by more
recent frost-action, lie on
solid rock (compare with
Photo 8). Man has spread
sea-sand over the area to
replace a poor soil with a
fertile one. On the right
we see cultivation in
unfenced strips.*

*Photograph 39
Ballyduagh, Co.
Tipperary. In this deserted
medieval village, the pale
square in the lower right
shows the site of the
manor house. Above are
outlines of houses with
gardens, and at the top of
the village street. In the
top left a ring of trees
surrounds the site of the
parish church; in the
bottom left there are the
ruins of a later
seventeenth-century house.
(See also Pl.31 J.K. St
Joseph)*

exports cow-hides, sheep-skins and furs. Much wine is imported. But the island is richer in pastures than in crops, and in grass rather than in grain. The plains are well clothed with grass, and the haggards [farmyards] are bursting with straw. Only the granaries are without their wealth. The crops give great promise in the blade, even more in the straw, but less in the ear. For here the grains of wheat are shrivelled and small, and can scarcely be separated from the chaff by any winnowing fan. What is born and comes forth in the spring and is nourished in the summer and advanced, can scarcely be reaped in the harvest because of the unceasing rain. For this country more than any other suffers from storms of wind and rain.'

Giraldus also offers detailed information on fish, amphibians, reptiles, birds and mammals, but this is so threaded through with medieval folk-lore that it is difficult to pick out fact from fable. He reports that salmon, trout, eels and lampreys are common in Irish rivers, but that many others, pike, perch, roach, chub, dudgeon, minnow, loach and bullheads are absent. Most of these do occur in Ireland today, but they have been introduced since Giraldus wrote. The Anglo-Normans did introduce the rabbit and the fallow-deer.

What Giraldus has to say about wheat failing to ripen is of particular interest, because a temperature curve shows he was writing at a time when mean annual temperature in England — and presumably in Ireland also — was rising to its thirteenth-century peak (Fig. 6.5).

During that peak the Anglo-Normans certainly grew good wheat crops on the manorial estates they established in south-east Ireland, but conditions for cereal crops became difficult again when temperature fell again in the late fourteenth century. It is not easy to pinpoint this effect, first because of the consequences of the Bruce invasion early in the century, when the warring armies 'between them left neither wood nor lea nor corn nor crop nor stead nor barn nor church, but fired and burned them all', and second because of the Black Death in the second part of the century, which reduced the population drastically — halving it according to some estimates.

It was thus between AD 1170 and 1350 that Anglo-Norman influence was most clearly stamped on the Irish landscape. At first the lightly equipped Irish soldiers could offer no resistance to the heavily armed and well-drilled invaders, who cut through the country smelling out the better lands like well-trained truffle-hounds. The Anglo-Normans were prepared to expend capital on the organization of their manorial farms, and were only interested in land from which they could hope to draw a dividend on their investment. Fertile and well-drained soils were what attracted them.

This was the first occasion on which financial considerations directly impinged on land use in Ireland. In the later periods of the Bronze Age there had been a fairly regular distribution of sites throughout the country. It is the same with place-names containing such

*Fig. 6.5 Graph to
illustrate fluctuation of
mean annual temperature
in England, by 50-year
averages, for the past 100
years. (After H.H. Lamb)*

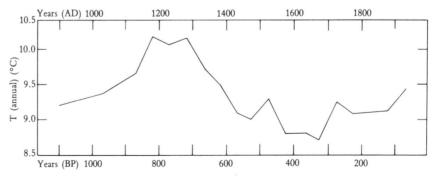

Fig. 6.6 An outline-map to show the distribution of the leading soil-types in Ireland today. Poorly drained soils predominate in the north and west. The more fertile soils chiefly occur in the south-east. (An Foras Talúntais)

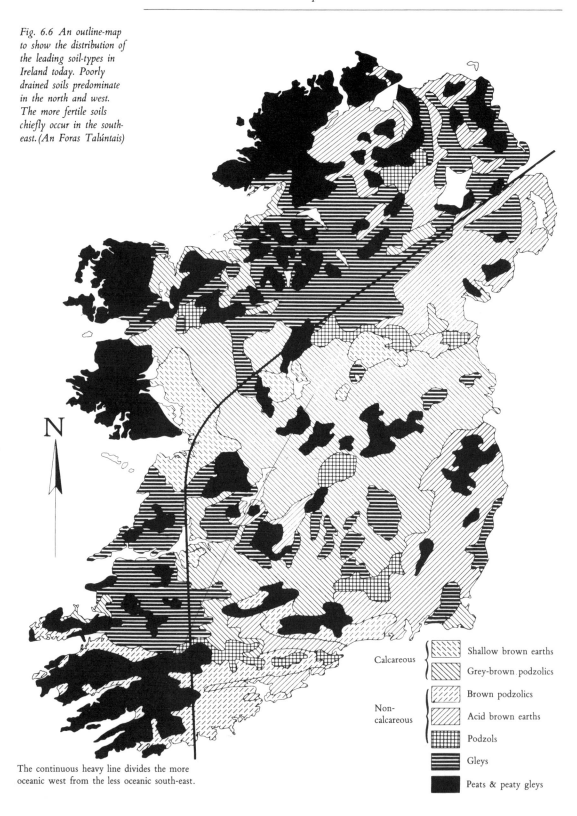

N

Calcareous
{ Shallow brown earths
{ Grey-brown podzolics

Non-calcareous
{ Brown podzolics
{ Acid brown earths
{ Podzols

Gleys

Peats & peaty gleys

The continuous heavy line divides the more oceanic west from the less oceanic south-east.

elements as 'rath' and 'lis', most of
which will stem from the early
centuries of the Christian era; these are
scattered throughout the country,
avoiding only higher ground, especially
in western areas. In Ireland for farming
at subsistence level there has always
been land enough for all, and the Irish
in the twelfth century, as at all times,
reckoned their wealth in stock,
principally in cattle. On the other hand
the Anglo-Normans were hungry for
commercial land, especially ploughland,
and they reckoned their wealth in acres.

Thus the distribution of Anglo-Norman
sites is very different, and the pattern
of the sites is so closely related to the
occurrence of good soils in Ireland
today, that it seems reasonable to
assume that the soils we know today
had developed by the time the Anglo-
Normans reached the country. In the
map of modern Irish soils (Fig. 6.6),
we see the immediate contrast between
the poorly drained soils of the north
and west (the gleys, peaty gleys and
peats — including peaty podzols —
shown in dark hues on the map), and
the more freely drained soils of the
south and east (brown earths, acid
brown earths, brown podzolics, grey-
brown podzolics, shown in lighter hues
on the map). A continuous line on the
map separates the two soil regions.

If we look at a meteorological map (see
Fig. 4.1a) that shows numbers
of rain-days, a very similar line will
divide a region with more than 175
rain-days to the north and west from a
region with less than that number to
the south and east. In other words in
Ireland today the soil will be
waterlogged if rain falls on at least half
the days in the year.

We can picture this as the edge of a
cloud. If climate deteriorates (and the
number of rain-days increases), the
cloud-edge will advance to the east and
south; if climate improves (and gets
drier), the cloud-edge will withdraw
north-westwards. Meteorologists tell us
that the Anglo-Normans arrived in

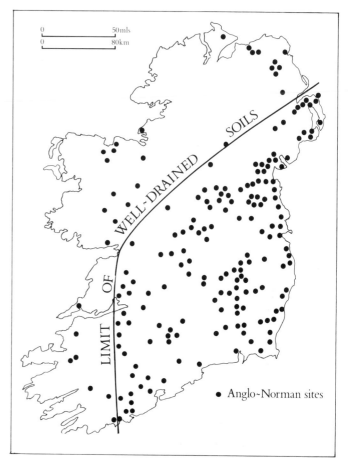

Ireland during a phase of very
favourable climate, but there is nothing
about the distribution of their sites to
suggest to us that better-drained soils
then stretched farther to the north-west
than they do today.

Wherever they found soils to their
taste, or a strategic point worth
defending, the Anglo-Normans erected
an earthen motte, later replaced by a
stone castle in places of especial
importance, and proceeded to settle
themselves into the surrounding
countryside (Fig. 6.7). On the whole,
as we have seen, they did not advance
beyond a line running from Skibbereen
through Galway to Coleraine, and
settled most densely in Leinster and east
Munster, an area of good land
interrupted by only one large island of
bad land, the uplands of the Wicklow

*Fig. 6.7 The distribution
of Anglo-Norman sites in
Ireland, and their
relationship to areas of
well-drained, fertile soils.*

Mountains, which were to prove a centre from which Irish forces would frequently emerge to harass the farms and towns of the surrounding lowlands. The basic Anglo-Norman unit was the manor (Fig. 6.8, Pl. 31), with perhaps 3000 acres (1200 ha), and here the lord would have his home-farm or stead, often protected by a moat, containing his house and his farm-buildings, with its surrounding fields. Radiocarbon has dated a moated house at Kilmagoura, Co. Cork, to AD 1225, and late-thirteenth-century coins were found in another at Rigsdale, also in Co. Cork. The parish church would be close by. Large farm units would be given to supporters, linked to the lord by allegiance as well as rent, to rent-paying individual farmers, and to borough communities of burgesses, with land in common, and their own court and other privileges. The holders of these larger units came from outside Ireland. The favourable climate had brought about a population explosion in most of western Europe, and in England, Wales and Flanders there were men anxious to get tenancies of good arable land in return for payments in money, in services and in kind. But the supply of such men was not inexhaustible, and

the lord would endeavour to retain the Irish work-force which had originally occupied the lands. Where possible he would reduce their status to that of villeins, who would be his property both in their persons and in their goods. Some got small parcels of land, paying rent but with no security of tenure, others held cottages but no land, and a third group, certainly Irish, the *betaghs*, had land without tenure held mainly by service. As their service-labour was largely communal, they tended to form a compact group, probably living in close association in houses clustered together in a 'clachan'. Even today we can find *Ballybetagh* as a place-name, and it is tempting to think that here we may have a link with the Anglo-Norman betagh villages or hamlets.

In the list of the Bruce devastations we can identify the units of the Norman farm — stead, barn, corn, crop and lea — and other documents spell out the round of duties of those who owed service. The corn was usually wheat or oats, and the service-tenants had to plough, harrow, sow, weed, scare birds, reap, tie, stook, cart, stack and thrash in the course of their duties. On

Fig. 6.8 The probable lay-out of an Anglo-Norman fourteenth-century moated manor at Cloncurry, Co. Kildare. (A.R. Orme, after J. O'Loan and P.J. Tuite)

the lord's land peas, beans and flax were also grown, but the poorer folk will have had meld and goosefoot in their rotation, which will have included periods when the land lay fallow.

It would be nice to think that on the manor in Ireland the normal practice of crop sequence — winter corn, spring crop, fallow — was carried out in neat enclosed fields, but it is more probable that the smaller tenants at least held separated strips scattered through large open common-fields, which cannot have made for efficient working. Such strips have a long history in Ireland and up till 150 years ago farms made up of such scattered strips could still be found; very often the plough furrow took on an arcuate form, and this shape also survives in some modern Irish field-boundaries (see Fig. 6.12d).

On the leas, if they had been shut up as meadows, the hay had to be made. The tenants had to scythe the grass, spread it, turn it and put it up in cocks, and then carry it to the haggard. It is probable that the scythe made its first appearance in Ireland in Norman times. As well as the meadows, there was 'pasture' and 'herbage', though what the exact difference was is unknown, and here the length of the grazing-period was carefully controlled. In the woods rights to hunting, cutting timber, grazing and the eating of acorns by swine were spelt out in detail; swine had to be ringed to stop them grubbing up the trees. There was usually a rabbit-warren and a dovecote. The lord had a water-mill, and if the tenants wished to grind their corn at home on a hand-mill, a fine had to be paid.

The colonists prospered for a time. Throughout Leinster and east Munster they took the flatlands, the rivers, the coasts and the Norse trading-towns, leaving the hill-country, the woods and the bogs to the Irish. A network of walled towns, castles and roads made the settlers secure and wealthy. Wool and hides were sent in large quantities

to France, Flanders and Italy. Woollen cloth, linen and furs were exported, and luxury goods — in food, wine, figs, raisins, walnuts, and in fabrics, satins, silks and cloth of gold — were imported. But the Bruce invasion, the Black Death and the deterioration in climate all combined in the fourteenth century to give the Anglo-Norman way of life a blow from which it never really recovered. Many of the colonists amalgamated with the Irish.

Fig. 6.9 Swine eating acorns. (After Röslin, 1562)

The plantations: AD 1550-1700

Before the Tudors came to the throne, the kings of England had been also kings of western France, and could afford to look on Ireland as a pleasant western annexe. The Tudors faced a potentially malevolent Europe, and malevolence grew as religious differences deepened. To the Tudors Ireland was the 'soft underbelly' of England, and appropriate steps had to be taken to secure the western flank.

What did Ireland look like to the Tudors? In Leinster they could see the well-kept Pale, and beyond the Pale the lands formerly loyal to the Crown but now in the hands of 'English rebels', lords of Anglo-Norman stock who had abandoned their allegiance, and adopted many of the ways of Irish life. In the foreground were the well-wooded Wicklow Mountains, still a stronghold of the 'Irish enemies'. In east Munster there were the fortified towns of Waterford, Youghal, Cork, Kinsale and a few others, and again the lands of the 'English rebels'. The great valleys of the Blackwater and the Lee were still filled with dense oakwoods. But this view stopped in west Munster, where the soil got poorer and the hills crowded more closely together. It was cut off again at the Shannon basin, where woods and bogs lay on both sides of the ill-defined river channel. If they looked north, Ulster was hidden by the broad belt of drumlins that stretched south-west from Strangford Lough to the headwaters of the Erne, and then followed the valley of that river north-west to the sea in Donegal Bay. Dense woods on the drumlin slopes and tops, and lakes, bogs and sluggish streams between them, made this very difficult country for the military man as it had also been in the Iron Age.

But in the Pale land-patterns were changing. In some communities the medieval strip-holdings with scattered plots in common fields still survived, but enclosure and the disappearance of small plots held by labour-service in favour of large leasehold farms worked by almost landless labourers were rapidly under way. The staple crop was wheat, but barley and rye were also grown.

Conditions were very different in the 'marchlands' beyond the Pale, and still more so in the Irish areas. There scrubby forest, lakes and undrained bog were still widespread. There was some tillage, mainly on a shifting or 'long-fallow' basis, in small plots cultivated with a spade. The lands were constantly redistributed to co-heirs, and so there was little incentive to intensive land-use, improvements or substantial buildings; even chieftains lived in cabins.

What impression of Irish farming and food can we form from the reports of Tudor observers, steeped in prejudice as most of them were? Cattle made the most impact. Milch-cows were prized; 'they will not kill a cow, except it be old and yield no milk'. Milk-products of all kinds continued to be eaten. Booleying was in full force; the people in summer lived 'in booleys, pasturing upon the mountain and waste wild places and removing still to fresh land. . . driving their cattle continually with them and feeding only on their milk and white meats [milk products]'; it was a good thing that 'in this country of Ireland, where there are great mountains and waste deserts full of grass, that the same should be eaten down and nourish many thousand of cattle'.

The other cattle were readily killed and eaten, and the large quantities of meat eaten without any accompanying bread was a constant source of surprise. Meat was eaten raw, boiled, roasted, and used as an ingredient in soup. Blood was drawn, and consumed after mixing with milk, butter or grains. Mutton, pork, hens and rabbits were also eaten. Venison appeared in pasties.

Wheat and rye were grown only on the better lands; barley was essentially for brewing and distilling; on poorer land and in the west oats were dominant. The heads of grain were singed, not thrashed; such a practice looked primitive, but considerable judgement was needed to hit on the exact second at which to jerk the grain out of the burning stem. Ploughs were hitched directly to the horses' tails; by modern standards this was a cruel practice, but in days when hanging and quartering, and breaking on the wheel, were matters of everyday routine, definitions of cruelty were rather different; the practice certainly reduced the wear and tear on the plough. Slide-cars were drawn in the same way. People constantly on the move had little use for vegetable gardens, and water-cress and wood-sorrel served as salads.

It was the easy-going wandering life of the Irish pastoralists that particularly irritated the Tudors, who thought that all would be well if the nomadic natives could be anchored on tillage-farms, where a more settled round of duties would tire them out and leave them less time for mischief. Able-bodied men should have more to do than 'follow a few cows grazing. . . for this keeping of cows is of itself a very idle life and a fit nursery for a thief'. If they were exhausted by working in the fields or gardens, they would have less energy for raiding; as it was 'when it is daylight they will go to the poor village. . . burning the houses and corn and ransacking of the poor cottages. They will drive all the kine and plow horses, with all other cattle, and drive them away.' To make wandering Irishmen into settled Englishmen was the goal.

The Tudors were businessmen and they decided they could not afford to take Ireland by a single massive onslaught. They would open up the country by cutting passes through the woods, bridging the rivers, building roads, and keeping the roads open by erecting forts and blockhouses along them. Military patrols and route-marches

would impede the formation of native alliances in these frontier-lands. Apart from the good lands in the east and south, and the coasts from Lough Foyle down the Irish Sea and round to Galway Bay, the geography of Ireland was little known, and extensive surveys would be carried out to find out exactly what the country held. Inter-clan wars and risings against English authority would occur from time to time; these would be ruthlessly put down, the 'Irish enemies' killed off or transplanted, and English settlers and English ways brought in in their stead wherever the land was of sufficient quality to support 'the English way of life'. The areas that were ultimately taken were essentially the same areas of good land that had appealed to the Anglo-Normans (see Fig. 6.6), with in addition the good land in Munster.

Irish resurgence was making life impossible for the open manor and the open village. The lord had to retire into the uncomfortable protection of the tower-house, while the ordinary folk either fled back to Britain, leaving their 'deserted village' behind them, or sought security in the walled towns, which continued to operate — like mini Hong-Kongs — in a countryside that was basically hostile, yet tolerated their existence for the trading-contacts that they brought. To give more shelter to crops, and to make it more difficult to drive cattle off the lands, efforts were made to surround the fields with stone-faced banks and ditches; to encourage timber the banks were to be planted with ash trees.

By 1515 the remaining territory under English control, apart from the walled towns, was now sadly shrunken to a coastal strip, which itself had to be protected on its inland side by a bank and ditch — the Pale — which ran from Dundalk through Kells to Kildare, and from there back east across the northern foothills of the Wicklow Mountains to reach the coast south of Dublin at Dalkey. Outside the Pale the remaining landlords of English origin

Fig. 6.10 The curved timbers necessary for ship-building had to be selected with great care; the picture illustrates the timber possibilities of variously shaped oak-trees. (After Duhamel du Monceau, 1764)

Fig. 6.11 Production (and export) of staves had begun before 1600. By 1615 staves were going to the Mediterranean for wine casks. After 1640 home demand for barrels to cask salt meat for export rose, and export fell away. When export of live animals was prohibited in 1665, demand rose sharply. Until 1710 the Irish woods could meet the demand, but in that year staves were imported for the first time. Until about 1765 Ireland could still meet half the demand, but after 1770 there were no more Irish staves.

no longer set their lands for money rents, but through share-cropping agreements advanced working-capital to their tenants, demonstrating in this — as in many other ways — their gradual adoption of Irish ways.

The first plantation came in the mid-sixteenth century when disturbances in Leix and Offaly, between the Pale and the Shannon, gave the English forces a chance to intervene. Victory was followed by the transformation of the area into King's County and Queen's County; the Irish were dislodged, their chief was pensioned off with 3000 acres, and the rest was parcelled out to settlers from England in lots ranging from 500 to 25 acres. The larger grantees had to pay a rent, perform military duties, manage the local water courses and fords, introduce tillage, build houses and supply timber. To prevent their land becoming sub-divided in the Irish manner, the grantees had to undertake to leave it in tail-male to their eldest son.

Lack of adequate survey gave rise to difficulties in division, and efforts were made to improve surveying methods. From such surveys we get glimpses of the landscape. Primary woodland was encountered round Athlone, where the map-maker recorded extensive forests of 'great oaks' in contrast to 'much small woods as crabtree, thorn, hazel, with such like'. In north Kerry some of the woodlands were clearly secondary as they consisted of 'underwood of the age of fifty or sixty years, filled with decayed trees, ash-trees, hazels, sallows, willows, alders, birches, whitethorns and such like.'

The method of plantation in Leix/Offaly produced a state-sponsored quasi-military colony. But new colonial ideas were developing as the Spanish *conquistadores* were carving up the Americas. Private enterprise could be encouraged.

The acquisition of Munster in 1585 came next, and after the Desmond

Rising had been crushed, and the native population virtually annihilated, about 600,000 acres (2500 ha) were available for new owners. Mouths were encouraged to open wide, and blocks of 4000 (1600 ha), 6000 (2500 ha) and even 12,000 acres (5000 ha) were offered, together with blue-print development layouts showing lots ranging from 1000 acres (400 ha) for the demesne to five and a half acres (2 ha) for the cottages. Edmund Spenser got 3000 acres (1200 ha); favourites like Sir Walter Raleigh received 20,000 acres (8000 ha), to whet his appetite for still greater plantations in north America; Richard Boyle, later Earl of Cork, subsequently purchased Raleigh's interest, and by later transactions, many of them extremely dubious, amassed an enormous estate.

In 1585 it was estimated that the plantation would bring 8500 English settlers, but in 1590 their number was reckoned at about 2000. They had brought ploughs and improved breeds of cattle and sheep with them, and undoubtedly raised the standard of farming in the region.

What with difficulties in securing settlers, difficulties in satisfying them when they did arrive, and the partially successful efforts of the original owners to regain the land, Munster in 1600 by no means presented the happy picture of contented English settlers farming enclosed fields on fertile farms protected by natural defences and near to the sea, a river or a town, that had been put forward by the prospectuses for the scheme. The comment 'Enclosures are very rare amongst them, and then no better fenced than an old wife's toothless gums. . . as for the arable land it lies almost as much neglected and unmanured [unworked] as the sandy deserts of Arabia' is probably nearer the mark.

But the plantation did throw the woods of Munster at the mercy of the new entrepreneurs, and the commercial exploitation of the forests began in earnest. From the woods a continuous stream of timber flowed out — trunks from good large trees for ships and houses, branches from these trees and smaller trees for barrel staves, and lop and top and all other wood for charcoal for iron and glass works (Fig. 6.10). It is hard to gauge the amount of large timber that was exported, but we can get some impression of the stave and charcoal trades from the information made available by Eileen McCracken.

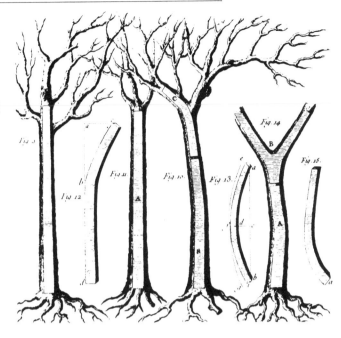

For barrel staves I have taken her figures, and tried to cast them in a crude graphical diagram (Fig. 6.11); much is conjectural, and for this I take full responsibility. As can be seen the production of staves made tremendous inroads on the oakwoods. Throughout the seventeenth century the number of

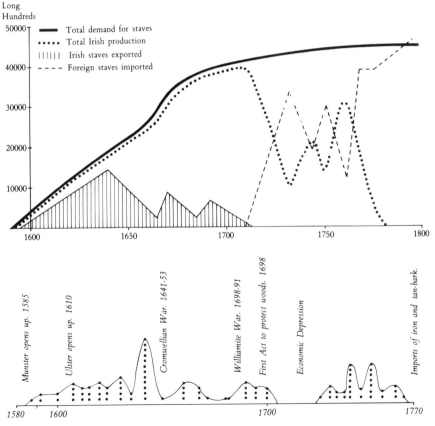

Fig. 6.12 Schematic diagram to show the times at which new charcoal-burning ironworks started to operate in Ireland. Each dot represents the opening of a works. The influence of military and economic events is clearly seen. The sharp decline after 1750 indicates the exhaustion of supplies of charcoal. (Based on data in McCracken, Irish Woods)

staves produced in Ireland rose steadily, and over-production led to eventual exhaustion of supply. After 1770 all needed staves had to be imported.

Mrs McCracken gives the years in which about one hundred charcoal-consuming ironworks started to operate, and again I have plotted these dates in a crudely graphical form (Fig. 6.12). Production started in Munster shortly before 1600, and such was the consumption of woodland that, after no more than a hundred years, parliament in 1698 was compelled to pass the first of a long series of acts both to conserve any remaining stocks, and to encourage the planting of trees.

While Ireland's woodlands were very greatly reduced, it did not follow that the fortunes of the entrepreneurs were correspondingly increased. Although Sir William Petty devastated the woods around Kenmare, his accounts show very little profit from the enterprise. Richard Boyle's figures for the Blackwater valley tell much the same story. The woods along the rivers of south-east Ireland were not only nearer to England, but were also safer; even here it was a constant struggle to recruit experienced managers of charcoal-kilns and superintendents of smelting-works, and the experts, even if they could be coaxed to Ireland, were always looking over their shoulders and thinking how much more pleasant it would be in the Forest of Dean, the heart of English iron-working. Richard Boyle (later Earl of Cork) summed it up: 'God ordained my ironworks to be an endless trouble to me.'

After 1593 there were nine years of general country-wide war until 1603, when an organized Irish army with foreign contingents was finally defeated by an Elizabethan army, and the independence and isolation of Ulster were brought to an end. Five hundred thousand acres were available for plantation, and this time the mistakes made in Munster were not repeated. Two thousand acres (800 ha) was the

upper limit on the blocks offered, and those who accepted had to bring in tenants from Britain, and build defences — a castle and a bawn — to protect their lands, tenants and goods. As a bait, the tenants were offered very generous leases. Roads and bridges were organized, towns and villages laid out and with growing commercialism markets, shops and local industries were established. A regular pattern of small enclosed fields for arable farming was established (Fig. 6.13). The Plantation of Ulster was more than the replacement of one group of farmers by another; it was truly an implantation of a different way of life, a difference that has maintained itself to the present day.

Like Leinster, Ulster has its upland areas of poorer soils, the Sperrins and the mountains of Donegal. The displaced natives withdrew to these areas where tillage was still more difficult, and there their nomadic habits became still more pronounced. Excessive sub-division of land as generation succeeded generation, and the constant fear of crops being burned or otherwise destroyed in raids and war, had brought about still further concentration on livestock, which escaped pillage if kept on the move. The seasonal booleying moves to summer pastures had always been strong, and the more drastic practice of *creaghting*, whereby whole communities and their livestock kept more or less constantly on the move, drifting from the protection of one lord to that of another, became more pronounced.

But when peace returned, agricultural output turned quickly upwards. Fish, hides and furs fell back in importance as exports, and cattle, butter and wool took their place. It may be that as the forests of Munster shrank, the numbers of cattle and sheep rose; certainly the ports of Youghal, Cork and Kinsale grew dramatically at this time. The bone content of some fifteenth-/ sixteenth-century ditches at Newgrange also demonstrated the rise in the importance of sheep at this time; sheep

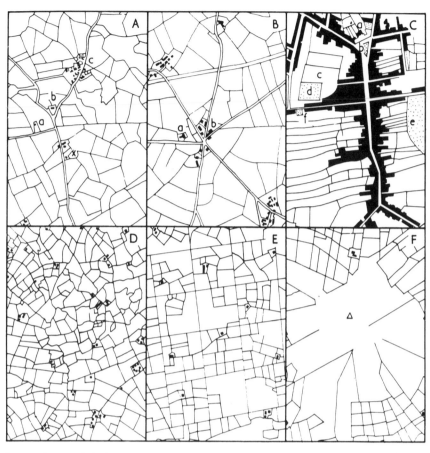

Fig. 6.13 Settlements and fields stemming from the Plantation of Ulster:
A *Clachan:* **a** *church house;* **b** *church;* **c** *clachan;* **x** *site of rath.*
B *Roadside hamlet:* **a** *church;* **b** *local post office.* C *Planned town:* **a** *technical institute;* **b** *open area;* **c** *brickfield;* **d** *fairgreen;* **e** *demesne;* **f** *linen factory.* D *Small irregular fields.* E *Regular fields with surveyed boundaries.* F *Fields laid out to accord with hill slope topography. (After Common and Glasscock)*

(or goat) provided almost one-third of all the bones found in the late medieval ditches, whereas in the prehistoric levels at the same site they only amounted to one-twentieth.

The drastic action that had been taken in Ulster was followed by land confiscations in Connaught, and the general hostility to these plantations, as well as to the strong central government in Dublin, provoked a further rising during the English Civil War in 1641. This led to a general countrywide war, which lasted for twelve years, before it was brutally terminated by Cromwell's victories. Two and a half million acres (well over a million hectares) were involved in the population shifts which followed; the Irish landowners were pushed to the west, to the wet and infertile lands beyond the Shannon; those of English

extraction whose loyalties to England were considered sufficiently safe were retained on the best soils in the south-east between the Boyne and the Barrow, and between these two groups a colonial buffer zone with ex-soldiers and new settlers straggled down central Ireland on lands of varying quality.

Once peace returned the country recovered quickly. An upturn in climate was bringing record harvests in Europe; Ireland concentrated on livestock. The markets and fairs that had been initiated in Ulster spread through the country, and with an improving road system cattle easily found their way either to the docks or the slaughterhouse. Sheep went to stock the English sheepwalks. Even when the English market was closed by embargo, alternative overseas markets were readily to hand. Sugar produced by slave labour was now pouring out of the West Indies, and meat was urgently required to feed the population there. Cork and its stock yards became the Chicago of Ireland, and heavily salted beef was crammed into barrels for the West Indian trade. As we have seen, the export trade in barrel staves faded away, as every barrel was needed for the trade. Generally it was a time of some prosperity. Petty reported that the general standard of clothing was equal to that of Europe. Chimneys were appearing in houses. Many people owned a horse. The emphasis on pasture rather than tillage left many people underemployed, and cottage industries, the spinning and weaving of wool and flax, were a source of supplemental income.

The short war that followed, from 1689 to 1691, was not altogether of Ireland's making, but she had to provide campaign fields for the 'Irish' army of James II and the 'English' army of William III. William's victory was followed by the reshuffling of at least one million acres (400,000 ha) of land, and when that was over only

15% of the land of Ireland was left in Irish ownership, and the ascendancy of the English landlord was complete.

What did Ireland look like in 1700, 150 years after the first plantation? The population had probably doubled, though it is difficult to give exact figures; Petty reckoned the population in 1672 at 1,200,000, and if we think of 1,000,000 in 1550 and 2,000,000 in 1700, at least our order of number will probably be correct. In 1550 people still trusted in castles (Photo 40), but these had been made obsolete by gunpowder, and in the seventeenth century the castle began to transform itself into a house (Fig. 6.14). In 1700 confident estate owners were beginning to build houses with large windows, through which they could admire the newly planted exotic trees in their demesnes (Photo 41). When these new pollens appear in our pollen-counts we bring the Destruction-phase (ILWd$_3$) to an end, and open the Expansion-phase (ILWe), when the slow process of restoring Ireland's woodlands takes its first tentative steps.

Fig. 6.14 Coppingers Court, Cork, as it may have been in the late seventeenth century.

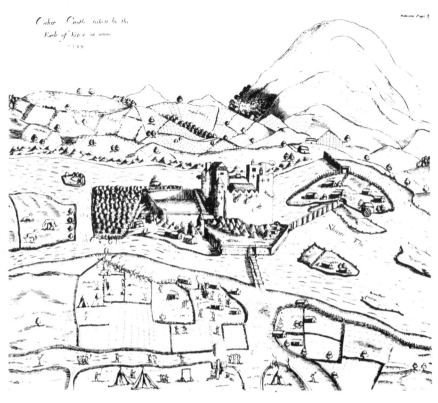

Photograph 40 Cahir, Co. Tipperary. This early 17th century engraving shows a landscape free of trees, except on the lower slopes of the Galty Mountains. The fields are enclosed by banks, walls and wattle fences; within some fields parallel lines suggest cultivation-ridges. The walls of the castle, like those of a tower-house, are pierced only by very small windows.

Photograph 41 Near Castlepollard, Co. Westmeath. By the mid-18th century the large-windowed mansion, with its planted trees and its formal gardens, has replaced the fortified castle and the tower-house. The adjoining land has been surveyed, and laid out in regular fields; further away there is uncleared scrub. Cultivation-ridges are prominent everywhere.

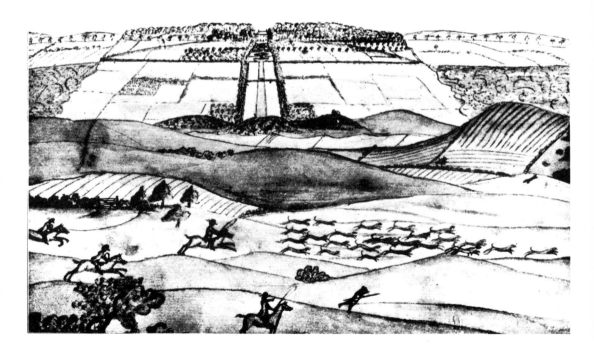

Though the road system still left a lot to be desired — 'the great rain has made the ways almost impassable, the horse road which is most old causeway being broken up and quite out of repair and the footway in the fields very boggy with abundance of ditches at that time full of water' — the stage coach was beginning to appear. Stock could move easily to market, and from there to the point of export. Banks to facilitate trade were coming into existence. The woods had shrunk out of all recognition, and been replaced by meadows and fields to support the larger population.

The potato was beginning to take its place in the Irish diet. When did the potato appear in Ireland? At an early meeting of the Royal Society in 1662 Robert Boyle spoke in terms that suggested that the potato had already saved thousands from starvation in Ireland; but it may be that he was indicating what the potato could do, rather than what it had already done, because at the same time his gardener was still struggling to produce the few potatoes needed to provide a delicacy in salads rather than an item of everyday diet.

References to the potato in Ireland do not become common until the 1670s, and then they suggest that the potato was still a garden, rather than a field crop. Dunton writes, 'Behind one of these cabins lies the garden a piece of ground sometimes of half an acre, and in this is the turf-stack, their corn — perhaps two or three hundred sheaves of oats — and as much peas; the rest of the ground is full of those dearly loved potatoes, and a few cabbages which the solitary calf never suffers to come to perfection.' At the end of the century the potato stood poised and ready to revolutionize life in Ireland.

Consolidation in the eighteenth century: AD 1700-1785

By comparison with the turbulent centuries which had preceded it, the eighteenth century was one of relatively uneventful development. By 1785 the population had doubled once more (see Fig. 6.16), and trade had increased tenfold. A vigorous programme of road-building (accompanied by the full establishment of a stage-coach system) and the construction of canals both integrated the country and centred it on its capital, Dublin, to an extent hitherto unknown. The last Irish wolf had been killed.

Unfortunately the now universal landlord-tenant relationship concentrated the new wealth in the hands of the landlords, who erected the palatial houses looking out on well-wooded demesnes that are still such a feature of the Irish landscape. Outside the demesne the lodgings of their tenants remained at their former miserable level. In the earlier part of the century the interposition of a middleman who took large blocks of land on long lease from the landlord, and let it in small blocks on shorter lease at higher rent to the tenant, ensured that such prosperity as escaped the landlord was siphoned off by the middleman, and little or none of it was enjoyed by the tenant. The middleman was not entirely useless, because he sometimes employed his capital in leasing dairy stock to tenants who could not afford their own, and so took them into 'clientship' in a way that had been widespread in early Ireland. In this way he exemplified that power to spring again from a cut-down stock that has typified much of Ireland throughout the ages.

The cottage industries based on wool and flax continued to provide valuable supplements to family incomes, and bleach greens became a feature of the Irish countryside. But Ireland was a backward agricultural country caught up in the rapidly developing British mercantile system, and when that system was shaken either by harvest vagaries or by wars, then the fortunes of Ireland fluctuated also.

The agricultural revolution was slow to reach Ireland. Already in the middle of the sixteenth century farmers in the Netherlands had eliminated the hitherto universal period of fallow. They replaced it with turnips and clover to feed increased numbers of stock, whose larger output of manure was used to fertilize the land for the corn crops. Animal and crop husbandry were now united in one system, capable of very intensive production. The weed problem was solved by the invention of the seed drill in 1700. With the young plants in neat rows, a hoe could be drawn between the rows, and the weeds eliminated while the crop was growing. Ability to survive a hard winter on scanty rations was no longer the criterion by which stock had to be judged; with animal feed assured, it was now possible to breed for production of meat, milk and wool.'

Eventually the wind of change did reach Ireland. A Linen Hall was founded in Dublin in 1711 to promote the growth of flax, and oversee the weaving and sale of linen. The Royal Dublin Society was founded in 1731, for 'the advancement of agriculture and other branches of industry and for the advancement of science and art'. The society circulated agricultural books, imported implements, and gave premiums for stock-breeding, tree-planting, spinning, weaving and a host of other activities. It did much to stir up an interest in agriculture among the landlords who formed its membership, and in the later part of the century the middlemen withered away, as many landlords took a direct and improving interest in the management of their estates. An improvement was badly needed; each year the Cork stockyards alone slaughtered 300,000 head of cattle, but the cattle were small, averaging only 4-8 cwt (200-400 kg) against the 10-15 cwt (500-760 kg) of contemporary English breeds.

If the quality of the cattle population was to be improved, controlled breeding was necessary. Improved pastures and hay and roots for winter fodder made it possible to carry bigger stocks, and here control was also necessary. Hedged fields prevented stock from wandering, controlled the degree of grazing and manuring, and provided shelter, while the ditch at the foot of the hedge improved drainage. Soon the landlords were hard at work, surveying and laying out new field alignments, digging ditches and throwing up banks, which were then made secure by the planting of hawthorns along them. They 'improved' their tenants' lands as well as their own, in places breaking up the old clachans and building new houses well separated from one another.

*Fig. 6.15 Some Irish field-systems: **a** large regular fields, Jordanstown, Co. Meath; **b** small regular fields, Ballykine Lower, Co. Down; **c** small irregular fields, Glinsouth, Co. Kerry; **d** curved strip fields, Nicholastown, Co. Kilkenny. **e** ladder farms, Foriff, Co. Antrim; **f** strips in common-fields, with surrounding ring of pasture, Dalkey, Co. Dublin, c. AD 1850. (After Buchanan)*

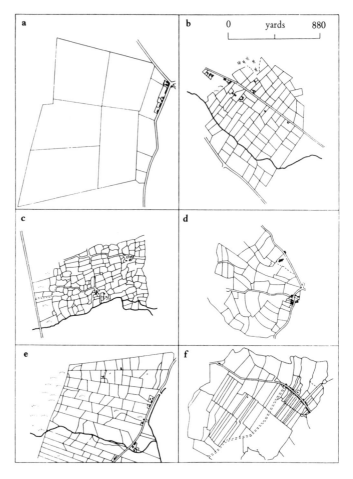

On flat ground the arrangement might be highly regular, on isolated hills such as drumlins the layout would be adjusted to the slopes, and on sloping ground a ladder pattern was often employed. After 1698 numerous acts of parliament promoted the planting of trees, and in 1735 the Royal Dublin Society began to offer premiums for such planting. These stimuli appear to have been quite effective, because by the year 1800 more than 130,000 acres (52,000 ha) of plantations had been added to what native woods survived, and between 1800 and the Famine another 210,000 acres (85,000 ha) were added. We had thus the paradoxical situation that while the landscape in the immediate vicinity of the estates was getting more and more densely crowded with trees, many of them exotic, the general countryside was getting barer and barer as the rising population got more and more desperate for fuel.

In the 1780s the pace of development began to falter. The new Corn Laws brought a swing to grain-growing against cattle, and the population was entering on that period of staggering growth that was to bring it from four to eight millions in the course of sixty years. We are very fortunate to have a record of what the country looked like in the immediately preceding years in Arthur Young's account of his *Tour in Ireland* in 1776-9. Like Giraldus Cambrensis, Young was from Britain, was human and not without prejudice; he was not very successful as manager of Lord Kingsborough's estate in Mitchelstown, he was conservative in outlook, he carried a large chip on his shoulder, but from his extensive travels and experiences we can build up a clear picture of the times.

In Cavan he found that Mr Clements had 'been very attentive to bring his farm into neat order respecting fences, throwing down and levelling old banks, making new ditches, double ones six feet wide and five deep, with a large bank between for planting'. He also approved of Lord Farnham, who had

farmed in Norfolk, and sowed his turnips and cabbages with a drill, and horse-hoed the weeds. The fields were drained, and liberally fertilized with dung, ditch-earth and lime. There was a herd of Lancashire cows, and although oxen were used for ploughing and general draft work, Lord Farnham also bred work-horses. The estate was well planted with Scots fir, silver fir, beech, oak and ash. 'Upon the whole Farnham is one of the finest places I have seen in Ireland.' Outside the demesnes the tree position was different; Co. Galway 'is perfectly free from woods, and even trees, except about gentlemen's houses'. Near the cities the position was worse; at Dunkettle, outside Cork, he reports 'Fuel; a very little coal, the rest supplied by bushes, stolen faggots, etc., as there is no turf in this part of the country.'

He also approved of Mr Oliver, of Castle Oliver, Co. Limerick, but not of his tenants who raised bullocks on farms of up to 500 acres. 'The face of the country is that of desolation; the grounds are over-run with thistles, ragwort, etc. to excess; the fences are mounds of earth, full of gaps; there is no wood, and the general countenance is such, that you must examine into the soil before you will believe that a country, which has so beggarly an appearance, can be so rich and fertile.' At the bottom of the scale we hear 'Great quantities of flax sown by all the poor and little farmers, which is spun in the country, and a good deal of bandle [narrow] cloth made of it. This and pigs are two great articles of profit here; they keep great numbers, yet the poor in this rich tract of country are very badly off. Land is so valuable, that all along as I came from Bruff, their cabins are generally in the road ditch, and numbers of them without the least garden; the potato land being assigned them upon the farm where it suits the master best. The price they pay is very great, from £4 to £5 an acre, with a cabin; and for the grass of a cow 20s. to 45s. They are, if anything, worse off than they were twenty years ago. A cabin, an acre of land, at 40s., and the grass of two cows, are the recompence for the year's labour; but in other places they are paid by an acre of grass for potatoes at £5. Those who do not get milk to their potatoes, eat mustard with them, raising the seed for the purpose. The population of the country increases exceedingly, but mostly on the higher lands; new cabins are building everywhere.' It is clear that in Young's time the potato had become a field, rather than a garden, crop, that it was the principal item of diet for the majority of the population, and that a rapid expansion of that population was making itself felt. What Young could not realize was that that expansion was going to produce a further sub-division of land into tiny potato-patches, and impede the orderly realignment of field boundaries, of which he approved so highly.

The landlords, like Lord de Montalt, at Dundrum, Co. Tipperary, might follow the advice of the Dublin Society and use Warwickshire and Shropshire ploughs, but elsewhere it was different, as at Castletownroche, Co. Cork. 'Four horses and three men to every plough, one to drive, one to hold, and another with a pole, bearing on the beam to keep it in the ground; but they do an acre a day, by means of leaving a great space untouched in the middle of each land, where they begin by lapping the sods to meet.' Such a plough-scene can have changed little since the fourteenth century, though two men are now sharing the job the ploughman alone did then (see Photo 29, centre). In the stony west everything was done with the spade. 'Upon asking whether they ploughed with horses or oxen, I was told there was not a plough in the whole parish, which was 12 miles long by 7 broad. All the tillage is by the Irish loy; ten men dig an acre a day that has been stirred before. It will take forty men to put in an acre of potatoes in a day.' He appreciated that spade cultivation was not necessarily to be despised as it could give a better return

than the plough; at Belleisle, Co. Fermanagh, he reports 'Much corn, etc. by poor people, put in with spades, which they call loys, because they have no horses, and one acre of oats dug, is worth one and a half ploughed; some do it on this account, though they have horses.'

Arthur Young saw Ireland from horseback or through the windows of a post-chaise. Were he touring today in a motor-car, he would be amazed at the hedges along the roadside, he would wonder where the masses of people had disappeared to, he would remark on the fanciful nature of many of the new houses, he would notice some trees, but much of the rest would still look familiar to his eyes.

The potato and the population peak: AD 1785-1850

It is not easy to pinpoint the cause, or combination of causes, that drastically accelerated, around 1785, the rate of population-increase in Ireland. We can picture that in 1741 the population was about three million, in 1785 it was about four million, while in 1841 — shortly before the Famine — when a census was taken, the figure was 8,200,000.

The death-rate was falling. As the 1840s approached medicine was improving, vaccination was adopted, and a chain of hospitals and dispensaries was spreading through the country. Food was improving in quality and also in quantity — there was no major famine (apart from the Great Famine) after 1740, and the improved transport system made the movement of food within the country more easy. The birth-rate was rising; more young people in the population meant more alliances, and the better diet may have raised the fertility rate.

Fig 6.16 Graph to illustrate population growth and decline in Ireland, AD 1690 to 1986. (After Connell and Gilmor)

In other European countries the population was also rising, but not as fast as in Ireland; the potato was being eaten in other countries, but not to the same extent as in Ireland, and it is difficult to resist the conclusion that the potato, not only by its dietary influence, but also by its social influence, was the chief cause of the fantastic — and disastrous — rate of population growth in Ireland.

The potato is one of the great food crops of the world, and alone of them finds conditions in Ireland entirely to its liking. The potato favours water-retaining soils, and these are not in short supply in Ireland, particularly in the west and south. Conditions for wheat are minimal, and those for barley little better; oats and rye are more at home. The summer temperatures are rarely high enough for the sugar-beet to produce its full potential of sugar, but they are more than enough for starch production by the potato, whose homelands are the Andean uplands of South America. Though 75% of the tuber is water, the food value of an acre of potatoes is greater than that of an acre of any grain crop. The potato yields starch, amino-acids and Vitamin C, and the consumption of 6.5 lbs (3 kg) per day provides an adequate diet. In Ireland an acre (0.4 ha) can be expected to yield about 9 tons, enough to feed six adult men for one year, and more than adequate to support a relatively large family. It is thought that the consumption per head may have reached 8 lbs (3.6 kg) a day.

For most of us forcible feeding in prison would seem preferable to thrusting half a stone of potatoes down our throats day in day out throughout the year. And for many this was all there was for months on end. We have only to read Arthur Young's litany as he perambulated the country; at Castletownroche 'They live the year through upon potatoes, and for half the year have nothing but water with them'; at Johnstown 'Their food is potatoes for at least eleven months of

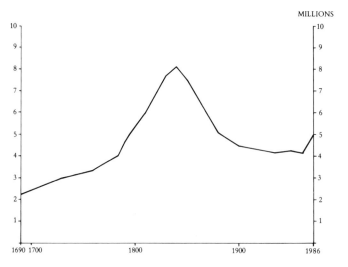

MILLIONS

the year, and one month of oat, barley or bere bread.'

For those with courage, there could be money in potatoes. W. S. Trench tells us how in 1846 he took 160 acres (65 ha) of rough mountain pasture worth one shilling an acre. He scattered lime over it and then ploughed it into ridges five feet wide; the potatoes were sown, guano was added as manure, and the ridges were further built up by hand. 'The potato grew to perfection in this rude description of tillage.' He expected to get a crop of potatoes worth £3000 'at the very moderate price of 3d. per stone', and be left with the land with its value raised twentyfold to one pound an acre, and ready to grow a good crop of corn or grass. But 1846 was the year of the blight, and he lost all.

In Ireland, as in other rural countries before farming was mechanized, the social pyramid was the land-owners, the tenant-farmers and the landless labourers. We have seen the land-owners in their elegant mansions, set in a tree-studded demesne, which was now surrounded by a wall, built as a relief-measure by the local labourers. The tenant-farmers lived in a modest way; in his *Topographical Dictionary*, Lewis tells us 'Farmhouses though varying in size are all built on the same plan, with an open chimney at one end, and at the other a small room separated by a partition, and serving both as a bed-chamber and as a storeroom. Few farm yards are attached to the houses, and these are very small and confined; the corn being frequently stacked on circular stages supported by upright capstones; barns are never used for any other purpose than thrashing, and are consequently built very small; the common farmer indeed is often unprovided with either stage or barn, and thrashes his grain in the open air.'

We can liken the social pyramid to a stratified bee-hive, in which the three layers ought to be in appropriate

Fig. 6.17 A nineteenth-century sketch from the Illustrated London News. *The cabins have mud walls and thatched roofs. In front of each cabin is a small 'garden', surrounded by low banks; here vegetables were grown. The background is completely free of trees.*

proportions. Unfortunately after 1785 the boards containing the base of the bee-hive burst outwards, and the labourers began to expand beyond the confines of the hive. The bee builds flimsy cells of wax, the labourers built their rickety cabins (Fig. 6.17) wherever they could find a sufficiency of square feet free from obstruction, and if possible one wall already provided — against a field-bank, in a ditch, against a rock-face. On the hillsides (far above the present level of cultivation) there were still patches of ground on slopes where lazy-beds could be laid out, and a cabin set up. With luck there would be blanket-bog not too far away, and an easier supply of fuel to compensate for the harder struggle on higher ground. On rougher ground, stones could be cleared away.

And as a last resort, there was the bog-surface itself. Both on the raised-bogs in the midlands, and on the blanket-bogs in the west, lazy-beds can be seen. Apparently only the thinnest skin of added sand or earth was necessary before the bog-surface could be brought under cultivation. Near the coast, sea-weed could be collected for manure.

In the east, sub-divisions of land at first sufficed to produce the necessary acre per family. In 1830 the Royal Dublin Society was offering premiums for schemes to divide up land so that there would be allotted 'to the greatest number of cottages a quantity of land not less than one acre, Irish', and also 'for the best account of actual experience of the quantity of land required to support a labourer's family with vegetables and potatoes, and to enable him to keep a pig and a cow all the year'. Those at a level higher up in the hive saw no reason to object to such fragmentation; the farmer by splitting some of his fields, and letting the land at £5 or more per acre automatically received cash to make the payment of his own rent secure, and the landlord was delighted to get prompt payment. Lest any suggestion should arise that the labourer should

acquire even a shadow of title to the land he rented, he often got it on *conacre*, or possession for eleven months only, which made its reversion clear beyond doubt.

But where to get the money to pay the rent? There can have been no sale for surplus potatoes; in Ireland potatoes are always a rags to riches crop. If the harvest was a light one, hunger might loom before the next harvest came round, and the pressure to eat the seed-stock might be impossible to resist. If the crop was a bumper one, there was no market for the surplus. Home spinning could bring in some cash, and if the dwelling was substantial a loom could be set up. Estate cottages in the east often had a special room for looms. A bonham could be purchased, and reared on family scraps for later sale as bacon. Sometimes the £5 rent would bring in addition to the acre of land the right to graze a cow for the year, and milk and butter would make a welcome supplement to the potato diet. Only at planting-time and at harvest was any serious labour required by the crop, and the able-bodied members of the family were able to migrate in search of paid work. But the more the population increased, the more candidates there were for the jobs, and the farmer had no difficulty in moving his wage-rate down.

A family, once some of the children had reached the age of seven or eight, was probably an asset rather than a liability. Capital outlay was almost nil. There were no agricultural implements needed, beyond a spade for everyone big enough to use one (Fig. 6.18). No farm buildings, because the potatoes could lie quite happily in a clamp in the field. A roof over the cabin, fuel for the fire, and straw to lie on were essential. Clothes were patched beyond all recognition, and handed down from one to another. Boots and shoes were for adults only, and then only on special occasions. If necessary, the potatoes could be roasted in the ashes of the fire, or boiled in a *fulacht fian*,

and eaten from the hand without
benefit of pot, plate, knife or fork. It
was subsistence-existence, in the fullest
sense of the word.

The larger children could assist in the
spade work. The others could gather
herbs to flavour the potatoes, tend the
cow and the pig, forage for manure —
because the potato was a greedy crop
— and, most important of all, scour
the countryside for fuel, leaving no
bush, bog or marsh unattacked.
Nineteenth-century writers take up the
tale where Arthur Young left off; in
Co. Dublin 'the hedges are demolished
without mercy, and, in many places
they gather the dung from about the
fields, and even burn straw'.

Both the raised-bogs and the blanket-
bogs were being heavily cut for fuel,
and even the swamps and marshes were
being robbed of their muds. The mud
was dug or dredged up, spread on the
surrounding lands, tramped underfoot
to a uniform consistency, moulded into
lumps, dried and burned. West Cork
today shows many small ponds; if we
look at them closely we can see the
still-jagged peat-cuttings that form their
margins; before the Famine they were
closed marshes; their open-water was
created by peat-cutting, just as on a
much larger scale the Norfolk Broads
are the product of medieval peat-
cutting.

It is hard to realize today just how
serious the struggle for fuel was. Even
in Arthur Young's time hedges and
fences were being stolen for firing.
How much worse must it have been
when the population was approaching
its maximum. The countryside must
have presented an extraordinary
appearance. There were the walled
demesnes with their trees, the oases in
a desert. The boughs of the trees hung
down over the walls, but inside the
walls there were mantraps to deter
timber-poachers. There were the
farmers' houses surrounded by shelter-
belts of trees, and the farmer would
have had a blunderbuss to protect

them. And then there was nothing, not
a tree, not a bush, to break the view of
the bare landscape dotted over with
cabins and endless potato-patches.

Everything was done with the spade,
and every region had its own variety of
spade. At one time a spade factory in
Cork used to produce at least seventy-
five different forms of spade-blade. As
we have seen, to use the spade rather
than the plough is by no means a sign
of inferior husbandry. The user of the
spade gives to his work the detail of
the gardener, rather than the broader
stroke of the plough, and yields will
usually be higher from the spade-plot

*Fig. 6.18 Drawing of
Irish labourer with spade
in one hand and shoes in
the other, c. AD 1850.*

Photograph 42a Glendalough, Co. Wicklow. In the early nineteenth century the valley was stripped of timber, as wood for fuel and charcoal for smelting. The monastic buildings stand out like ruined teeth in a bare gum.

Photograph 42b For this similar picture the photographer had to move up from the floor of the valley. Its left-hand slopes now carry secondary oakwood, pines and exotics have been planted on the right, and there is young plantation on the low ground between the two lakes. Only the top of the Round Tower (now restored) and part of one church can be seen.

than the ploughed field. If excess of labour has allowed wage-rates to drop below a certain level, it will be cheaper for the farmer to use teams of men with spades, rather than the plough, with its attendant cost of keeping the draught animals.

And hand-in-hand with the spade went the cultivation-ridge or 'lazy-bed', and we have seen that this method of cultivation is of high antiquity in Ireland. Though lazy-beds today are largely confined in distribution to the poorer west and in crop to the potato, they were formerly in use throughout the whole country, and a wide range of crops was raised on them. The width of the bed, and the height to which it was built up, varied both with the nature of the soil and the requirements of the crop to be grown. The plough was sometimes used in the first laying out of the bed, but after that the spade took over, and the shape of the bed might be adjusted to the needs of the crop at various stages of its growth. After the bed had been in use for some time it was divided down its centre; and what had been the ridge-crest became the new furrow.

As I have said before, the general connotations of the word 'lazy' are quite inappropriate here, because the careful management of the cultivation-ridge is a sophisticated method of coaxing the best out of a soil that is often wet and unpromising to begin with. The water content can be improved by suitable proportions of ridge and furrow, and the fertility can be raised by manuring, and a low-grade soil can often be brought to a reasonable level of productivity.

In the west the lazy-bed (Photos 43, 44, 46) ruled all, and the plough was unknown. In the early years of the nineteenth century a detailed survey of the boglands of Ireland was made, and Alexander Nimmo, a Scottish engineer, very sympathetic to the plight of the peasantry, did a lot of work in the south-west. Speaking about the barony

of Iveragh in south-west Kerry he says there was not a single plough or proper spade in the whole area. All cultivation was done with 'an implement the iron blade of which is about five inches broad, and nine long, with a socket making an obtuse angle with the blade, into which a long wooden handle is fitted: the socket does not cover the base of the handle, which is fitted on by a wedge and nails: the edge admits of the appliance of the right foot only; the handle has no cross piece to draw it back or turn it. The implement admits not in any way being used as a lever,' and may in its action be rather considered a peculiar kind of plough

Photograph 43 Aran Islands, Co. Galway. The soil for these cultivation-ridges has been made by bringing in sand and seaweed, and spreading them on bare limestone rock.

Photograph 44 Carrownaglogh, Co. Mayo. Cultivation-ridges going back at least to the earlier Bronze Age, are revealed when blanket-bog is cut away.

than as a spade. It appears particularly adapted to the cultivation of sloping and stony ground; but its effect in digging or removing the soil being small, it is used in conjunction with a small triangular kind of shovel, which is fitted with a handle similar to the spade and employed for spreading the earth, which has been previously stirred by the spade in the trench, over the intervening beds; this being the universal mode of cultivation, at least in this part of Ireland.' He goes on to say that the implement is 'totally unfit for the purpose of cutting turf', and that 'if the cultivator is still to be kept without a plough, cart or team, at least the spade should be as highly improved to him as the instrument will admit.'

Nimmo's language is somewhat stilted, but he does give a picture of poverty and hard work. The same 'implement' appears in Scotland as the *cash-crom*, where it was used by groups of men to turn over the soil, in the way that a plough would have been used in less populated parts. In the west of Ireland we can picture groups of men turning out of their clachan to the arable common-field each morning, ten to the acre if lazy-beds were to be set up,

forty to the acre if potatoes were to be planted. There was no special factor controlling the shape or size of the field, and a number of people would own either separate blocks within the field, or, much more sensibly, rights on a certain number of lazy-beds in the field. Here we see a version of the common-field sysem that had flourished on the better land of eastern Ireland when the mouldboard-plough appeared, and may go back to still earlier times. Cultivation in common withered away in the 'planted' east of the country, but may well have survived in the native west, and blossomed out again into the *rundale* system when eighteenth-century population pressures developed (see Fig. 6.16).

In rundale there was the common arable field, and nearby the clachan, a cluster of modest houses with outbuildings and small enclosures. Around the perimeter was the outfield, used for pasture and periodic cultivation, and perhaps farther away the meadows, the mountain-grazing and the bogs, all of which were shared in common.

With a balanced community such a

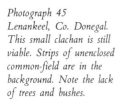

Photograph 45 Lenankeel, Co. Donegal. This small clachan is still viable. Strips of unenclosed common-field are in the background. Note the lack of trees and bushes.

system was viable, and could stand limited expansion. More potatoes could come into the arable field, and the productivity of the outfield could be raised. But once population-growth exceeded a certain rate, the system had to collapse. Holdings and rights fragmented under succession in severalty. As the potato expanded to take up the whole of the arable field, it left no aftergrass to feed stock and to receive the dung in return. If stock numbers were reduced, the total amount of manure available for the arable field fell. Ultimately if all were not to be reduced below the subsistence level, there had to be movement, either to higher levels up the hill-slopes, to the east, where potato-patches could still be rented to the further detriment of the existing fields, or out of the country altogether, to England or America.

The population of an overfull bee-hive can be relieved in two way. Swarms can carry large numbers away in search of new feeding-grounds, or disease can decimate the colony. Long before the Famine the swarms of emigrants had begun to leave Ireland, and by 1830 the rate of population-growth was

beginning to slacken off. But this was not enough, and when in 1845 potato blight finally caught up with the potato in Ireland, disaster was inevitable. During the Famine years (1845-51) about 800,000 people died, and twice as many emigrated. The heart was knocked out of Ireland, and the population continued to fall without interruption until 1930, when it was only 4,000,000, and Ireland was one of the emptiest countries in Europe (see Fig. 6.16).

Photograph 46 Near Manor Kilbride, Co. Wicklow. The house-foundations of a long-abandoned clachan lie beside an extensive area of old cultivation-ridges; the varying shapes and proportions of the ridges show that a variety of crops was being grown in them.

The aftermath of the Famine:
AD 1850-1903

If we were to look back to 1850 BC, we would see a well-wooded Ireland, and in clearings we would see a Bronze Age population enjoying a standard of life equivalent to that of anywhere in western Europe. If instead, we look back to AD 1850 we see a ruined landscape, almost destitute of any woody growth, and with the fertility of much of its soils grossly depleted by endless repetitions of potato crops. Those of its people in whom any element of *élan vital* had survived had only one goal — to seek a higher standard of living elsewhere. And it is on the foundations of that ruined landscape that much of what we see around us today has been built.

One thing was clear: the land had to be rebuilt into larger units, which might have some hope of economic survival. Some holdings fell back into the landlord's hands when the former tenants emigrated, and he rapidly repossessed himself of others by means of eviction if the tenants fell into arrears with their rents. For the landlord himself was now facing ruin. Relief measures, both indoor and outdoor, had been organized for famine victims, and these were charged on the local rates; not only had the landlord to pay his own dues, but if his tenants failed to pay, and their valuation was less than £4 — there were vast numbers of such tiny holdings — then he had to pay their dues as well; for him it was only good sense to buy the family emigrant tickets to America, and demolish their cabin, lest another occupant should revive his liability for rates. Programmes of tree-planting were abruptly terminated. Many estates collapsed under the strain, and in 1849 legislation made it possible for estates encumbered by debts to pass into new hands. But whereas many of the older landlords had lingering strains of paternalism towards their tenants, the newcomers had not, and for many small land-holders it was out of the frying-pan into the fire.

After 1850 things improved rapidly. Increasing population and increasing prosperity in England meant good prices for Ireland's farm produce; the tenant farmers prospered on their larger farms; continued emigration of younger men meant that the services of those that remained were in demand and wages rose; at the top the landlord was happy. A railway boom was opening up the country; before the Famine there were 105 km of rail; twenty years later there were over 32,000 km. Imported manufactured goods and food-stuffs could reach all parts of the country, with the result that shops thrived while local industries decayed.

But the essential dichotomy between the more favoured and more accessible east, and the poorer and more distant west persisted. And paradoxically it was the east that provided the bulk of the emigrants; in the west a still dispirited population lacked the initiative to go further than seasonal work in Britain, and the population obstinately remained at a level that was too high for the local resources.

The self-perpetuating flame of Irish resistance to British domination that had been encouraged to flare up by the Act of Union in 1801, had almost flickered out during the distresses•of the Famine, but it gradually warmed to life again, and England was forced to adopt, through the person of Mr Gladstone, a policy that has been aptly described as 'a nauseous mixture of slaps and sops', the slaps being the coercion of political unrest, and the sops being the bringing about, as a first step, of co-partnership between the landlord and tenant, and, as a second, of transfer of ownership from landlord to tenant. The Land Act of 1870 was the first important sop: if a tenant surrendered his farm he was entitled to be compensated for any improvements he had made; if he was put out, for any reason other than non-payment of rent, he was entitled to compensation for disturbance; if he wished to purchase his holding, he could borrow money from the state.

The all-too-brief good times ended abruptly in the middle seventies, when bad weather brought crop failures on a massive scale. Prices for what modest home produce there was did not rise, because the new generation of large cargo steamers was carrying in cheaper produce from overseas. Rents could not be paid, evictions started up again, and political agitations accompanied them. A further dose of coercion was accompanied by Mr Gladstone's second Land Act, that of 1881, with its famous 'three Fs' — fair rents, fixity of tenure and free sale. A few years later it was supplemented by an act by which the State would advance the whole of the purchase price of a farm, and be repaid by annuities, and about 25,000 farms soon changed hands.

From 1850 on the process of realigning field boundaries, enclosing new fields and planting their boundaries with trees and bushes had gone steadily on, but landlords were no longer able to afford new plantations of trees on the scale that had obtained before the Famine; planting was balanced by cutting to finance it, and the acreage under plantations remained the same. The Act of 1881, which brought nearer the transfer from landlord to tenant, had disastrous effects on the attitude of the landlord to his estate; he could no longer see it as something to be husbanded so that it could be passed on in tail-male in perpetuity, and he decided to turn his estate into money while the going was good. As always, timber was turned to a source of cash, and many landlords sold their stands of timber to travelling sawmillers, who came over from England and moved across the country from estate to estate, again leaving devastation in their wake. As a footnote we may add that the woods that survived this cutting enjoyed only a brief respite before they vanished in World War I, and when that was over, 200,000 acres of woodland had disappeared, and less than half of one per cent of Ireland was covered by forest.

Photograph 47 Cappaghmore, Co. Galway. A successful small farm on low-lying limestone.

The grim cycle came round again in the late eighties. Poor yields at home, cheap imported foreign goods, rent arrears, evictions, violence, coercion, and more Land Acts. Tenant protection was further extended, and more money was made available for farm purchase.

Economic conditions improved again in the nineties, and from this time on the more favoured east was economically viable, and was beginning to develop the appearance that we know today. Some trees had survived on some estates, the trees that had been planted in the field-banks were growing to maturity, and while the total number of trees was still minute, the view across the landscape did contain some trees, and the ghastly dreariness of immediately post-Famine times was fading away, though numerous house ruins and shrunken clachans were still evidence of the vanished population.

The west remained on the precarious edge of subsistence, and special attention was given to its improvement. In 1891 a Congested Districts Board was set up to help those western regions where the density of the population manifestly outstripped the local resources. The Board built roads, bridges and harbours, and much of the modern tourist traffic enjoys the benefits of its activities. It stimulated fishing, gave agricultural advice, and encouraged cottage industries. Added income was vital, and this came from the cottage industries and seasonal earnings in Britain, now made easier of access by the new roads and railways. But as the historian, Professor Louis Cullen, points out, even before the Board had been set up, emigration rates from the west and the age of marriage had both started to rise. These were positive moves, portending better than the palliative remedies of the Board. New cash sent home in remittances from emigrants may well have exceeded new cash generated by the Board, and the modernization made possible by the new money probably tended to promote more emigration in search of still

higher standards rather than to stem it.

Foreign food products were now flooding into the English markets, and it was no longer sufficient for Ireland to produce in quantity, she must produce in quality also. In 1894 Horace Plunkett founded the Irish Agricultural Organization Society to promote joint purchases and sales, and to bring the dairy industry to a level where it could meet competition from Denmark and New Zealand. He followed this up in 1899 by securing the creation of a government Department of Agriculture and Technical Instruction to raise the general standards of farming in Ireland.

1903 marks a turning point in the history of the Irish landscape. In that year the new department established its first forestry centre, and assumed responsibility for the management of its first block of woodland. Here we have the first step at national level to restore to Ireland a substantial area of woodland — and the first step drastically to alter the appearance of the Irish landscape. It was also the year of the culminating Land Act — the Wyndham Act — which, when there had been added to it the power of compulsory purchase, made the completion of Gladstone's ambitions possible. Entire estates, not just piecemeal holdings, could now be offered for sale, and very generous financial terms made easy purchase possible. When the possibilities of the Act had worked their way through the system, Ireland was indeed a land of small farmer proprietors.

7

MODERN IRELAND:
AD 1903 to 1986

When the transfer of land was complete, all vestiges of early Ireland and of feudal Ireland had disappeared. In their stead authority was represented by institutions of government, both at national and at local level, and the land was held by farmer proprietors who clung with a vice-like grip to their small units of inefficiently worked fields. Even today half the Irish farms are of 12 hectares (30 acres) or less. But at least at the national level the landscape could now be viewed and managed on a country-wide basis, rather than operated as a patchwork of estates, farmed at various levels of interest and efficiency.

It was realized that the soil was a matter for nation-wide concern, and soil investigation units were added to the Geological Survey. The absolute deficiency of timber had to be rectified, and a State forestry programme was initiated. Because of the virtual absence of coal, the winning of peat on an industrial scale had already attracted attention by the middle of the nineteenth century, and one hundred years later this operation was placed on a national basis.

The soil of a country is its most important single resource. Unlike other resources such as oil or metallic ores, the soil is — or should be — inexhaustible, and no nation can afford to ignore its management. In Ireland, because the humid climate encourages soil deterioration, such management is a matter for special concern.

In coastal districts since at least the twelfth century man has been drawing shelly sand and seaweed from the shore, and spreading it on his fields to improve both the fertility and the drainage of the soils. It was only this practice that made farming possible along much of the western and southern fringe. Here the soils had first degenerated to peaty podzols, and had then become smothered by blanket-bog. As population pressures grew in the late eighteenth century much of the peat was cut for fuel, to reveal the poorest of soils. But if the soil was stripped down to the iron pan, and the latter was broken up with crowbars, it was again possible for water to move downwards. Sea sand and seaweed were added to the soil, which was then replaced as a surface layer; over the years the otherwise idle hours of winter were spent in drawing and spreading more material, until in some places as much as a metre had been deposited. Sometimes the sand was first used as bedding for cattle, where it absorbed large quantities of dung and urine. In the Aran Islands such soils were built up on bare rock. In this way a first-class soil replaced a very poor one (see Photo 43). Today the practice has been largely abandoned, but the improved properties of the man-made soils remain; the prosperous onion-growing that is carried on in the vicinity of Castlegregory in Kerry is entirely based on the soils that were laboriously built up by past generations.

As the twentieth century opened, another agricultural revolution was taking place, this time consequent on the introduction of the so-called 'artificial' fertilizers, which made it possible directly to replace calcium, potassium, nitrogen and phosphorus in the soil. External and internal wars then distorted this gradual development. World War I, and especially the two years after it, were among the most hectic periods of agricultural prosperity in Ireland's history, surpassing even the best years of the Napoleonic wars. Food and timber were in unlimited demand. The soil's reserves of fertility were heavily drawn on, while timber stocks were butchered. With the aid of artificial manures the first could be relatively quickly replaced, but it was a matter of many years before the scars the second left on the landscape could be healed over. The difficulties of the post-war crash were intensified by military activities at home, first against British forces and later on an internecine level, but the first Dublin government was strongly in favour of agriculture, and prices in general were kept low to encourage agricultural exports. The aftermath of the Great Depression of 1929 was intensified in Ireland by an 'economic war' with Britain, which pushed agricultural prices down still further. But if agriculture came under fire, the protective tariffs, which were part of the campaign, provided the screen in whose shelter the industrialization of the south of Ireland was born.

World War II again created demand for agricultural products, but on this second round government control of prices and other matters was more rigorous, and the bonanza of 1914-18 was not repeated. Once again production was increased at the expense of reserve-fertility, and once again there was wholesale felling of park trees, hedgerow trees, woodlands and plantations, creating a new generation of landscape scars. The end of hostilities left the land of Ireland in such poor shape that intervention at government level was necessary. The European countries whose lands had been ravaged by war were in the same position, and received generous American aid through what came to be known as the Marshall Plan, and although Ireland had been neutral, she also was helped. Large grants for field improvement both by the cutting of drains and by the removal of tree stumps and large boulders were made available, but through the enthusiasm of contractors and other interested parties, grandiose schemes were often embarked on which expended money on a scale far beyond the benefit that might be expected. To restore the calcium that had been leached from the soil, ground limestone was made available at subsidized prices; the innovation brought about the final demise of one characteristic feature of the Irish landscape, the lime-kiln, where small quantities of limestone had been burned with peat or coal, at least since the eighteenth century. To restore the other nutrients an ambitious and expensive scheme was launched, whereby by undertaking to pay an annuity over a period of years, in the same way as the land purchase annuity was being paid, a farmer could have the necessary amount of fertilizer applied to his fields.

Part of the American grant was used to found an Institute of Agricultural Research, *An Foras Talúntais*, and this has been of the greatest importance to further agricultural development. The institute launched a national soil survey to discover the real capacity of Irish soils.

Great areas of blanket-bog were planted, or marked down as areas for future afforestation. In North Mayo, where the blanket-bog is remarkably extensive and continuous, the generation of electricity in peat-fired power-stations was begun (Pl. 33). World War I had created a demand for native fuels, and considerable experimentation sought to generate electricity efficiently from peat. In 1946 bog development was nationalized, and by 1970 135,000 acres (55,000 hectares) of bog, nearly all raised-bog, were yielding over four million tonnes of peat per annum. Today the burning of peat provides 20% of electric current generated. Elimination of unnecessary handling has been the goal, and more than three-quarters of the total is won by tearing up the surface with a harrow, allowing the debris to dry, and then sweeping it into a ridge along the bog, from which a light railway carries it to the power-station. The dry ridges are protected by enormous lengths of polythene sheeting, and seen from a distance the shimmering ridges create the illusion of a vast and unexpected lake. If the windmill has disappeared from the Irish countryside, the steaming cooling-towers of the bog-side power-stations have added a new feature. At the outset of the programme it was decided in principle that the exhausted boglands would be turned into farmlands or forests. Today we have the cutaway bogs, and no one knows what is the best thing to do with them. Will they revert to wetlands, or wilderness areas? It will be difficult to make them commercially viable.

Large-scale peat-harvesting has so far been confined to extensive areas of raised-bog. Now 1200 hectares (3000 acres) of blanket-bog in north-west Mayo are about to be invaded by machines. Minor bog areas, both raised and blanket, too small for big machines, are being attacked by 'bog misers', small-scale dredgers or tractor-mounted macerators, and no bog will be safe from them. Every day it becomes more imperative to give inalienable protection to at least a few of the bogs that are still intact. Gallant efforts are being made to raise money to purchase such bogs, but it is a little ironic that the chief thrust is coming from the Netherlands, a country that has already destroyed all its bogs.

Like the peat bogs, the water resources have also been harnessed to generate electricity. But here alas the topography of the country creates dilemmas. The rain that falls on the mountainous rim of the country either falls quickly to the sea by numerous small streams, or debouches onto the central low-lying area, where it waterlogs the soil, if indeed it does not cause flooding. The hydroelectric engineer wishes to retain the water in the soil, so as to maintain a steady flow in the rivers for the benefit of his turbines, the farmer wants to get the water off his land and out into the sea as quickly as possible. The Shannon is the country's greatest source of hydroelectric power; the farmer is constantly calling for a major drainage scheme, even though much of the land liable to flooding is of poor quality. We have seen that in early Littletonian time part of the Shannon basin was occupied by large lakes, and it would not be impossible to restore these to some extent, and greatly increase the storage capacity of the hydroelectric system. Unfortunately this is a zone where politics and economics overlap. It was proposed to develop the River Boyne for hydroelectric purposes, and expensive preliminary works were undertaken; then the decision was reversed, and it was agreed to undertake a major drainage scheme, though even the simplest of cost-benefit-analyses would have shown that the money expended on drainage would never be recouped by increased agricultural output. But the sight of a great excavator crawling up and down a river bed, even if it is ruining the landscape by degrading the river to the status of a half-filled canal, destroying its fish and piling up raw spoil-banks along its margins, is a much greater winner of local rural votes than the idea of a distant power-station bringing benefit to faceless city-dwellers. The concept of an unspoiled wetland as a local, national and even international resource is one which is equally difficult to sell to the rural voter.

But by the middle nineteen-fifties post-war developments were beginning to run out of steam, the country was stagnating, and the tide of emigration was beginning to flow again. Revitalization was necessary, and this was provided by the Whitaker Plan for Economic Development, which was

Photograph 48 Near Dingle, Co. Kerry. When large rocks have been pushed aside, and the soil re-distributed, and fertilizer spread, great areas of new grassland will arise. In the process much evidence of earlier human activity will disappear.

Photograph 49 Blanchardstown, Co. Dublin. The Irish landscape today. (Ordnance Survey)

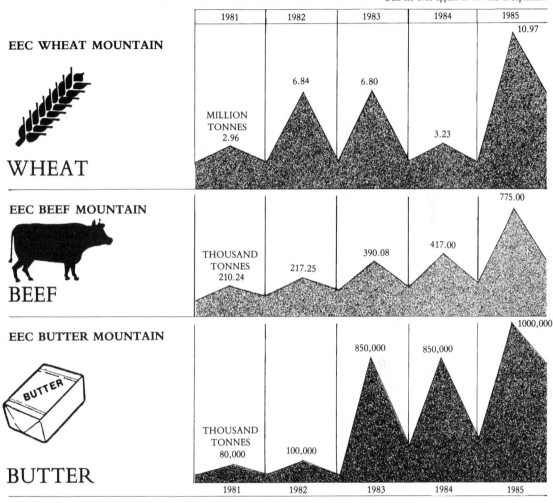

Fig. 7.1 Diagram to illustrate progressive growth of EEC overproduction

Date for 1985 applies to the end of September

| 1981 | 1982 | 1983 | 1984 | 1985 |

EEC WHEAT MOUNTAIN

WHEAT

MILLION TONNES 2.96 — 6.84 — 6.80 — 3.23 — 10.97

EEC BEEF MOUNTAIN

BEEF

THOUSAND TONNES 210.24 — 217.25 — 390.08 — 417.00 — 775.00

EEC BUTTER MOUNTAIN

BUTTER

THOUSAND TONNES 80,000 — 100,000 — 850,000 — 850,000 — 1,000,000

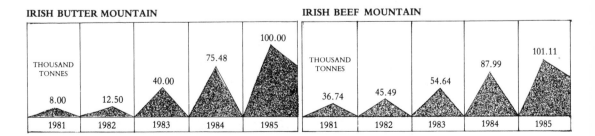

IRISH BUTTER MOUNTAIN

THOUSAND TONNES

| 1981 | 1982 | 1983 | 1984 | 1985 |
| 8.00 | 12.50 | 40.00 | 75.48 | 100.00 |

IRISH BEEF MOUNTAIN

THOUSAND TONNES

| 1981 | 1982 | 1983 | 1984 | 1985 |
| 36.74 | 45.49 | 54.64 | 87.99 | 101.11 |

accepted by the government in 1958. It was to transform the Irish scene. We still prize Arthur Young's record of late-eighteenth-century Ireland, and the detail he gives of new and old farming practices. T.W. Freeman first published his very valuable *Ireland: a General and Regional Geography* immediately after the war in 1950, and a second revised edition followed in 1960. The book presents an Ireland that had drifted along almost unchanged since the twenties, but which in the next twenty-five years vanished almost as completely as Young's Ireland has gone. In the book the Grand Canal still carried commercial loads, and only two pleasure boats had ventured onto the Shannon; today there are 300 cabin cruisers. Freeman's *Geography* will stand beside Young's *Journal* as a record of a vanished time.

The Whitaker plan stressed the need to capitalize on Ireland's greatest natural resource, the grassland which covers 80% of Ireland's utilized agricultural area, and to boost cattle, sheep and milk production. But the main thrust was in the industrial area, and the challenge of free trade was accepted. A second seven-year programme was adopted in 1963, and was equally successful. In the sixties economic growth was faster and more sustained than in any previous period in Irish history. Living standards rose by more than 50%, and the tide of emigration was reversed. Private motor-cars rose from 250,000 in 1958 to 700,000 in 1970. But somewhere along the line, as John Healy has pointed out, the people's eyes turned away from the *country*, as a land to be cherished, and looked instead to the *economy*, as a source of privilege.

In the period such growth was not unique to Ireland, nor entirely achieved by Ireland's own efforts. Much of the momentum was derived from the general economic upswing that Europe enjoyed in the sixties. But the golden age ended in 1971 when the United States would no longer issue gold metal

in exchange for paper dollars, and sustained economic progress faded away as monetary instability developed.

1973 brought two further developments, as different from one another as the two poles of a magnet. Accession to the EEC came first, and another agricultural bonanza was launched. Farmers received steadily increasing prices for their products, the Common Agricultural Policy swallowed up all that was produced, financial institutions fell over one another to press loans on the farmers, land prices rocketed to heights that defied all reason, farm buildings proliferated on all sides, and no one stopped to think that 'with eager feeding food doth choke the feeder'.

With the EEC milk price 40% above world level, it was so easy just to shovel the butter into cold store, and not think of adding value to the milk by developing alternative dairy products; the EEC makes special grants for such development, and Ireland was allotted IR£35 million; only one-seventh of this has been taken up. It is also easy just to push the sides of beef into intervention, without much attention to quality, and not think of butchering and packaging. Ultimately there had to be a limit to what the storage caves of the Common Market could engulf.

This transient prosperity masked the other development of 1973, the creation of a cartel by the world's most important producers of oil. At first increased energy costs were absorbed easily as prices for farm products continued to rise. But international prosperity and above all economic expansion were dealt very deadly blows. The cartel has collapsed, oil prices have fallen dramatically, and energy costs must fall. But no one thinks that the extinction of the cartel will restore the *status quo* of 1973. Today the Common Agricultural Policy is also on the point of collapse. Excess production will have to be penalized.

8
THE FUTURE

In 1986 we can no longer pretend that we do not hear the rumbles, ever growing louder, of discontent with the Common Agricultural Policy. The policy can no longer be sustained or defended, either on financial or on moral grounds. One half of the world should not produce excess food, which it cannot eat and cannot afford to sell, while the other half of the world starves. But if the policy is scrapped, what will Ireland do then, poor thing?

One change is most urgent, and that is a radical revision of the agricultural grant system. The EEC has called a halt to grants to increase milk production, and a severe quota system is in operation. As a result a good dairy farmer in eastern Ireland can now produce his restricted quota of milk from fewer acres than he is using for this purpose at present; what is he to do with his surplus land? The cynic says 'nothing, as in that way loss can be avoided'. But even today farmers in western Ireland are still receiving EEC grants to reclaim hill land and turn it into grassland which they will use to feed dairy cows.

However, very much less land, as well as very much less milk, is what the EEC wants. The high agricultural prices that the CAP has produced have encouraged farmers to improve their efficiency, and less and less land can produce the same amount of food. John Lee of An Foras Talúntais has been looking at this question, and he reckons that by the year 2000 — only fourteen years away — the EEC will have 5 million hectares of surplus grassland and

up to 10 million hectares of surplus arable land, an area almost twice the size of Ireland. Pressure will confine production to the best quality land, and here Ireland has some share.

Grassland suitable for milk production is concentrated in the high rainfall areas of Ireland and the west of Great Britain. Ireland has 9% of the best grassland in the Community, and here dairying should hold its own. But the rain that is welcome for grass makes problems for tillage. Because of poor soil-drying conditions, the Irish farmer has to carry out tillage operations on days that are less than favourable, with resultant damage to the soil structure and increased machinery costs. The swing to winter wheat will continue because it is easier to work heavy soils in autumn than in spring. None the less, Irish cereal yields in quantity — though perhaps not in quality — are well above the EEC average, but the country only has 4% of the best arable land in the community.

Ireland is traditionally a land of potatoes, though yield at 26 tonnes per hectare is below the EEC average, and far below Holland at 36 tonnes, Belgium at 31 tonnes and the UK at 30 tonnes per hectare. Ireland's potato farmers will have to give great attention to quality and packaging if they are to hold even the home market.

At present because the price of sugar is at an artificially high level in the EEC, sugar beet is a profitable option for Irish farmers. In order to prevent the erection of a sugar mountain, acreage under the crop is restricted by a quota system, and there is no prospect of expansion here. In any case in a rational world sugar production would be left to the West Indies and areas of similar climate, which might then enjoy some prosperity instead of being pushed down into misery by the subsidized production of sugar elsewhere.

These trends obviously have important implications for the Irish farmer and the Irish landscape. In 1986 the State will spend more than £20 million on long-term development aids to agriculture. These want to be looked at with a new eye. In 1986 the State will spend £9 million on arterial drainage, in addition to the £47 million it spent on such drainage in the four preceding years. Almost none of this money has gone on further improvement of good land; the bulk went to achieve a modest improvement in very poor land, and neither Ireland nor Europe wants more poor land; they have more than enough of it already. What then to do with the poor land we already have?

This is not a new question. The debate on what to do with the wet soils of western Ireland has now been in progress for more than a century. Most authorities agree that of the 20 million acres (over 8 million ha) of land in Ireland about 6 million (2½ million ha), say one-third of the whole, are unfit for profitable agriculture; the bulk of this unprofitable land lies in the west. In 1845 Griffith in his Valuation Report said that half the unprofitable land should be planted with trees. In 1883 Gladstone invited a Danish forester, Howitz, to report on the possibilities of reafforestation in Ireland; his report echoed that of Griffith — 5 million acres (2 million ha) were more fitted for forestry than anything else, and 3 million (1.2 million ha) of these acres lay along the western seaboard. The matter still remains unresolved. From modest beginnings, and despite the set-backs of two world wars, the annual rate of planting has been pushed up to 20,000 acres (over 8000 ha) per

annum, though the final target is not yet decided on. Much of the planting hitherto has been on the uplands above the recognized limit for cultivation, or on blanket-bog, but sooner or later the main question must be answered — Are the low-lying poorly drained soils of western Ireland to be taken boldly out of marginal agricultural production and transferred instead to timber production, where the yield can be expected to be generous?

Recently attention has been focussing on the 'drumlin belt', a broad swathe running from coast to coast through Down, Armagh, Monaghan, Fermanagh, Leitrim and Sligo. Drumlins are low, elongate, isolated hills built up of glacial till, which make very poor farmland. Because the till of which they are built up was rich in clay and was extruded under heavy ice pressure, it is very dense in texture. Water cannot easily percolate through it, and soils are wet and very difficult to drain. The sloping flanks are in many cases too steep for farm machinery to manoeuvre easily. Leitrim is the worst off of all the counties. Only one-tenth of the soils are well-drained; six-tenths are poorly drained, and much of this is on steeply sloping drumlin sides. The remainder is bog, lake or river, occupying the low ground between the drumlins. Farms are small, and the vast majority of them cannot produce a family income which is comparable to that of a family of industrial workers. Population loss by emigration has been heavy. Much of the land is held by unmarried elderly folk, both men and women.

It would seem impossible for agriculture, even if efficiently practised, to give an adequate return for investment here. But there is no doubt that trees grow well on drumlin soils, and large-scale afforestation has been proposed. Big EEC grants for tree-growing have been offered, but to date only minute amounts of these have been taken up. A major problem is that expenses come early, but the generous returns come late. Poor though his land may be, the Irish small farmer has a passionate attachment to it, and it is almost impossible to acquire parcels of land to build up into adequately sized units for commercial forestry. Proposals for long leasings have not been taken up either.

There may be some psychological block here. For more than a hundred years Ireland has been a treeless country, and every viewpoint shows a wide expanse of landscape. Transfer an Irish farmer to the Black Forest, and he may suffer claustrophobia. The Irishman wants to lean on a gate, and look out over rushy fields with wandering bullocks; he does not want to sit in a cottage, blanked off by conifers, even though his capital is augmenting itself around him as he sits.

Frank Convery of University College, Dublin, has been looking at the position in Leitrim in some detail, where A. O'Rahilly has been growing trees for some time, and has a first crop approaching maturity. There is no doubt that spruce from the west coast of North America, *Picea sitchensis*, will grow well in Leitrim, the only question is does it grow too rapidly? Will its wood produce planks of necessary strength? Windthrow may be another difficulty, as when the trees are approaching maturity the soil may not have sufficient strength to anchor the roots. But acquisition is the main problem, as blocks of some extent have to be built up.

If an adequate pilot scheme can be shown to be successful, then the project will take off as there are several sources of funds, such as pension schemes, to which growing timber is an attractive investment. And there is no doubt that Europe needs wood. After oil, wood is the largest single import, by value, into the Community.

But it is not a case of trees anywhere you can get land sufficiently cheaply, a policy which has tended to colour the activities of State forestry. The land should be 'good forestry land' below 240 m in elevation, and much care should be taken of the young trees in their first critical years. Because of windthrow, peat — either as upland blanket-bog or cutaway lowland bog — should be avoided. To maintain landscape variety, small blocks of hardwoods, such as oak, should be scattered through the conifers. The hardwoods will take much longer to come to maturity, but will pay handsomely when they do.

When tillage is concentrated in drier south-east Ireland, the dairy herds are on the good grasslands, and forests have been established wherever they can form profitable wood, what is to become of the rest of the landscape, and of its people? This is a problem that is not confined to Ireland, but exists equally in many parts of rural Europe. There is an especially close parallel between the problems of Brittany and Ireland.

In Ireland in 1900 everyone was rejoicing that the tyranny of large estates was over, and that the land now belonged to the small farmers of Ireland. But less than a hundred years later the horrid thought is beginning to arise that perhaps there was something to be said for large estates, such as still survive in England. There they no longer belong to greedy landlords, but to shrewd insurance companies or pension funds. These owners offer parcels of land on leases, and so make it possible for a young man to begin farming, first by being able to get land, and second get it without crippling himself by having to borrow the money necessary to purchase it. In Ireland it is still next to impossible to rent land on a lease of sufficient length to make improvements, and if land can be bought, it will be in small parcels at too high a price.

On the other hand, small parcels are no longer so objectionable, now that farming is specialized, and everyone has a motor-car. Ireland is the land where nobody walks; cows are intelligent creatures, and learn to obey the horn of a tractor just as well as the bark of a dog. The farmer no longer has pigs, his wife no longer keeps hens, and the milk comes in cartons from the supermarket, so why live on the farm? It is much nicer for the wife to live in a ribbon-development outside a town, with municipal water and sanitation, and the possibility of company, while the husband goes off in his car to visit his scattered parcels of land.

The poorer soils of Ireland must face not only use at a less intensive level, but also habitation at a still lower level. And beyond the move of farmers to the local town, there is the drift to the Greater Dublin area (see Photo 49), or out of the country altogether.

Greater Dublin now holds 35% of the population of the Republic, and is set to grow much larger; Paris holds only 20% of the population of France. Even more of Ireland's land will fail to produce an income which will allow the life-style that the Dubliner has achieved, and every country dweller has come to expect. Unfortunately the life-style is supported, not by Irish productivity, but by foreign borrowing. Either new income sources will have to be found for the countryman, or an income subsidy will have to be paid, if considerable areas in Ireland are not to become 'wilderness land'.

Tourism is a source of income, but not one that can be indefinitely expanded. France has established an elaborate system of *gîtes*, that is self-catering holiday accommdation on *bona fide* farms. I say *bona fide*, because in Ireland an establishment describing itself as a 'farmhouse' may prove on arrival to be a bungalow outside a small town. Such *gîtes* have great attraction to the visitor with a special interest, such as natural history or archaeology, and these visitors are increasing in number.

But if we are to attract tourists to our countryside, we have to put an end to

our penchant for disfiguring it by erecting ugly buildings, by polluting its waters or by scattering it with litter. The United Nations have designated 17% of Ireland as areas of outstanding natural beauty; for how long will we hold that position?

Are we prepared to pay a direct subsidy to chosen western farmers to stay on the land, and work it at a deliberately low level so as to save the landscape from falling into desertion? Could we pay them a salary as litter-wardens, and give them power to inflict on-the-spot fines to those who desecrate the countryside? Can we give them mobile cranes, to collect abandoned motor-cars (Pl. 32)?

It may seem curious to talk of encouraging low-level output, even in a restricted area and with a definite purpose, since low-level output is our national disease. We expect a European standard of income from an Irish standard of output. Twenty-two countries are members of the Organisation for European Co-operation and Development, and these have recently been ranked in order of international competitiveness; Ireland stands sixteenth in the list, with the UK only two places ahead at fourteenth. An economic commentator recently observed that we cannot expect a higher standard of living in 1990 than we enjoyed in 1980; but do we need or deserve a still higher standard of living when the Third World is starving? Can we reproach the Third World for causing damage to their agricultural land by cutting down forests, when we are busy polluting our land, our lakes and our rivers and sweeping away our field monuments, for the sake of short-term gain?

Our landscape will continue to deteriorate unless the Irish people will put aside the Golden Calf, and turn again to the husbandry of their Four Green Fields.

Bibliography

This bibliography does not attempt to be comprehensive, but endeavours to suggest sources for further reading. Emphasis is concentrated on recent publications as far as possible, and many of these themselves contain detailed bibliographies of the sphere of interest in question. References to articles in *Proceedings, Journals,* etc., give only the year of publication and the volume number; they do not give page references.

GENERAL

AALEN, F.H.A. 1978
Man and the Landscape in Ireland
Academic Press

COMMON, R. (ed.) 1964
Northern Ireland from the Air
Queen's University, Belfast

Atlas of Ireland, prepared under the direction of the Irish National Committee for Geography
1979 Royal Irish Academy

FREEMAN, T.W. 1960
Ireland (2nd edn.)
Methuen

GILLMOR, D. 1971
A Systematic Geography of Ireland
Gill and Macmillan

KIELY, B. 1985
The Aerofilm Book of Ireland from the Air
Weidenfeld & Nicolson

MOODY, T.W. & MARTIN, F.X.
(eds.) 1984
The Course of Irish History
(revised edition) Mercier Press

MOULD, Daphne D.C. Pochin 1972
Ireland from the Air
David & Charles

NOLAN, W. (ed.) 1986
The Shaping of Ireland: The Geographical Perspective
Mercier Press

ORME, A.R. 1970
The World's Landscapes — Ireland
Longman

PRAEGER, R. Ll. 1937
The Way that I Went
Allen Figgis; Methuen

STEPHENS, N. & GLASSCOCK, R.E.
(eds.) 1970
Irish Geographical Studies
Queen's University, Belfast

1. GROWTH OF THE ROCK FOUNDATION

DAVIES, G.L. Herries, & STEPHENS, N. 1978
Ireland, a Geomorphology
Methuen

HOLLAND, C.H. (ed.) 1981
A Geology of Ireland
Scottish Academic Press

JENNINGS, J.N. 1985
Karst Geomorphology
Basil Blackwell

MITCHELL, G.F. 1980
The search for Tertiary Ireland
J. Earth Sci. R. Dubl. Soc. 3

NAYLOR, D. & SHANNON, P.M. 1982
The Geology of Offshore Ireland and West Britain
Graham & Trotman

WHITTOW, J.B. 1974
Geology and Scenery in Ireland
Penguin

2. THE ICE AGE

BOWEN, D.Q. 1978
Quaternary Geology
Pergamon Press Ltd

EDWARDS, K.J. & WARREN, W.P. 1985
The Quaternary History of Ireland
Academic Press

McCABE, A.M. & HIRONS, R.K. 1986
Field guide to the Quaternary of South-East Ulster
Quaternary Research Association, Cambridge

SUTCLIFFE, A.J. 1985
On the Track of Ice Age Mammals
British Museum (Natural History)

3. THE END OF THE ICE AGE

GODWIN, Sir Harry 1975
History of the British Flora
(2nd edn.) Cambridge University Press

JESSEN, K. 1949
Studies in Late Quaternary deposits and flora-history of Ireland. *Proc. R. Ir. Acad.,* B, 52

MITCHELL, G.F. 1965
Littleton Bog, Tipperary: An Irish vegetational record
Geol. Soc. Amer., Special Paper 84

PENNINGTON, W. 1974
The History of British Vegetation
(2nd edn.) English Universities Press

SINGH, G. 1970
Late-glacial vegetational history of Lecale, Co. Down
Proc. R. Ir. Acad., B, 69

4. RESPONSE TO WARM CONDITIONS

DEVOY, R.J.N. 1985
The problem of a late Quaternary landbridge between Britain and Ireland
Quaternary Science Review, 4, No. 1

MOORE, P.D. & BELLAMY, D.J. 1974
Peatlands
Elek Science

O'ROURKE, F.J. 1970
The Fauna of Ireland
Mercier Press

PREECE, R.C., COXON, P. & ROBINSON, J.E.
New biostratigraphic evidence of the post-glacial colonization of Ireland and for Mesolithic forest disturbance
J. Biogeogr (in press)

ROHAN, P.K. 1975
The Climate of Ireland
Stationery Office

SLEEMAN, D.P., DEVOY, R. & WOODMAN, P.C. 1986
Post-glacial Colonisation of Ireland
Irish Biogeographical Society, Cork

WEBB, D.A. 1943
An Irish Flora
Tempest

WEBB, D.A. 1983
The flora of Ireland in its European context
J.Life Sci. R. Dubl. Soc., 4

WOODMAN, P.C. 1978
The Mesolithic in Ireland
BAR, Oxford

5. THE FIRST FARMERS

CLARKE, D.V., VOWIE, T.G. & FOXON, A. 1985
Symbols of Power
HMSO

EDWARDS, Ruth Dudley 1981
An Atlas of Irish History
(2nd edn.) Methuen

EOGAN, G. 1984
Excavations at Knowth
Royal Irish Academy

EVANS, John G. 1975
The environment of early man in the British Isles
Paul Elek

HERITY, M. & EOGAN, G. 1977
Ireland in Prehistory
Routledge & Kegan Paul

NORMAN, E.R., & St JOSEPH, J.K.
1969
The Early Development of Irish Society
Cambridge University Press

O'KELLY, M.J. 1982
Newgrange: Archaeology, Art and Legend
Thames and Hudson

REEVES-SMYTH & HAMMOND, F.
1983
Landscape Archaeology in Ireland
BAR Oxford

SWEETMAN, P. David 1985
A Late Neolithic/Early Bronze Age pit
circle at Newgrange, Co. Meath
Proc. R. Ir. Acad., 85, C

6. RISE AND FALL
OF POPULATION

BELL, J. 1984
A contribution to the study of
cultivation ridges in Ireland
J. R. Soc. Ant. Irl., 114

CULLEN, L.M. 1981
*The Emergence of Modern Ireland,
1600-1900*
Batsford Academic

ELLIS, S.G. 1985
Tudor Ireland
Longman

GRAHAM, B.J. 1985
Anglo-Norman Settlement in Ireland
Group for the Study of Irish Historic
Settlement

HUGHES, K., & HAMLIN, A. 1977
*The Modern Traveller to the Early Irish
Church*
SPCK

LYONS, F.S.L. 1973
Ireland since the Famine
(rev. edn.) Charles Scribner & Sons

MacCARTHY-MORROGH, M. 1986
The Munster Plantation
Clarendon Press

McCRACKEN, Eileen 1971
The Irish Woods since Tudor Times
David & Charles

YOUNG, A. 1780
Tour in Ireland
(edited by Hutton, A.W., 1892) George
Bell (republished by Blackstaff
Press 1983)

7. MODERN IRELAND

FANNING, R. 1983
Independent Ireland
Helicon

FitzPATRICK, H.M. 1965
The Forests of Ireland
Society of Irish Foresters

GILLMOR, D.A. (ed.) 1979
Irish Resources and Land Use
Institute of Public Administration

MURPHY, J.A. 1975
Ireland in the Twentieth Century
Gill & Macmillan

WHITAKER, T.K. 1982
Economic development - the Irish
experience
Irish Times, 28.9.82

8. THE FUTURE

AALEN, F.H.A. 1985
The Future of the Irish Rural Landscape
Geography Department, Trinity College,
Dublin

BLACKWELL, J. & CONVERY, F.J.
1983
*Promise and Performance: Irish
Environmental Policies Analysed*
Resource and Environmental Policy
Centre, University College, Dublin

CONVERY, F.J. 1986
*Farming and the Environment: Cost and
Opportunities*
Resource and Environmental Policy
Centre, UCD

CRUICKSHANK, J.G. & WILCOCK,
D.N. 1982
*Northern Ireland: Environment and Natural
Resources*
Queen's University of Belfast and the
New University of Ulster

FLATRÈS, P. 1986
La Bretagne
Presses Universitaires de France

LEE, John 1986
European Land
Farm & Food Research, 17

LEE, Joseph, 1984
Reflections on Ireland in the EEC
Irish Council of the European Movement

LEE, Joseph, (ed.) 1985
Ireland: Towards a Sense of Place
Cork University Press

O'CARROLL, N. 1984
The Forests of Ireland
Turoe Press

INDEX